A publication of the

AMERICAN ASSOCIATION FOR HIGHER EDUCATION
National Center for Higher Education
One Dupont Circle, Northwest
Washington, D.C. 20036

G. KERRY SMITH, *Executive Secretary*

The American Association for Higher Education, AAHE,
promotes higher education and provides a national
voice for individual members. AAHE, founded in 1870,
is the only national higher education organization
open to faculty members, administrators, graduate
students, and trustees without regard to rank, discipline,
or type or size of institution. AAHE is dedicated to
the professional development of college and university
educators, to the achievement of their educational
objectives, and to the improvement of conditions
of service.

1870–1970 CENTENNIAL ANNIVERSARY

agony and promise

CURRENT ISSUES IN HIGHER EDUCATION

1969

G. Kerry Smith, EDITOR

ASSOCIATE EDITORS, *Joseph Axelrod,*
Tom Erhard, Mervin B. Freedman,
Lewis B. Mayhew

agony and promise

Jossey-Bass Inc., Publishers
615 Montgomery Street • San Francisco • 1969

AGONY AND PROMISE
Current Issues in Higher Education 1969
G. Kerry Smith, Editor

Library of Congress Catalog Card Number 73–92897

Standard Book Number SBN 87589–049–0

Manufactured in the United States of America
        Composed and printed by Hamilton Printing Company
        Bound by Chas. H. Bohn & Co., Inc.

JACKET DESIGN BY WILLI BAUM, SAN FRANCISCO

FIRST EDITION

Code 6917

THE JOSSEY-BASS SERIES IN HIGHER EDUCATION

General Editors

JOSEPH AXELROD *and* MERVIN B. FREEDMAN
San Francisco State College

22637

Preface

Kenneth Boulding has compared the present period of history to the bridge of San Luis Rey: "We are walking a very narrow tightrope over a very deep chasm, with some kind of promised land on the other side, and we could very easily fall off. That is why this is both a dangerous and a very exciting time." Boulding's analogy, presented in the 1966 edition of *Current Issues in Higher Education,* is as fitting now as it was then. If anything, the situation is more dangerous; for the stout-hearted and the adventurous, it is also more exciting.

Whether the upheavals on campuses and in the cities should be interpreted as deep shocks that will generate renewal or as signs that we have passed the point of no return is not answered in these essays. But these essays leave no doubt that social and campus unrest represents a serious challenge, if not a threat, to leaders in all areas of American life. What the country is now experiencing may fall short of an all-out revolution, but it is certainly more than just a passing fad.

In an effort to respond to the challenge of the past five years (we are now in the year VI After Berkeley), the leadership in higher education has been forced to consider sweeping changes. Whether the changes now being made or those in the making will prove adequate remains to be seen. It may well be, as many have pointed out, that our society simply expects too much from our colleges and universities. They have wound up with more than they can handle. The most demanding problems of the time— social, ecological, or moral—crowd the campus gate. How shall the keepers of what David Riesman calls "the secular cathedral of our time" decide which problems to accept and which to reject? And who, in the final analysis, are the keepers? Or are there any keepers any more? Can academia safeguard its chalice and serve megapolis at the same time? Should it try to become a template of what the larger society could be? How neutral can it be? Can it stay behind a moat or should it move in the direction of a store-front college in the inner city? What admissions and support policies should be used for the disadvantaged, the unprepared, the ethnically different, and the militant?

These and other wide-ranging questions are discussed in *Agony and Promise,* along with key developments that relate to them—the upheaval at San Francisco State and other institutions, the search for relevance and personhood, the life style of psychedelia, the radical challenge to authority and scientism, the lash and backlash, the urgency of black power, and the long unwinding of the war.

The ivy walls have been breached. It is no longer possible to consider the problems of colleges apart from the problems of society. A general conclusion to which these essays lead might be formulated thus: change, in some form, is inevitable; change for the worse is often alluringly easy; change for the better takes hard work. Or, as Robert McAfee Brown sums it up in the title of his contribution, "No Promise Without Agony."

G. KERRY SMITH

September 1969
Washington, D.C.

Contents

Contributors

WILLIAM M. BIRENBAUM, President, Staten Island Community College

HARLAND BLOLAND, Assistant Professor of Higher Education, New York University

HOWARD R. BOWEN, President, University of Iowa

ROBERT MCAFEE BROWN, Professor of Religion, Special Programs in Humanities, Stanford University

SEYMOUR ESKOW, President, Rockland Community College

JAMES FARMER, Assistant Secretary for Administration, Department of Health, Education, and Welfare

MERVIN B. FREEDMAN, Professor of Psychology, San Francisco State College

JAMES M. GAVIN, Chairman of the Board, Arthur D. Little, Inc.; former Army general who served as the United States ambassador to France during the Kennedy administration

JAMES M. GODARD, Project Director, Southern Regional Education Board

ANDREW M. GREELEY, Program Director, National Opinion Research Center, University of Chicago

CHARLES V. HAMILTON, Chairman and Professor of Political Science, Roosevelt University

DALE HECKMAN, Research Assistant, Center for Research and Development in Higher Education, University of California, Berkeley

HAROLD L. HODGKINSON, Project Director, Center for Research and Development in Higher Education, University of California, Berkeley

STANLEY J. IDZERDA, President, College of Saint Benedict

JOHN C. LIVINGSTON, Professor of Government, Sacramento State College

ROBERT MACNEIL, Reporter, British Broadcasting Corporation

WARREN BRYAN MARTIN, Project Director, Center for Research and Development in Higher Education, University of California, Berkeley

ROLLO MAY, Psychoanalyst, author, and lecturer; former counselor at Michigan State College and at College of the City of New York

LEWIS B. MAYHEW, Professor of Education, Stanford University

L. RICHARD MEETH, Dean of the College, Park College

HANS J. MORGENTHAU, Albert A. Michelson Distinguished Service Professor of Political Science and Modern History, University of Chicago

EDMUND S. MUSKIE, United States Senator from Maine

HELEN H. NOWLIS, Professor of Psychology and Research Consultant on Student Affairs, University of Rochester

ALLAN W. OSTAR, Executive Director, American Association of State Colleges and Universities

WARREN ROVETCH, President, Campus Facilities Associates, Boulder, Colorado

JAMES A. SHIFLETT, Executive Director, Community Arts Foundation, Chicago

ROBERT SMITH, Professor of Education and former Acting President, San Francisco State College

GEORGE G. STERN, Professor of Psychology, Syracuse University

FREDERIC C. WOOD, JR., Associate Professor of Religion, and Chaplain, Vassar College

agony and promise

PART ONE

University and Society

Section I

Politicization of the University

The American university has become politicized. None of the essays of Section I deny this statement. As Harland Bloland states the problem in the second essay of the Section: "The issue is no longer whether [universities] should attempt to influence public policy at all—but rather in what kind of policy question they should become actively involved. . . ."

In the opening essay of the Section, Hans Morgenthau points out that for the individual faculty member, the matter may already be beyond choice: "The transformation of [the] universities into gigantic service stations for the government and the big corporations" has already taken place; faculty members have in fact become "the agents of the political values and interests identified with the . . . powers that be." But Morgenthau's central point goes beyond the university. Political activity on the part of the citizenry, he asserts, has become meaningless; reform is no longer possible—either through the democratic process or through revolution. (In the discussion following the presentation of his paper, in response to a question about revolution, he replied: "The idea that you can—as our criminal law still pretends— overthrow the American government by force is the most utopian idea anybody can have.")

The title of William Birenbaum's essay, "Lost Academic

Souls," is a play on words. According to Grayson Kirk, quoted at the outset, the university that becomes politicized does so at the cost of losing its soul. Birenbaum contends that politicization is not the danger; the danger lies in the abuse and misuse of the enormous power the higher education establishment now possesses. Birenbaum shows how that power could be used wisely if those who possess it could be persuaded to share it.

Just who constitutes the higher education establishment? For readers who may wonder about the place of the federal government in that establishment, Allan Ostar's essay will be of great interest. He asserts that American higher education "is now standing at a crossroads and the direction it takes will be determined by the policies the federal government adopts. . . ." Ostar is persuaded, moreover, that the long-range future of American higher education will, in fact, be determined by the federal government during the term of the present Washington administration.

The four essays of Section I provide insight into the American university's major dilemma today: whether to assume responsibility as an agent for social reform or whether to protect (and increase, if possible) its status, power, and financial interest in America's governmental-industrial complex.

JOSEPH AXELROD

~⟨ 1 ⟩~

STUDENT-FACULTY PARTICIPATION IN NATIONAL POLITICS

Hans J. Morgenthau

There can be no doubt that much of the campus unrest which we are witnessing today in aimless emotional explosions and destructiveness is the result of the experience of the meaninglessness of "legitimate"—or what we might call "conventional"—political activity. This experience of the meaninglessness of political activity is a general experience. When we look at the national scene, we are struck by how little it frequently means just how we vote or who is elected. Take the classic case of the 1964 presidential elections. Most of us thought that here was as clear-cut a case of two different personalities, two different political philosophies, and two different political programs as one could wish. But those who voted for the loser were pleasantly surprised to find that his political program, at least on the international scene, was in good measure executed by the victor who had opposed that political program in the election campaign.

I happened to listen recently—for a couple of minutes only—to a talk by Senator Goldwater. The first question was how Senator Goldwater felt about President Johnson executing his program, and Senator Goldwater smiled with great satisfaction and said, "Well, he did it after he had read my speeches."

I personally doubt that very much, but, in any event, Lyndon Johnson did in good measure what Senator Goldwater had advocated. Time and time again, every four years, we hope and work for a change in national policies one way or the other; and we find afterwards that except for the style of government and the attractiveness or lack of attractiveness of the personalities involved, everything remains, by and large, the same. Thus, we have today in the academic community a widespread feeling that it really does not make any difference how you act within the system—that if you want to bring about real changes, you have to oppose the system itself.

What I want to point to in particular is the ominous character of the presence of such a widespread feeling. For once large and articulate groups within the population begin to doubt that they can make a useful contribution to American political life within the established system, and once they arrive at the conclusion that in order to make such a contribution, they must oppose the system itself, then, obviously, the system itself is in a serious crisis. When we speak of alienation and of the anarchic tendencies among the student population, we are referring to particular instances of this opting out of the American system itself.

Two years ago I gave a lecture at Stanford University, an institution whose fame did not result primarily from its radical tendencies, and I had lunch in a fraternity house where there were a number of clean-cut, unbearded, well-washed and bathed students—people who look exactly like one thinks the sons of the vice-presidents of banks and of corporation lawyers might look. I was taken aback by the tenor of the conversation at lunch, which centered around two questions: first, shall we evade the draft, or, second, shall we allow ourselves to be drafted and refuse to go to Vietnam? If this is the attitude of students who you may say are predestined to become the pillars of society, who are born into the establishment and whose material and personal advantage lies in playing the game of the establishment in order to be able to rise within it, then, something must be fundamentally wrong, not only with the techniques of the political process in this country, not only with the modalities of participation, but with the very ethos of Amercan democracy. For those are not the people whom one encounters frequently in the forefront of student revolt—I mean the ill-adjusted, if not the pathological, who find in taking over the leadership of a disturbance an opportunity to play a role and to achieve something. Those students at Stanford did not need this kind of an outlet. By remaining within the grooves of the establishment, they could have made their impact, they could have become aware of their own selves and of their own importance. They could have amassed the values that American society cherishes most, such as material benefits, social status, political influence. But the exact opposite took place. They seriously, voluntarily, and with conviction, opted out of the American system—in a sense, one may say, out of American society.

Thus the problem of student and faculty participation presents itself today in a different and much more serious and fundamental light than it would have, say, four or five or six years ago, because the issue of student and faculty participation raises in an acute and specific sense the very issue of the survival of American democracy.

Let me turn for a moment to the connected issue of faculty participation in national politics. Here we are in the presence of a more subtle and quite different problem. Many members of our faculties participate inconspicuously—you may say almost naturally—in the national political processes by serving the powers that be. It is, of course, an obvious fact that an institution of higher learning in any period in any society, being a product of that society, will support the values of that society. American institutions of higher learning reflect the values and interests of American society as Russian universities naturally and inevitably reflect even more stringently the interests and values of the totalitarian society of the Soviet Union. This is inevitable and this has always been so. But what is new is the transformation of especially the more prestigious universities into gigantic service stations for the government and for the big corporations. Without the research and experimentation that go on in universities, the government and the big corporations could not operate as they do and would have to change radically their ways of operating. This cooperation between universities and the powers that be, both public and private, naturally and inevitably and organically draws faculty members into the political processes that defend the status quo. Faculty members thus working, without really being aware of it, for the government or for the private powers that be become—again, without being aware of it—the agents of the political values and interests identified with the public and private powers that be.

The Vietnam war in this and in other respects, I think, has been an eye-opener. It has been the great event, the very crisis, in the modern history of America to sharpen and bring to the fore those basic problems of American society. This crisis—in which the academic community, faculty and students, on the one hand, and the national policy, on the other, find themselves—can only be understood in the overall context of the crisis of modern democracy; and I want to point very briefly to a few issues.

Take, for instance, the enormous complexity of modern political issues as compared with the issues of, say, fifty or a hundred years ago, which makes it for everybody concerned much more difficult to participate in a meaningful way in the political process. Take the way in which the issue of race relations posed itself a little bit more than a hundred years ago. It posed itself in terms of the abolition of slavery, the legal status of the black people, and that issue was easily understood by the man in the street and easily resolved one way or the other. Take a look at the way in which the issue of race relations poses itself today, in what infinitely greater social, economic, and moral complexity, the issue of integration, the issue of creating at least an approximation to equality for black Americans. The answer to those issues cannot be a simple yes or no as it was a hundred years ago in the case of slavery. How do you vote if you have a position with regard to those issues, that is, how do you translate that position into a vote at election time, and how do you try to influence the elected officials so that they follow the policies to which you are committed?

Take, in the military field, the issue of the antiballistics missile. The enormous complexity of this issue makes it completely impossible for the man in the street even to understand the issue. He may be emotionally for defense, or he may be emotionally against defense, or he may emotionally be in favor of unending nuclear arms competition with the prospective enemies of the United States, or he may be against it. But the issue itself is so complex that even the policy-makers shift from one position to another within a couple of weeks and confuse the issue even more.

In the field of labor relations, fifty years ago the issues were simple. Are, for instance, the prohibition of child labor and a limitation of the working hours of women violations of freedom of contract—yes or no? Or should labor unions be treated as criminal conspiracies? The man in the street had simple answers to questions such as these.

Look at the enormous complexity of industrial relations today. What is more important and more fatal to public participation in the democratic process is the impossibility—if you are not an out-and-out partisan—to take a stand for one or the other solution of the issue that can be translated into votes or legislative enactments.

So, aside from the particular frustrations the academic community has experienced, and aside from the particular temptations and corruptions to which the academic community is prone, you have here a general crisis of the democratic process, which results from the gap between the ability of the man in the street to take a position and to translate this position into effective political action, on the one hand, and the nature of the issues upon which the political community must act, on the other.

Thus, the particular frustrations we as academics experience are in a vaguer and more general sense shared by the public at large. Since the academic community suffers particular frustrations in which the general public does not share, it may well have a particular responsibility to clarify the issues, to keep itself away from those temptations and corruptions to which I have referred, and within the small compass of its possible activities, you may say, to create a center of commitment to the truth as applied to the national issues of the day.

One might, at least, hope that from the renewal of this kind of commitment to the truth in matters political, there might occur a revitalization of the democratic process that would stifle those frustrations and their more dangerous expressions that we see on the American campuses today.

～ 2 ～

POLITICIZATION OF HIGHER EDUCATION ORGANIZATIONS

Harland Bloland

A recent headline of the *Chronicle for Higher Education* stated: "Academic Turmoil Grows Over Moves to 'Politicize' Universities and Associations." Referring to heated debates that had occurred during the 1968 meetings of the Modern Language Association and the American Historical Association in New York City, the article bearing this caption attempted to summarize the opposing views of academic scholars on the appropriateness of the politicization of their associations and of universities. The term *politicization* was defined roughly as the involvement of academic organizations in political controversies.[1]

---

[1] Malcolm G. Scully, "Academic Turmoil Grows Over Moves to 'Politicize' Universities, Associations," *The Chronicle of Higher Education,* January 13, 1969.

The debate is, of course, a meaningful and important one —but it must (and frequently fails to) take into account the fact that academic organizations already are politicized in at least one important sense. Universities and associations have been, particularly in the 1960s, very directly engaged in political activity. The purpose of this analysis is to clarify the nature of this activity and to suggest that the issue is no longer whether higher education organizations should attempt to influence public policy at all— but rather in what kinds of policy questions they should become actively involved in the future. A distinction is made here between two types of political controversies in which universities and associations have participated or may soon participate. These two types are narrow political issues—those issues that touch directly on the basic educational or scholarly objectives of the higher education enterprise—and broad political issues—those controversial policy questions that affect other institutions and groups in the society as directly and profoundly as they affect academic institutions and groups.

The following remarks deal most directly with academic voluntary associations—although they have important implications for the predicament of the university as well. The reasons for focusing on associations here are several. They are generally less complex organizations than universities: their membership is more homogeneous, their structure less diversified, and their goals more narrowly circumscribed. As a result, one can see in the behavior of associations patterns that are less clearly manifest (although equally significant) in the behavior of universities. In addition, there has been a tendency in the 1960s for associations to play an increasingly important role as links between the academic community and the federal government, and, in fact, to serve as vehicles for the expression of academic views on public policy.

Many academic associations have attempted, in the last decade, to achieve an effective voice in the shaping of public policy that directly affects their primary purposes as academic organizations. Their efforts to participate in the formulation of higher education policy are viewed here as the narrow politicization of these associations.

The process of narrow organizational politicization has been an inevitable concomitant, it would seem, of widening and deepening federal involvement in higher education since World

War II. As more and more critical decisions regarding higher education have come to be made within federal agencies and Congress, there have been strong incentives for national organizations of academicians to defend scholarly and educational standards in the political arena against politically-determined decisions regarding research priorities, acceptable research procedures, and the distribution among higher education programs of federal support. In addition, of course, as the cost of all aspects of higher education has soared, these associations have been pressed to the task of encouraging adequate educational support from the only institution now capable of providing that support in sufficient amounts: the federal government.

In recent years, university administrators have acted through Washington-based associations such as the American Council on Education and the National Association of State Universities and Land-Grant Colleges to promote federal support for a wider range of university activities to counteract what they view as imbalances created within universities by the concentration of federal funds on research in the scientific disciplines. On the other hand, recent cutbacks in federal allocations for science (particularly basic science) research and congressional threats to the research autonomy of federally-funded scientists have stimulated scientific learned societies to expand their relations with government. Social scientists, too, have looked to their associations to defend their work autonomy from a growing tendency toward the regulation of government-financed social research.

On the whole, such narrow political activity on the part of higher education associations has not been a subject of great controversy among association members themselves. Few academicians have, for example, vigorously disputed the appropriateness of using their professional organizations to promote federal support of basic research or to defend the research autonomy of faculty members supported by federal agencies.

Rather, conflict among association members has arisen in the last few years over questions that have been defined here as broad political issues. Controversy has occurred primarily within national associations representing university faculty members, as adamant factions within these organizations have attempted to involve them directly in policy issues of broad public import. Clear examples of such issues are, of course, the war in Vietnam, civil rights, and police brutality toward demonstrators in Chicago.

Since 1967, particularly, there have been overt efforts within the American Sociological Association, the American Physical Society, the Modern Language Association, and many other major learned societies, to establish a public organizational position on the Vietnam war. In virtually every instance, the issue of whether to commit the society, as a professional organization, to such a broad policy view has created heated debate among the members; and, in most cases, proposals related to Vietnam have been defeated—at least for the time being. The memberships of a number of these learned societies have agreed, however, not to hold association meetings in Chicago in the near future. And there are indications that more academic associations will begin to take public stands on this and other broad political questions.

It seems important to consider here why efforts in the direction of the broad politicization of higher education organizations have stirred so much academic controversy, and to suggest some assets and liabilities for the higher education enterprise of broad political activity of associations and universities.

The impetus to use associations as vehicles for the articulation of member views on broad political issues grows out of a deep concern among some members of these organizations that scientific specialization—and the extensive ties between academic institutions and the federal government—have subverted the traditional and potential role of higher education organizations as the locus of vital social and political criticism. Advocates of the involvement of educational organizations, as such, in the broad political process argue, on the one hand that the dependence of university scholars on federal support for their research has introduced a new tendency among academicians to "play it safe" in their role as commentators on national policy, and has reduced their incentive to engage actively in controversial social causes. On the other hand, it is argued that scientific specialization has tended to remove academic scholars from a sense of responsibility for the possible social and political implications of the knowledge they advance.

Thus, the active participation of organizations such as learned societies in broad political controversy is seen as a means of drawing the higher education enterprise into a more relevant and responsible role in relation to the pressing policy problems of modern society, and of counteracting the present tendency for such organizations to serve as the passive instruments of federal policy.

In the terms of this argument, limiting academic associations to participation only in narrow political issues simply strengthens the bonds between these organizations and the federal government and further insulates the academic community from its true moral responsibility as the locus of criticism of the society's ills.

The basis for the frequent defeat (so far) of proposals committing associations to a position on Vietnam has been essentially this: The engagement of academic associations in broad political activity seems to many faculty members to fall outside of the essential purposes of the scholarly societies as they define or interpret these purposes. It is widely argued that since the basis for membership in learned societies is a shared commitment to scholarship or to a discipline, rather than to any ideological principle, it cannot be assumed (and is not, in fact, the case) that the members of a disciplinary society share ideological views on many of the wide-ranging and complex political issues of the day. For the learned society to take a public stand on broad political affairs could be, in many instances, a source of destructive divisiveness among its members. (And if views on policy issues are often widely diverse within higher education associations—with their relatively homogeneous memberships—they can be expected to be even more varied within the differentiated structure of the university.)

Inherent in this argument is the assumption that scientific knowledge—while certainly relevant to political problems—and often highly influential in their solution—"does not directly and clearly provide the answer to any complex political issue." [2] Thus, sharing a single disciplinary perspective on public affairs does not necessarily lead a group of scholars to the same answers to policy questions, as public policy statements by disciplinary associations may suggest.

Furthermore, many academicians fear that association activity in broad public affairs is a threat to the professional status and autonomy of these organizations. According to this view,

[2] Don K. Price, "Purists and Politicians," *Science, 163*, January 3, 1969, 28.

ideological statements on broad policy issues undermine the claim of academic organizations to a basic commitment to the objective pursuit and transmission of knowledge. If expertise is not a consistent basis for the behavior of these associations, public faith in them is reduced, and belief in their legitimacy as social critics and policy advisors in the narrower sphere of their special expertise is attenuated.

Those who resist broad politicization argue that academic institutions do not now function merely as passive instruments of the established political and social order. Rather, they assert, these institutions continue to serve, in a vital sense, as centers of dissent and criticism. As such, their autonomy must be carefully guarded; and one critical way in which they can take steps to preserve this autonomy is to participate as effectively as possible in the shaping of policy which directly affects their professional interests. Narrow politicization can thus be seen, from this perspective, as a means of enhancing the independence of academic organizations as loci of detached, scholarly research and social criticism.

The arguments cited above concern specifically the appropriateness of public organizational stands on broad policy issues. The case in favor of broad political activity for academic organizations assumes that in order for academicians to fulfill their social responsibility, they must use their professional organizations as vehicles for the articulation of their political views. I would not suggest here that academic organizations can or should ignore pressing political and social problems of whatever scope. However, deep concern for, and interest in public affairs does not seem to require overt political action on broad policy issues on the part of these associations as organizations. If the traditional purposes of scholarly associations are to be interpreted in such a way as to assure the relevance of the work carried on within them for the solution of social problems, this broadening of focus might most effectively take place through the enhanced use of the association as a forum for careful analysis of broad political controversies and for the consideration of the significance of specialized scientific knowledge for their solution.

A trend in this direction is indicated by the creation within a number of scholarly societies of special committees or groups which concern themselves with public policy. Examples are the American Institute of Physics' Committee on Physics and Society, and the American Political Science Association's Caucus for a New Political Science—both of which are stimulating within their parent bodies increased attention to partisan issues and social crises, and a greater responsibility for the use of scientific knowledge in the clarification and resolution of critical policy problems.

In addition, it seems highly appropriate to expand the range of issues raised for consideration by all association members at their professional meetings—encouraging wider interest in the relevance of scholarly research for contemporary social affairs, and informing members on the various facets of major social issues with which they might otherwise be unfamiliar. The association (or university) might thus serve, more than it has previously, as a forum for the analysis of broad policy issues, drawing on disciplinary perspectives and skills to shed light on these matters.

This is not to suggest that social action is inappropriate to individual members of the academic community—as scholars and as citizens. As individuals, academicians are provided with a wide variety of avenues—other than through their professional associations—for the public expression of their policy views. They are, for example, increasingly employed as consultants to government on broad questions of national policy. I would propose, however, that academic organizations can function most effectively as contexts for the scholarly examination of social issues, thus helping to prepare their members for more informed participation in the political process.

Academicians who wish to be politically active through organizations also have the clear alternative of joining organizations which have basically ideological or political purposes. Certainly, the possibility for individuals to join different types of organizations in the pursuit of their varied interests is a characteristic feature of this pluralistic society.

To stress, in conclusion, the advantage of retaining some degree of organizational neutrality in relation to contemporary social crises, it should be emphasized that higher education associations and institutions have a unique role to perform in a rapidly changing technological society. They require freedom from the necessity to commit themselves on each of the constantly shifting policy dilemmas of the day so that there can be developed, in this scholarly context, an overview, or a broader perspective, on social and political affairs—an overview which policy-makers, responsible for immediate solutions to a bewildering variety of policy questions, cannot possibly sustain.

LOST ACADEMIC SOULS

William M. Birenbaum

In November of 1965, Grayson Kirk, President of Columbia University said:

> The responsible student knows that a university would suffer irremediable damage if it allowed itself to become embroiled institutionally in a partisan fashion in any subject of current controversy. . . . If any university becomes politicalized in this fashion, it will have lost its soul.

In December of 1968, Sidney Hook, distinguished professor of philosophy at New York University, said:

> We cannot believe that the mission of the university is to lead mankind to a New Jerusalem. Any attempt to do so would destroy, among other things, the university's role to serve as intellectual sanctuary when the winds of popular passion blow.

> . . . The goal of the university is not the quest for power or
> virtue, but the quest for significant truths. . . .

Kirk now spends most of his time raising money for a
university which, apparently, has "lost its soul," and Hook is now
passionately blowing around the country politically organizing
the troops in behalf of his own New Jerusalem.

"You shall know the truth, and the truth shall make you
free." The connection between knowing the truth and some version of how men should live has always guided those who would
lead the university. In behalf of such a connection self-righteous
men established Harvard, Thomas Jefferson argued his case for
a new university in Virginia, Congressman Morrill persuaded the
national legislature to create a whole new breed of educational
institutions, and every university in this country today that is
"politically" realistic reaches out for its nearest urban base.

When the early medieval scholars broke through the walls
of the monastery to flee to the streets of the cities, the church must
have issued a press release warning against lost souls. Bologna,
whose colors march first in our academic parades, was originally a
storefront operation, housed in rented halls and cold lofts through
which the winds of popular passion certainly blew. The retreat
from the streets of the city into the Oxonian superblock campus
was no retreat from the politics of the time. The enclave campus,
purposely designed to disrupt the orderly flow of city life, was but
one expediential version of the connection between the quest for
truth and how men should live. The reconstruction of the monastery's wall around Oxford's superblock was an attempt at party
discipline, a redevelopment act as politically charged as the Model
Cities Program. It is this counterpoint to medieval politics that
we Americans, as skillfully imitative as the Japanese, replicated
in such absurd places as the remote prairies of southern Indiana
or the inaccessible Adirondack foothills surrounding Ithaca. From
embattled parapets overlooking the plains of Harlem or the South
Side neighborhoods of Chicago, ancient knights cry out in behalf
of their souls, besieged by the motley hordes wanting in, searching
for souls of their own.

Other brave knights have stoutly defended their special
privileges and vested interests before. The walls did not keep the
sciences out. The walls did not keep the technologies out. The

walls did not keep the tradesmen and the farmers out. The walls did not keep the new professions out. The walls did not keep the immigrant masses out. The walls did not keep the Manhattan Project out. The walls did not keep Hitler out. The walls did not keep the GIs or the Fulbright Program out. The walls did not keep the trade unions out, or the industrial recruiters or the ROTC credits. The walls will not keep the poor, the black, out.

Our colleges and universities stand in no clear and present danger of *becoming* politicized. They always have been politicized. They are now. The clear and present danger is a sharp new exposure of the misuse and abuse of the substantial power they have come to possess. Not only are the brick-and-mortar walls crumbling—the archaic versions of how we should build the university in the modern city—but also under attack are the credit-hour version of law and order; the outmoded versions of due process represented by oligarchical curriculum committees and self-perpetuating boards of trustees; and the doctrine of segregation upheld by politicized academic departments and culturally biased admission thresholds. The qualitative gaps between those who teach and those who are taught have been markedly reduced by the character of the new knowledge and the technologies available for getting access to it. About all that can be said now about the college student and his teacher is that one of these adults is younger than the other, that each knows something the other does not, and that both are in deep trouble. The sheer quantity of what there is to know now magnifies the ignorance of both. They share a new kind of equality, and it is the reality of this equality that now shakes the walls to their very foundations.

Monopoly power is the antithesis of egalitarian and democratic politics. The essence of monopoly power is the control of the production of the goods and services essential to a people's survival. To survive in an economy based on the technology we have developed now requires for most some kind of education beyond the twelfth grade. To survive effectively in a political state of the kind to which we subscribe now requires some kind of education beyond the twelfth grade. To survive spiritually and culturally in an affluent middle-class society of the kind our wealth and technology promise for all now requires some kind of education beyond the twelfth grade. For better or for worse, what we call higher education in this country virtually holds monopoly power over the production of educational goods and services beyond the twelfth grade. Indeed, the colleges and universities exercise what amounts to a monopolist's influence over educational production below the twelfth grade.

Under the circumstances of the new knowledge and the urbanization of America's people, the link between education and survival is irrevocably political. Admissions policies (decision-making about who will be kept out) have political consequences. The quality of what happens to the people who get in has political consequences. The act of granting a degree (the terms under which one may get out) is a political act.

Freedom itself is a political concept. It means, if nothing else, a particular distribution and use of and access to power. The adjective *academic* when placed in front of the word *freedom* merely specifies particular purposes in behalf of which some of the power is to be mobilized. From Jefferson to Horace Mann, from Dewey to Robert Hutchins, our establishment's leaders have always talked about education for freedom. It is no longer possible to educate the youth of this nation for the life of free men in institutions that organize and use survival power in keeping with anti-freedom principles. The antique traditions, naturally, no longer make sense to city-bred youth, exposed earlier in life to the messiest problems of a citified adult world. Resist the power of the church or of the state? Autonomy, sanctuary, objectivity, neutrality? What do these slogans mean now when uttered by an institution that has itself become one of the principal power centers on the American landscape, without whose active collaboration the military, government, industry, and the professions cannot shoot off their rockets, make the peace, produce the cars, or heal the sick?

At a much earlier time, perhaps the best defense of academic freedom required the organized centers of learning to build walls between themselves and the worldly arenas of action. But the science laboratory compels a new relationship, intimate and friendly, between thought and action. The modern city compels a new connection between thought and action. The new knowledge converts both the city and the urban center of learning into imperative action laboratories, without the use of which no significant learning can be produced. This is the meaning of *relevance* now. Pot, sex, Vietnam, ghetto, choice, crime; our students now respecting the ancient traditions we teach them, consult the original texts, the original sources of the knowledge. What shall we say to them as we form our own unions to enlarge our paychecks and reduce our teaching hours, as we accept the royalties from our own books and the honoraria from our own consulting sorties? This is the meaning of *relevance* now. Student and layman, taxpayer and newspaper reporter, poor black and middle-class white, politician and churchman, all see through the hypocrisy now. Knowing for sure that we have the power, the red-blooded American thing for them to do is to challenge the terms on which we use (or misuse) it. Trying so hard to play the game themselves, they understand very well the game we are playing. The best defense of academic freedom is no longer an unrealistic assertion of an impossible autonomy, plaintive cries of a tattered slogan about neutrality. The best defense of academic freedom now is intelligent participation. This is the meaning of *relevance* now.

As the walls come tumbling down, the citizens of the New Bologna will undoubtedly complicate life inside our academic places. More frequently than ever before we will be compelled to venture forth into the streets of the New Bologna. They are not safe streets. University presidents and professors may get mugged there, or even worse, shot down. But our educational institutions, finally being but frail human creations, finally depend upon what we frail humans decide to do with them. We must expect change, and honor change by the way we think about it and feel about it in our hearts. If we expect to reduce the academic crime rate and restore academic law and order, we must be prepared to share the process of academic law-making with those we expect to govern. If we are sincere in our invitation to the new masses to play the old American game, we must respond sincerely to their plea for a participatory role in the redefinition of the ground rules by which the game is to be played now. If we really mean an integrated America, we must invent fresh mechanisms for integrating the new knowledge into the curricula, and think afresh about the kind of segregation we enforce on the campuses between two-year and four-year undergraduate students, between the teachers and the taught, between the dead-ended career and vocational programs, and the open-ended professional and graduate ones, between black and white, between the governed and the governors, between the academic monastery and the secular city.

Finally, we must stop fighting the environment our incredible intellectual achievement has produced. Because we must live in the cities, because the cities are essential to our continued intellectual progress, we must restructure our institutions to honor and understand the mentality required for successful city life, a citified mentality. To do this we must methodically break down our own walls, and launch vast new programs aimed at the disruption of our own un-American academic monopolies.

First, the old demarcation line separating the jurisdictions of the higher educational system from the lower makes less and less educational sense. It is no longer at seventeen or eighteen that the demands of the postschool, adult world begin to take hold of urban youth. The process of education must correspond more realistically to the process of growing up in the city. Growing up in the city respects the reality of human biological development, the significant psychological and cultural events which begin to occur when a person crosses the line from childhood to adolescence. "College" and "high school" are no longer viable educational categories.

Second, the rejuvenation of the decaying urban communities requires a substantial transfer of power from white to black, from the more powerful to the less powerful. This transfer must engage and involve the deployment of our best and most sophisticated intellectual, technical, and administrative talents. The confrontation between the experts and the people in the context of a power transfer is the most important event in the life of both the campus and the city. This event must be enacted democratically, if education for freedom is really among our higher purposes.

Third, the superblock campus is a physical representation of monopoly—insular, monolithic, and exclusive. It centralizes buildings, activities, and power for the purpose of its own defense rather than disperses and diffuses its resources in order to equip the people with the power to defend themselves. The urban campus must be in the city. The city itself is the relevant place for learning.

Fourth, people work in places of learning, and learn in places of working. We must find new ways to honor the experience of those we seek to educate. The reorganization of our curricula around problems magnifies the importance of the student's experience in the eduational process. As Aristotle said: "What we have to learn to do, we learn by doing." The city and the new knowledge invite doing as a part of learning, acting as a necessary part of thinking.

Fifth, the differences between the upper and lower ranges of performance on the tests we use to admit students are far greater than the actual genetic and biological differences among the same sample of humans. We have not begun to educate people to the outer limits of their capacities. Educational systems, not human beings, are failing. We must confront this reality.

Finally, the most squandered, underutilized, misused, and abused educational resource in our colleges and universities is students. We must ask ourselves what setting, what network of relationships achieves the best environment for learning. The authoritarian, patriarchal response to this question is now untenable. Student freedom is an essential educational methodology.

Jacques Cousteau concludes his brilliant documentary film on the life of sharks with a sequence showing a brave diver on the floor of the sea holding out bait in his hand to attract the sharks. At first, a few come and nibble cautiously at the bait. They become bolder and more aggressive, and then more come. Then more, until scores of sharks are dashing and slashing at the bait. Of course, the bait is not enough to feed them all, and soon there is a frenzied competition in which the sharks wildly strike at each other, at anything that moves or crosses the path between them and the bait. The turmoil is vicious. The diver is hastily drawn up to the surface to escape the deadly, primitive chaos.

We are encouraging cannibalism on the campus. Our ancient methods are devouring our present, urgent purposes. The Columbias, the NYUs, the San Francisco States, the Chicagos have descended to the bottom of the sea. They hold out the bait. It is not enough. No mother-ship floats on the surface of American life now ready to haul the brave academic divers back to safety. Are we lost souls, or fearless explorers? One thing is for sure: the truth is hidden somewhere there at the bottom of the sea—where we are, with the sharks.

$$\sim\!\!\!\triangleleft\ 4\ \triangleright\!\!\!\sim$$

HIGHER EDUCATION
AND NATIONAL
POLICY

Allan W. Ostar

National policy decisions affecting higher education, decisions that will have a profound influence on the future of higher education for a long time to come, are now in the process of being made. The issues boil down essentially to the questions of who should go to college; who should control the colleges; who should pay for college; and who should be involved in making national policy concerning higher education.

Those of us over forty have an idealized concept of the answers to those questions. We grew up with the idea that education at all levels is essential to the development of our society and that society has an obligation to support education. Society, in the past, generally has accepted its responsibility to support edu-

25

cation, largely through voluntary contributions and through taxation.

According to a book on fund-raising by Professor Scott Cutlip of the University of Wisconsin, the first systematic effort to raise money on this continent was for a college—Harvard College, of course. Since student fees were expected to provide only a small part of the cost, in 1641 the Massachusetts Bay Colony sent three clergymen to England to solicit money for the college so that it could, among other endeavors, "educate the heathen Indian." One of the three returned with five hundred pounds; one became a rector in England; and the third wound up hanging from an English gallows. Thus ended the first organized attempt to convince society of its responsibility for the support of higher education.

But even with that less-than-fortunate beginning, we have never given serious consideration to the idea that the student is the primary beneficiary of higher education and therefore should pay all or most of the cost—until recently, that is. I refer to proposals for the so-called Educational Opportunity Bank put forward by Professor Zaccarias of MIT, and incorporated in recommendations for national higher education policy by the Carnegie Commission on the Future of Higher Education and the federal committee headed by Alice Rivlin. The proposals essentially would shift all or most of the cost of higher education to the student, which he would pay by borrowing on his future income. Critics of the plan call it the Student Life Indenture Plan, or SLIP.

Just as philanthropy has been a primary source of support for private colleges and universities, state and local taxes have been a primary source of support for public higher education. Both, of course, benefit by federal assistance. The principle of public responsibility for the support of higher education was firmly established under the Northwest Ordinance. As the frontier pushed westward, among the first acts of the territorial legislatures was the provision of free state institutions that would be open equally to all. The most eloquent statement I have seen in this regard was made in 1865 by John B. Bowman, first regent of what was later to become the University of Kentucky. Said Regent Bowman:

I want to build up a people's institution, a great free university, eventually open and accessible to the poorest boy in the land, who may come and receive an education practical and suitable for any business or profession in life. I want to cheapen this whole matter of education, so that under the broad and expansive influences of our Republican institutions, and our advancing civilization, it may run free, as our great rivers, and bless the coming millions.

My hidden reason for introducing this statement is to put the Republican party on record in favor of universal educational opportunity and low tuition.

The platform of the Republican party during the presidential campaign included support for tax credits for educational expenses and giving greater operational responsibility for education to the states, perhaps in the form of bloc grants. This was good campaign material, but I doubt that either of these goals will be actively pursued. The second might, but probably for elementary and secondary education and not higher education. Once any administration—Democrat or Republican—is in office and has its staff in place, it begins to establish national priorities and these naturally take precedence over the party platform during election time. The tax credit plan would take a billion and a half dollars or more out of the federal treasury for use largely by middle-income families. The administration might well see more urgent needs for that money and want to spend it for its own programs. The same might be true for bloc grants.

I began by suggesting that critical decisions affecting the long-range future of higher education are now in the process of being formulated. They will be made during the term of the present administration. I do not want to suggest that the federal government—and I include Congress—has the sole power to make these decisions, but it will certainly have the major voice. That should not be surprising when you consider what has happened to the federal role in financial support of higher education. Just after World War II, it amounted to about two hundred million dollars. Today it is more than three and a half billion dollars, and the Carnegie Commission suggests it will be 13.22 billion dollars within ten years.

Former U.S. Commissioner of Education Francis Keppel

liked to refer to the federal government as a junior partner in the
higher education enterprise, but this perception of the federal
role may no longer be valid. The Wescoe Committee, formally
known as the Advisory Committee on Higher Education to the
Secretary of Health, Education, and Welfare, in its report released selectively last August, analyzed the development of federal
participation in higher education since World War II, and looked
ahead, concluding that the federal government has "moved inadvertently into a position of primary responsibility for the destiny of higher education."

Higher education is now standing at a crossroads, and the
direction it takes will be determined by the policies the federal
government adopts in deciding how to allocate its resources to
higher education.

What are some of the alternatives? The first alternative is
to continue on the present course of supporting mission-oriented
or categorical programs, academic facilities, and student aid. The
second is to channel funds to higher education primarily through
the individual student. The third is to provide support directly
to the institutions themselves. These three alternatives are not
mutually exclusive, but the critical question is which approach
and philosophy will be predominant.

The Wescoe report succinctly evaluates the assets and liabilities of categorical support and other programs now in existence. It notes that World War II established a partnership
between the government and the universities which produced
scientific and technological advances essential to national security
while strengthening the scientific resources of these institutions.
The GI Bill and present student aid programs represent a thrust
toward the reduction of financial barriers to a college education.
Grants and loans for academic facilities and housing have helped
ease the stress of growth for a large number of institutions. On
the liability side, however, the Wescoe Committee describes present federal support without clear goals or a comprehensive set
of related policies as resulting in

> distortion of academic development, disruption of institutional
> integrity and the imposition of burdensome, sometimes incon-
> sistent, administrative regulations. Want of concern for the
> impact of federal funding on individual colleges and universi-

ties as institutions has left some unaided, others selectively assisted, and a few heavily committed to federal programs. Some institutions receiving no aid face extinction; those receiving selective support suffer internal distortions, while those heavily dependent on federal aid have become prisoners of unstable financing.

An unfortunate side effect of heavy emphasis on project-grant support and the fragmentation of federal programs involving higher education is the development of Washington representatives to facilitate more effective participation in federal programs. Some of the large universities have established their own offices in Washington at considerable expense. Others have entered into contracts with private commercial firms that promise to help colleges and universities get more federal money—for a substantial fee, of course. Others have joined together to maintain Washington offices on a cooperative basis. Competition is getting keen for the available dollars, and Washington is becoming filled with the babble of many voices speaking for higher education.

Each of the major aircraft companies has a Washington office to promote and handle contracts with the Department of Defense. Will each of our more than two thousand colleges have to do the same? Is educational service in the national interest to be handled in the same way as contracts for the production of missiles, with institutions competing with each other for federal assistance? This may be one consequence of too much reliance on the project-grant approach to support for higher education, and it poses a distinct threat to institutional identity and integrity.

The president of a major state university recently remarked that federal project-grant support was turning his institution into a holding company for academic entrepreneurs. The loyalties of his faculty no longer were to the goals and objectives of the institution, but to their research projects and to the federal agencies that supported them. The recent sharp cutback in federal project support, however, has forcefully brought home to the faculty the need for stable and continuing support through the institution.

To facilitate the development of clearly stated goals and a coherent set of policies on the part of the federal government, the Wescoe Committee recommends the creation of a National

Council of Higher Learning in the Office of the Secretary of Health, Education, and Welfare.

The second alternative involves the channeling of federal funds to higher education through the student. One plan which has considerable political appeal would provide tax credits for educational expenses. This sounds good to middle- and upper-income parents who are hard-pressed to meet the rising costs of sending their children to college, particularly to those that charge high fees. Actually, however, the plan was conceived as a means of channeling federal funds to colleges and universities without worrying about constitutional restrictions on the use of federal funds for religious or racially-segregated institutions. One of the originators of the tax credit plan, Roger A. Freeman of Stanford University, explained the way it would work: "Tuition tax credits are not intended to help the taxpayer as such but to help him support the college of his choice." To get the federal money, colleges would raise their tuitions; the parents would pay it, and deduct an amount from their federal tax bill. Nobody gets hurt, except low-income families, students working their way through college, and veterans on the GI Bill who would have to pay the increased tuition without much of the benefit of the tax credit. Also, it would cost the U.S. Treasury a billion and a half dollars a year which would have to be made up either through increased taxes or by reductions of other programs of assistance to higher education.

A more recent proposal is the Educational Opportunity Bank, or Student Life Indenture Plan. Some of the proponents of this plan see it as a means of encouraging colleges and universities to charge all or most of their costs to the student, who would pay them by borrowing from the federally-sponsored bank and repay a portion of his income for thirty or forty years. Since the student pays the bank back, why do I categorize this plan as a device to channel federal funds to higher education through the student? Because the plan must provide for a student to "buy out." Therefore, it would be advantageous for students going into higher paying jobs to buy out, leaving the bank in the actually unsound position which would require federal subsidies.

The thrust of both the recent report of the Carnegie Commission on Higher Education, headed by Clark Kerr, and the report of the HEW Committee on Federal Support for Higher

Education headed by Alice Rivlin, is to expand equality of opportunity by allocating a substantial part of federal higher education funds directly to the students. Both Kerr and Rivlin have acknowledged that this will enable institutions to raise their tuition more readily. The inevitable consequence, of course, is an escalation which would require ever-increasing student financial aid funds to enable students to meet the ever-increasing costs of going to college. This trend would lead down the road to the point where the student would bear the primary burden for the support of higher education. If this becomes the accepted principle, why then should state legislators and private donors provide funds for college and university instruction? Affluent students presumably would have no difficulty paying the full cost of their education. Others would be given access to a national student loan bank so that they too would be able to pay the full cost. The only difference is that the affluent would be able to set about building a career and establishing a family debt-free, while everybody else would start with the equivalent of an educational mortgage ranging up to thirty thousand dollars or more, or have a long-term indenture on their future earning. If the spouse also went to college, the debt would be double.

Among the arguments in favor of channeling funds through the student are that it would provide students with freedom of choice in selecting their colleges; it would promote diversity; and it would give students greater power in the area of educational decision-making. Critics have suggested that students do not gain freedom of choice merely by having enough money. The institution still exercises freedom of choice in its admissions policies. Since this approach might well eliminate the need for publicly supported institutions, diversity would no longer be maintained. All colleges, as economist Milton Friedman suggests, would operate on a free market basis. The argument that channeling funds primarily through the student will eliminate governmental control is refuted by the present position of Congress to withhold federal funds from students whose actions it deems are contrary to the national interest.

In response to the position that students should pay a much greater share of educational costs, Howard Bowen, economist and president of the University of Iowa, estimates that "in real economic terms" the student already is paying about 75 per

cent of the cost of going to college when you take into account
foregone earnings. "My analysis," says Bowen, "leads me to the
conclusion that the recent rise in tuitions in both private and
public institutions should not continue, and that proposals involving the further escalation of tuitions are essentially unsound."
He proposes a national program based on aid to students to help
them meet college costs, and aid to instiutions to help keep college charges from rising.

Let us now take into consideration the third alternative,
which is to provide federal support directly to colleges and universities. Increasingly, higher education is becoming united in
the pursuit of this goal.

Last March a panel of college and university presidents
representing every type of institution appeared together before
the U.S. Senate Subcommittee on Education to discuss the Higher
Education Amendments of 1968. This historic occasion brought
together representatives of the American Council on Education,
the American Association for Higher Education, the American
Association of Junior Colleges, the American Association of State
Colleges and Universities, the Association of American Colleges,
the Association of American Universities, and the National Association of State Universities and Land-Grant Colleges.

They agreed that the immediate role for the federal government was to perfect and provide adequate funding for existing programs, particularly academic facilities. The second basic
objective of the federal government, they suggested, would be to
do everything in its power to help all institutions, public and
private, to keep their charges down. Third, they called the subcommittee's attention to the fact that every major higher educational association is represented on the panel as believing that the
next major move the federal government must make in its support of higher education is general institutional support. The
trick, of course, is to gain consensus for a specific proposal, and
that process is now under way.

In November, representatives of the seven major associations called a press conference to launch their drive for institutional support. University of Wisconsin President Fred Harvey
Harrington pointed out that many of the nation's colleges were
"near the breaking point" where they might have to raise tuitions
and fees drastically. Participants in the press conference concluded

that with unprecedented enrollments and constant pressure for new areas of service, the financial needs of colleges and universities have reached a critical stage. Needed is a substantial new program of institutional grants by the federal government to complement, not supplant or diminish, present programs in order to protect the essential integrity of colleges and universities.

During the past year, most of the seven associations have issued their own statements urging federal support for general institutional purposes. The American Council on Education recently released its statement, which said that such support was the "principal unfinished business of the federal government in the field of higher education." The council said that a program of institutional grants can have the following immediate effects:

1. It can provide a broad base of support for institutions to strive toward greater quality.

2. It can provide a broad base of support for other approved institutions to strive toward the quality that inadequate previous resources have denied them.

3. It can help institutions, public and private alike, to slow down the trend toward increased student fees—a trend that is in direct contradiction to all our efforts to provide broader access to higher education for all our young people.

Two pieces of legislation for institutional support are now being considered by Congress. One is known as the Miller Bill because its principal sponsor was the late Representative George Miller of California, who was until his death Chairman of the House Committee on Science and Astronautics. Its formal title is National Institutional Grants Program. It is designed to channel funds to all types of institutions on a formula basis for the support of education and research in the sciences, including the social sciences. The bill initially was developed by the National Association of State Universities and Land-Grant Colleges in cooperation with the American Association of State Colleges and Universities, and the spokesmen for higher education that testified on the bill all supported it in principle, but with certain suggestions for changes in the formula.

Last year, Representative Daddario's Subcommittee on Science, Research, and Development conducted extensive hearings on the Miller Bill that were largely exploratory. Prior to the current session of Congress, the subcommittee revised the original bill and increased the initial authorization from 150 million to 400 million dollars. This would indicate strong interest by the subcommittee, and the hearings that were held during the past two weeks appear to have strengthened its interest.

The declaration of purpose of the revised bill as introduced by both majority and minority members of the committee states, in part:

> Experience has shown that the project grant and contract system, almost the sole means through which the federal government now secures the research it requires from institutions of higher education, is inadequate. It is, therefore, essential to provide, as a supplement to other forms of support, an element of stable, long-range funding for research and instructional programs in the sciences to the institutions of higher education in such a fashion as to preserve their independence, integrity, and freedom of inquiry.

While most members of the higher education community who have testified on the bill would prefer an institutional grants program that would cover the humanities as well as natural and social sciences, political experience suggests it is best to begin in an area where federal participation has long been recognized and accepted. Implementation of the principle, if successful, could later be extended to the arts and humanities.

There is clear indication that the bill, as revised by the House committee, will be introduced in the Senate this week by several influential senators.

A second major institutional grants bill was introduced in the Senate by Senator Harrison Williams of New Jersey and twenty-seven other senators. This bill would authorize 1.5 billion dollars for the fiscal year beginning in 1970 for the support of comprehensive community colleges, and increase to 2.5 billion dollars by the fiscal year ending June 30, 1973. Initially, it would provide 10 million dollars for the development of state plans. The purpose of the bill is to assist the states in providing postsecondary education to all persons in all areas of each state for the purpose of strengthening, improving, and developing comprehensive community colleges.

Senator Williams, in introducing the bill, commented that the comprehensive community college represents a new level of education in the country—a level quite different from secondary education and higher education. He added that "education is not a private privilege; it is a public responsibility."

It has been assumed that the House Subcommittee on Education would not be particularly enthusiastic about general institutional aid. But the best case I have seen for institutional support was made by Representative Edith Green of Oregon, chairman of the subcommittee, and I end with a passage from her article.

As we move toward 1980, I would propose that educators begin to press for a policy of general federal aid to higher education with as few strings attached as is politically possible. Obviously, this demand will necessitate a favorable federal response before it can become a reality in terms of long-range practice. But the time to begin to campaign is now. We must convince ourselves and the federal agencies that colleges and universities know what they need and know how best to spend their incomes.

It seems to me, also, that to request this kind of a policy in federal spending will require forbearance on the part of all higher educational institutions. They must hold out for aid to meet their priorities as they conceive them. Federal money simply must not become a force to mold American education into conformity.

I do not intend to say that national purposes are of themselves inimical to the internal direction and goals of our colleges and universities. Students of the University of Iowa grow as individual researchers in work on space satellites. Students and faculty at Stanford benefit enormously from the government-sponsored Electron Accelerator. Yet I believe that public and private universities should maintain their own direction and let government come to them for the brains and programs which government needs. If the procedure works the other way round—government funding for specific governmental needs—then the universities and colleges lose the precious power to determine what is best for them: given their students, their faculties, their facilities, their long- and short-range purposes. . . .

If higher education bends its purposes to fit only the needs of the nation—as interpreted by one or more federal agencies with a great deal of money to spend—then the educational goals of diversity, excellence, and nonconformity may be in danger.[1]

[1] Edith Green, "Through A Glass Darkly: Campus Issues in 1980," in G. Kerry Smith (Ed.), *Stress and Campus Response* (San Francisco: Jossey-Bass, 1968).

Section II

University and
Community

    One might expect a sense of community to become increasingly important to members of the standardized, impersonal culture that now dominates our society; a sense of community, after all, is one of the means by which they can achieve what they most seek—identity and intimacy. In the first essay of Section II, Stanley Idzerda points out that if our society were really pluralistic, the development of "community" would take place naturally. But the majority of our citizens today, he asserts, reject most forms of communal identity.

    Whatever the direction of society, Idzerda's argument continues, it is nonetheless possible for a college to develop community—"community of older and younger peers, sharing in the development of each other's specifically human attributes." Idzerda presents the principles upon which such a model can be built. And he expresses the hope that if such colleges were successful, then college students, as they matured and as their lives came to center in the off-campus world, "might help create community outside the colleges."

    As one thus envisions "community," he sees strong understandings existing between the campuses and the great mass of adults. But Robert MacNeil, in the second essay of Section II, deplores the fact that such communication does not now exist. He places the blame on the journalist. Criticizing the profession for its "igloo of cliché," MacNeil asserts that in both print and broadcast the journalist has presented a distorted view to the public of what American college youth today stands for and how it behaves. And the reason, MacNeil goes on to say, is hardly ignorance or stupidity; the reason is that the fourth estate "is too much a part of the establishment. . . . It is a defender of the status quo." He suggests a new role for the journalist: "to be the link between the academicians, who have the discipline and the leisure and the creativity to make critical observations of the environment, and the great mass of people who do not have the ability or the detachment to make sense of it all."

The final essay of Section II, by Seymour Eskow, presents a new model for the community college. He paints it not as a service but as a force—a force for building a sense of community. But among the obstacles the two-year college faces, he makes clear, is the nineteenth-century rhetoric of the four-year colleges and the universities. Hurdles also exist, of course, within the junior college establishment itself. But the essay does not dwell on the obstacles. Its main message comes through its vision of a truly "community" college.

JOSEPH AXELROD

~⟨ **5** ⟩~

BUILDING COMMUNITY IN A PLURALISTIC SOCIETY

Stanley J. Idzerda

There is general agreement that our society is increasingly "pluralistic"; also, the groundswell of interest and discussion in "community" has been building for at least a decade. If pluralism is defined as a condition in which diverse religious, ethnic, racial or other groups cleave to their own traditions within their own group, while at the same time they live together within a single economy and polity in harmony and mutual forebearance, then quite clearly a pluralistic country like ours, by definition, has a whole range of "communities" to which people belong. Therefore, there is no issue.

But the proposition we have just stated makes too many typical assumptions about the content of pluralism and community. While we use pluralism as an ideal or as a model, all the evidence is that there is less pluralism today than fifty years ago, and most of the evidence seems to say that we are not interested in pluralism in the strict sense of the term. In his acute essay, "Education and Pluralism," Thomas F. Green of Syracuse University shows quite clearly that what we call our growth in pluralism is nothing of the sort; when we declare ourselves a pluralistic society we really mean that we are becoming an open society, a polity in which one's race, ethnic background, family connections, and regional affiliations make less difference each year; indeed, the whole educational system is geared to turn out people who can and should transcend their own particular background, people who can enter any aspect of national life without any personal wrench at all. The chief criterion of belonging to the open society is to be able to function productively with anybody, anywhere in the country. This means not pluralism, but assimilation to the needs of a national economy within the framework of representative secular democracy. The Gross National Product and the Democratic Way of Life thus bound a vast landscape in which we are free to do what we wish without the narrow, parochial, limited and constricting aspects of belonging to, or being identified with, some special group which limits our options or hinders our self-fulfillment in the mobility race.

An overwhelming majority of our college-age population (and their parents) want the open society and implicitly reject most forms of communal identity which might interfere with the opportunities of an individual to become whatever he wants to be. Social scientists have disputed the merits of the melting pot or assimilation view of American life; in one sense, these disputes do not matter, for that is the path Americans as well as many other modern peoples have taken.

At the same time, there is a great outcry about the price one pays for the open society. We have dispensed with or outgrown the consanguineous family and the nuclear family; we now have the atomistic family. We strive mightily to get out of material or spiritual ghettoes. We are intense about the significance of our individual, subjective destiny in the city of man. Each of our lives is a page out of a book by Harvey Cox. This is modernity; this is our life in the Secular City.

These might be worthwhile attributes for contemporary life, but they have one interesting result: the individuals benefiting from these opportunities and the freedom of the open society feel quite alone and they do not like it. The response to the loneliness is twofold: First, one attacks that very neutral and productive nonideological WASP-like group they hoped to become, namely the establishment; second, there is incessant chatter about love, concern, real relationships with others. In a word, we hunger for community, even while we make choices which militate against community.

As I have already suggested, the educational apparatus is at the center of those efforts to create the open, or as we seem to prefer to call it, the pluralistic society. We learn how to learn, to adapt, to cope with information, to be objective, and how to "communicate" with all comers. Most of what we learn must be value free, for strongly held values might bring on conflict with competing values. Then we could not have the proper fit in an open society, where performance in a neutral environment is the ultimate desideratum, where indeed the value-free computer will finally give us the most reliable answers to our needs and our questions.

Under such circumstances, transfer from one college to another becomes easier each year, because each one is so imitative of others. Each has the same orotund rhetoric introducing its catalog, but the rest of the catalog has little relationship to that introduction. Each introduction speaks with the accents of the aristocratic and apostolic intentions which colleges one day may have possessed, but the rest of the catalog deals in knowledge-purveying for any who wish it, for any use they deem necessary, including the further purveying of knowledge.

It seems self-evident that a good part of the students' motivation for attending college is to be able to share the fruits of an open society. They find the college the very model of that society. For instance, over the past twenty years, colleges have been dropping local habits, rituals, specific styles of life, and special commitments because they seemed outmoded or irrelevant. A century ago, those dropped traditions might have been replaced with new

rites and symbolic actions more suited to the times. Today they
are replaced with nothing, for we find it difficult to conceive of
that special set of habits or outlooks on one campus which might
bind us together and perhaps set us off from others. Each person
partakes of the neutral knowledge machine and belongs to nothing; many complain of collective apathy or anomie. Many retreat,
not to aristocratic or apostolic goals, but into radical subjectivism
or to the practical decision to wait until they get out to lead authentic individual lives. Some find the tension between their subjectivism and the knowledge machine so great that they revolt
and try to destroy the knowledge machine or to change the people
who tend it. Sometimes the revolt makes the tenders of the machine remember that they are not dealing with personnel, or
people, nor even individuals, but persons. When that realization
dawns, then something like communality or community may be
considered as a possibility.

I suggest that the college need not be a perfect simulacrum
of the larger society. It may be a model or a template of what the
larger society *could* be—a society in which each person is seen
as free and autonomous, as a knower and a valuer who is quite
aware that he does not know who he is until he knows to what
or to whom he belongs, and why. In a college with this intention
the student may discover what makes him a unique, nonreplicable
person at the same time that he discovers he cannot live in a
private universe. He may find that it is really worthwhile to join
the human race, and he may learn that before we make the decision to join that abstraction we call humanity, we must learn
how to live with small groups, some of whose values and habits
may be quite special and life enhancing. The college then may
not feel obliged to develop totally interchangeable units of mankind; rather, it may find that it must be a community, a group
of persons whose acts together and whose life together make a
colloquy as well as dialogue possible. Such a community would
not be afraid of internal conflict, because conflict can be rewarding and growth-inducing if communal intimacy is based on something more than propinquity on a two-hundred acre plot called
a campus.

Such a community cannot have separate administrative,
faculty, and student cultures, each based upon mutual ignorance,
amused toleration, or adversary-type confrontation. Rather it

would intend to be a group of older and younger peers, sharing in the development of each other's specifically human attributes in a life of learning based upon that fragile and carefully wrought set of attributes and habits we call scholarship. Such a developing community would realize that the practice of scholarship has as its goals the quickening of the life of the person, the development of his capacity for valuation, and the deepening of his moral and aesthetic sensibilities.

So perceived, scholarship would not be an inert acquisition, but would be a set of outlooks and habits acted out in the daily lives of those who seek to grow within it. It would be the exchange of thoughts, and insights; the reliance upon the traditions of the race and the making new of traditions which new challenges and circumstances call forth. So scholarship could, and does, lend to civility and creativity, for to be able to learn and think and act with all our powers means that we become artists with our own lives which we share with others. One might aver that this surely cannot be done with the pimply, subjective, apathetic or sullen crew we call today's college student. Some might say that to call an undergraduate a peer in learning is sentimentality. I suggest that those who call it sentimentality have not seriously taught freshmen lately.

Beyond the life of learning is the life of campus interaction. We are being forced to change our ideas about governance lately. First, the faculty wanted a piece of the action, and then the students dared to think that they, too, ought to participate in decisions that affected their lives. I think that few campuses where communal government has been tried have regretted the results. They may find life more complicated, less certain, and infinitely messier. But they also find that when communality of goals, purposes, and action is assumed, then more persons at all levels of responsibility become more responsible and sense that their lives are more fruitful. Can you imagine what might happen to the larger society if these expectations are brought to it? Can you imagine what might happen if students from such colleges were truly aware of their vocation to be fully human and to belong to their local community as well as to the human race?

The word *vocation* comes trippingly to the tongue in our society, yet it is borrowed from a religious context, and it reminds me that church-related colleges might still have a significant role, if they can leave off moaning about their dreadful condition and the multiple threats to their existence. I live and work in a Benedictine women's college, where most persons share to some degree or other an awareness that we are a continuing part of a fourteen hundred-year Benedictine tradition of scholarship, worship, and service. We also share the Benedictine familial habits of hospitality, modesty and gratitude. Of course the traditions and the habits are not always completely realized, but they continue to make their demands upon us, and all of them conduce to self-fulfillment and to community. I was first attracted to the college because I had never seen so many beautiful students gathered together in one place; suddenly I realized that what I took for beauty was more a reflection of happiness, of a common life, gratefully shared.

Now, I do not suggest that all church-related colleges emulate the Benedictine model. There are many mansions, many modes of spirituality, many outlooks which may reflect truly what a church-related college wishes to be and to bring to its small community, and then, as a felt obligation, to the larger world. Most church-related colleges are too small, too poor, and too obscure to attempt a fruitless imitation of what the larger and wealthier colleges are doing. One might conclude, then, that they will remain without significance in the mainstream of higher education. Not so. If each of these colleges can create a true community of interests, activities, and convictions on their campuses, they may change permanently the lives of many of their students. These students may become full persons, capable of independence, of actions based upon reflection, and of belonging to their fellow human beings. Such students sent out to the larger open society may have an ultimate significance. They might help create community outside the colleges, and something like a pluralistic society may one day come to pass.

6

ROLE OF THE FOURTH ESTATE

Robert MacNeil

I would like to consider whether all of the fourth estate—TV as well as the public press—might not respond better to the needs of society in these disturbing years than it now does. Early last summer, CBS bestirred itself to make a documentary called "Hunger in America," an emotional and vivid treatment, which caused the then Secretary of Agriculture, Orville Freeman, to protest self-righteously but eventually to modify his policies. The broadcast was effective but it produced nothing like the legislative impact of the recent public conversion of Senator Hollings of South Carolina. Eight months after the CBS program and just when the *New York Times* was publishing a detailed study of poverty, the senator discovered for himself that people in poor rural areas really were hungry. It seems incredible. It is difficult to conceive of anything more important for America to do than to make sure that its own people are adequately fed. It astounds me that priorities can become so muddled. Over thirty thousand

Americans have now been killed in Vietnam defending this country from an exceedingly abstract threat to its well-being and Senator Hollings has just discovered that there are hungry people in his own state.

So, an important role for the fourth estate—the public press, including television—should be to keep our elected representatives reminded of what the priorities are. But apart from the CBS and *New York Times* efforts, how much space has the press and television given to the question of hunger in America?

There are other urgent subjects. *Time* recently did a cover story on failures in American medicine. But that story has been ripe for years. The fact so often quoted is that America falls behind many other countries in preventing infant mortality. Now infant mortality is not a mysterious or fashionable disease. If you have a case of infant mortality in the family you do not talk much about it at cocktail parties. Infant mortality does not attract highly motivated fund-raisers or stimulate charity balls. But if the essence of American pragmatism is to solve solvable problems, then the priorities are again wrong. Cancer and arthritis are largely unsolved problems and it is marvellous that we are spending millions attempting to solve them. But infant mortality is a solved problem, requiring only basically adequate medical attention during pregnancy and childbirth. Yet we let it persist. For reasons of economics or fashion, we are pursuing dramatic goals in many fields while forgetting to apply uniformly throughout American society what we already know. And the media, the journalists, are too often as guilty as any other part of society of tolerating this perversion of our energies. NBC did a heart-rending documentary a few years ago about which of many needy patients would have his life saved by the artificial kidney machine and which would die for lack of it. Yet, in the spring of 1966, when I suggested to NBC a documentary on the state of American medicine (mentioning incidentally the facts on infant mortality), the suggestion was ignored.

The trouble here, I believe, is that journalism, print and broadcast, is too much a part of the establishment in American life: in business or politics or whatever. It is a defender of the status quo. It is not playing a sufficiently detached or independent role. It is not taking a long enough or cool enough look at society. It is too much a part of the society it observes. But I think that

America today is in such a state of moral confusion as to demand
what one might call a more existentialist role for its journalists.

The crises in American life are apparent. But one phenomenon which should be of special interest to people in the
universities, is what is going on in the minds of the students. It
is evident that this just-maturing generation finds many of
America's cherished goals despicable and is willing to do anything to make the system within which we pursue those goals look
ridiculous. Untrapped as yet by the domestic imperatives, they
find our materialistic pursuits absurd.

Now it is very unlikely that this generation has been specially chosen to stumble on absolute truth, but their extreme
ways of making their points do not automatically mean the dis-
affected young are all wrong about American society. I don't see
my profession exercising enough intelligent curiosity about the
student movement. It strikes me as a momentous historical phe-
nonemon that virtually an entire fresh generation in the world's
most powerful nation is utterly contemptuous of the way that nation is run and what it stands for. But when this extraordinary
phenomenon is covered by public media, we see only its violent
manifestations. We see the young outraging middle-class America
with nihilism or sex or drugs, or often simply with deflating
humor. And when journalists do make an effort to empathize,
they are spurned as too square, too alien, too much part of the
system even to be treated courteously. I think the students are
right about this. We—the fourth estate—*are* part of the system.
We bring to reporting their activities our own values, which are
largely the values of our audience. Unless we infiltrate the hippy
fringes of journalism, we are part—our newspapers, our magazines,
our TV stations—of what the young despise. And if it is like that
for young adults of our own race, economic class, and cultural
background, how deep must the alienation from our journalism
be for the poor white or the ghetto Negro?

Obviously, I am not suggesting that we must create a new
social caste for the fourth estate, living untouchable lives like the
embalmers of ancient Egypt. I just wish we were a little more untouchable than we are; that as part of an American journalist's
consciousness, he felt that moral concern, at least a moral objectivity, were essential to his profession.

We still live in a professional environment of inherited

cliché. We impose order on the disordered facts by squeezing them
into journalistic molds which are clichés. It is not only the mechanics of journalism, however, which are dominated by cliché,
but our professional image of ourselves. We acquire very early a
cliché that tells us to assume a hard-bitten, cynical approach to
the world, tempered now and then with a kind of mawkish sentimentality which passes for emotion. The cliché the American
journalist lives by also requires him not to be too intellectual.
Even the journalism schools have not eroded this anti-intellectual
bias in the profession: in some quarters they may have increased
it. And in all these cliches there is another implicit: that is that
the American journalist is not considered morally objective. It is
not thought to be part of his business to go beyond the systema-
tized prejudices which make up the conventional morality of the
moment. Obviously journalists have neither the time nor the
audience to indulge themselves as moral philosophers; but they
could be more engaged.

I have a feeling that the generation that is now busily tear-
ing the universities apart and fighting the police is moving this
country into a new era, morally and intellectually, and it may be
a very good moment for the fourth estate to ask, as the students
are, where we are going.

Material achievement is approaching a plateau on which
great ingenuity will be required of both consumer and persuader
to generate wanted goods. Internationally, something like security
has been in sight even though the Vietnam war has interrupted
the slow escape from the Cold War in Europe. In this generation,
America's greatest shame, the Negro condition, is at last being
faced. Economically, the society is undergoing a subtle but rapid
conversion to a form of modified socialism.

It is the failure to understand the imperatives behind these
and other changes—the moral and political necessities behind
them—that causes much of the discord and violence today. All
conditions of Americans show this failure to comprehend the
changes and it will be the role of the fourth estate to help them:
to help the embattled policeman to understand that he is not
judge, jury, and executioner but only the apprehender of suspects;
to help people like Mayor Daley and Vice-President Agnew understand that looting and arson are not capital offenses; to help
the National Rifle Association understand that gun worship is

not the highest form of civilization; to help the threatened urban white understand that he carries some of the historical guilt for the oppression of the blacks and that he must share his country with them; to help certain senators to see that there are people in this land of plenty who are—quite literally—hungry.

The fourth estate will not achieve this by living in its igloo of cliche. Newspapers and television will have to be willing to broaden the scope of their operations, to look at American society as a broader concept than crime, or race, or the economy; to have questions asked more often about where it is all going, about how well the society is realizing the ideals upon which it was founded. In short, with a population better and better educated vocationally, but apparently not equipped to comprehend the evolution of society, there must be a supply of better information to make the society basically comprehensible to itself. The schools and universities have only a vague contact because society comprises the people who have left. The churches do not seem able to contribute dynamically to an understanding of the forces loose in American society. The theater and the film industry are not deeply engaged. What else is there of an institutional nature? Elected officials are not trustworthy alone as guides, since it is the tradition of American democracy to be sceptical about a politician's visions.

So it must be up to our profession to be the link between the academicians, who have the discipline and the leisure and the creativity to make critical observations of the environment, and the great mass of people who do not have the ability or the detachment to make sense of it all. This has always been the journalist's role, of course, but it is all so much more complicated today that he must be a more complicated fellow to fulfill it.

What is needed, I think, is a more open line between the thinking community in the universities and the fourth estate if a greater part of the content of journalism is to be raised above the sensationalization and trivialization of new thought and the stereotyped handling of complex events. This can be achieved by several means. The academic community can deliberately foster a less patronizing attitude toward us, the popularizers. More universities can establish schools of journalism and in these schools try to elevate the concept of journalism, concentrating less on vocational skills (which in any case are quickly acquired on the job) and more on broadening the knowledge and outlook of the future journalists. Then I think there could be much wider use of schemes like the Nieman Fellowship in which a few mature journalists, over thirty and doing well in their profession, can go to Harvard for a year's intellectual nourishment. I would like to see such renourishment become the pattern in journalism as it is now in some other industries. Few professions exhaust one's intellectual resources as quickly as thoughtful journalism. The conscientious journalist today, unless he has had an unusually comprehensive education, soon finds gaps in his knowledge of the physical and political sciences, philosophy, religion, history, and economics. And psychologically, thirty-plus is the right age for a reflective pause in a career. I think universities would do a great service to the fourth estate and the American public by encouraging or organizing the endowment of many more such fellowships.

Finally I think people in the universities could help considerably to raise the tone and content of American journalism if they would, as so many academics do in Britain, practice more journalism themselves. It is not uncommon for eminent British figures in philosophy like Bertrand Russell or history like Hugh Trevor-Roper, as well as economists and scientists, to write for popular consumption in the daily press and to appear on television. I think the experience would have a salutary effect on your industry as well as ours. If I may be forgiven for abusing American hospitality by making a criticism, I think the American academic world might benefit from the discipline of having to write plain, robust English. Even subjects like philosophy and sociology requiring a specialized vocabulary can benefit from the effort of making an occasional rendering in the vernacular. Specialized jargon can often be the refuge of the unclear mind; few ideas are so complex that they cannot be expressed in plain English. So, I would like more cross-fertilization between the thinkers and the popularizers to help the fourth estate break out of its clichés, to help it comment more thoughtfully and subtly on today's environment. It is to the credit of the fourth estate that Senator Hollings discovered that there are people in his state who are hungry. But it is also an indictment of the fourth estate that it took him until February, 1969, to discover it.

7

COMMUNITY COLLEGE

Seymour Eskow

The question, "What does society expect of higher education?" is obviously designed to prompt the counterquestion, "Which society?" The Kerner Commission speaks of two societies: what does each expect of us, and if their expectations are not compatible, to which do we respond? And those of us who are on the phone suspect that there are a lot more than two societies. We are advised or implored or confronted by the Old Guard and the New Left, by the Manufacturers Association and the Great Books Society—seemingly by all the economic, social, and intellectual interests and factions and subcultures of our community, each with its own definition of the mission and the means and the clientele and the boundaries of higher education. Who, then, speaks for society?

And who answers for higher education? When state authorities, trustees, administrators, faculty members, and students

are engaged in a struggle for power, what agency or office or body
is able to marshal the resources of our colleges to answer the calls
of society clearly and quickly? And if it is our students who are
defining the expectations of society, who speaks for the students?
The activist and the hip students have captured the media as well
as the administration building, and they may indeed be the best
of the young, the leaven that will raise our society from the hang-
ups of technology, racism, and war—but our campuses continue
to be populated by other students as well—those who care about
proms and pennants, and upward mobility, and vocation. There
are still a surprising number of students who enjoy linear books
and departmentalized disciplines and feel no compulsion toward
immediate involvement in community affairs or other approaches
to relevance. Perhaps what has really changed is the intensity and
the resonance of the claims made upon us, and the bewildering
social context in which they are made. Now, as ever, the catalog
of demands is endless and contradictory: American society expects of its schools—everything.

There must continue to be sectarian institutions: colleges
free to choose the clienteles they will serve, the life-styles they
will endorse, the value systems they will support. The public community college, on the other hand, cannot easily or in good conscience refuse to acknowledge any petition. We come out of that
impulse in American life that created the public library, Chau-
tauqua and lyceum, the mechanics institute, agricultural extension, the land-grant college and, of course, the idea of a common
school: pragmatic, populist, mediating institutions that hope,
variously, to serve the individual and society by making culture
and learning and training widely available. Now society seems to
be asking for universal post-secondary education, and the public
community college is volunteering to do the job.

When the community college refuses an assignment, we
plead poverty or ignorance, not principle. Since we have found
no principle of exclusion, we propose to recognize all of the
talents and the temperaments in our communities, and to build
institutions and curricula and learning strategies that are responsive to all. State University of New York's motto, borrowed from
Carlyle, summarizes this fond intention this way: "Let each become all that he is capable of being." Contemporary versions are
borrowed from Rowan and Martin and the youth culture: "Whatever turns you on" and "Do your own thing."

Criticisms that refer to jack-of-all-trades, that list the dangers of attempting all things to all men, that build on supermarket and cafeteria metaphors are pertinent here. Cafeterias don't have to be overlit barns; they can be designed to make conversation and intimacy possible. And the supermarket is a delight, particularly for the self-motivated and independent: you can browse and sample and be surprised, or explore one department in depth. In any event, the specialty shop and the exquisite little restaurant cannot satisfy all of our hungers or all of our hungry. But merchandising metaphors are not satisfactory. A more useful metaphor is the city: we accept the fact that the city is here, try to mirror the city in our institutional forms and environment, defend the civilities of the city against pastoralists and nostalgia. Educational problems and failures are like city problems and failures: we have curricular slums and pockets of intellectual poverty. The best minds of our nation live in the fashionable academic neighborhoods. But we in the community colleges live and work in the other America. We are trying to bring something of value to those not rich enough, or able enough, or motivated enough, or ready enough for the other institutions. We are trying to find ways of reaching and teaching those who are not moved or touched by the versions of learning offered elsewhere. At this moment we need help more than we need satire and metaphors. If only our friends in the senior colleges and universities would drop the rhetoric of "rigor" and "standards" and "discipline" for a little while and work with us! We need their help to multiply the options we offer, to create a dense and pluralist urban milieu for all the citizens of our communities. If we work together toward the ideal we all share, we can change the future.

The community college of the future will form coalitions of concern and service with the other agencies of the community: with the public schools, with whom we shall share teachers, students, and instructional media; with the school and public libraries in our region, pooling our collections and clients; with business and industry, health and social agencies, whose work stations and personnel will provide classrooms and teachers away from campus; with community theater and the symphony orchestra and all of the cultural apparatus of the locality.

Our future campuses will recognize the context of the communities in which they are built, the presence or absence of opportunities for learning elsewhere. Some will become complex centers of new communities whose libraries, classrooms, and theaters will be shared by the young student, local agencies and groups, and the general citizenry. Others may have no elaborate central campus, but will permeate the community, sharing libraries and theaters already existing, renting or building classroom space where it will be accessible to the subcommunities of a region. Some will do both. The community colleges will try variations of the cluster college concept, searching for administrative forms that create small and diverse communities coexisting within the framework of the mass institution.

The community college will create agencies and institutes to provide guidance, training, and cultural opportunities for subgroups in the community. Many of our current collegiate premises and practices, useful in other times and for other students, will be scrapped or modified. The pressure for full-time and continuous attendance will be abandoned, and many students will alternate between work and college and day and evening attendance. The women whose children are in school will be increasingly visible in our classrooms during the day, particularly if we build child-care facilities, so that the fiction that adult education occurs only during the evening will disappear. For many of our students, degrees and credits will be irrelevant and hence will be discarded. For the others, we shall see the uselessness of fixed sequences and requirements; indeed, we may find nothing but good resulting when we permit the literary or artistic student to delay or waive the mathematics or science course that turns him off.

Despite the promise of a cybernated paradise furnishing to all necessities and luxuries without human labor, the community colleges will continue to offer occupational education in the future for those students who find it meaningful. The colleges may finally drop the rhetoric of "transfer" and "terminal" curricula which —even now—no longer helps very much. We shall try new, more flexible mixes of general education, vocational education, and work experience, including apprenticeships.

We shall face up to the probability that the liberal arts are now a collection rather than a curriculum, and if the senior colleges will give us their help, we shall try to find new ways to coherence. We shall have to learn more about our student subcultures, their learning styles, and the teaching strategies that are appropriate for those styles. Community service, study abroad, independent study, inquiry and textual analysis, programmed materials—for whom are they right and for whom are they irrelevant? Perhaps the matching of students and modes of learning will be the job of the new breed of counselor in the college of the future.

We cannot now be sure whether our teachers of the future will learn these new teaching strategies on our own campuses or in graduate school. When our teachers come from graduate classrooms that themselves use the new instructional styles, that themselves demonstrate the excitement of inquiry and the Socratic dialogue, then our own classrooms will inherit the fruits of such developments.

Is this vision hopelessly Utopian?—to bring to each community in America a vital center of culture and learning, drawing its sustenance from all elements of the community linked to the larger powerhouses of learning throughout the country, its lines of communication open to all of the citizens of the community, undertaking to put them in touch with those ideas, issues, men, and experiences that might lend order, meaning, and color to their lives.

Section III

Black and Urban

The six essays of this final section of Part One deal with two overwhelming problems in American society and with their impact on American higher education: the racial crisis and the deterioration of the American city. The basic tone of Section III is set in the first essay, by James Farmer: "things are wrong, something is wrong, somewhere we have failed. . . ." Farmer argues that if our civilization does not move toward genuine pluralism, it will not survive.

In the two essays following Farmer's, Charles Hamilton and James Godard discuss major problems in curriculum planning and admissions policy. Their essays focus on black studies programs and on minority group access to higher education. Both authors deal with their subject in its immediacy, giving many practical suggestions, and they also touch on some of the wider facets— for example, the erosion of conventional academic standards, which many administrators admit is the problem that "worries" them most. Colleges and universities are increasingly applying quite new standards—that is, yardsticks other than the traditional criteria for judging excellence—in reaching decisions about admitting students, hiring faculty, approving new curricula, defining how academic credit may be earned, and awarding degrees. Clearly, this is more than a black studies or minority group problem. The entire system—with its traditional definition of courses and credits, admission and graduation requirements, faculty quali-

fications, and control of program approvals—the entire network of conventional "standards" is being called into question.

The next three essays concentrate on other, equally important dimensions of the American urban campus. Warren Rovetch's essay stresses the importance of merging campus and town planning, and presents the new principles that the creative city campus planners are now following. The two final essays are about San Francisco State College, drawing lessons from the 1968–1969 events on that campus that might be useful to administrators and faculty elsewhere. Mervin Freedman's thesis is that the problem of San Francisco State is the problem of all urban campuses—indeed, the basic problem of American urban society generally. What happens at San Francisco is therefore, in a sense, prophetic. Robert Smith, in the essay that ends Section III, presents thirteen "perceptions" (as he calls them) gleaned from his experience as the acting president of San Francisco State who refused to cast his lot with the chancellor and trustees or yield to the pressure of general public opinion.

JOSEPH AXELROD

~{ 8 }~

FROM POLARIZATION
TO PLURALISM

James Farmer

It would be a disservice to the nation and to its peoples, all of
them, to expect any magical, simple panacea-like solution to
the enormous and tormenting problems which confront us. We
are going through a phase—I trust it is a phase—in our nation
where the polarization is more severe than ever before, where the
tensions are greater than at any time in the nation's history since
the reconstruction days following the Civil War, and when the
confusion is greater than it has ever been, among both white and
black all over the country. Hardly anyone knows where to turn,
many grope and substitute rhetoric for programs and the nation
as a whole is now groping beyond the rhetoric searching for programs. Even when a particular victory is won for human dignity
and freedom, it is often seen only as a single separate event and
its total underlying meaning is not understood. For example, we
might say that the hot dog which was so hard fought for and so

dearly won in the early sixties was a lot more than a hot dog, but the nation never really understood that and I am not sure that most of us who were activists in the movement understood the full meaning of that hot dog.

The hot dog was a symbol. It was a symbol of decency and dignity. It was a symbol of the dreams of man, a symbol of the dream deferred, of human dignity and equality.

When those brave, those courageous, those beautiful black college kids in the South were sitting in at the lunch counter demanding coffee and hot dogs, they were not hungry and they were not thirsty. What they were really asking for, in short terms, was a right to sit there and be served like anybody else because they were dignified human beings. But, in more profound terms, they were asking for complete equality in the land. They were asking for the right to tread the earth with the same dignity with which others tread.

The nation gave us the hot dog in the Civil Rights Act of 1964. The hot dog was very easy to give and very simple, but it did not, partially because it did not understand the demand, give us what the hot dog symbolized—the right to overall dignity and decency.

We did improve the upward mobility of many black people in the country, specially those who are in the middle classes. The black Ph.D. has many people and many institutions vying for his services. The college graduate who is black has it easier than he had it in the past and that is partly because of the efforts of the hot dog movement. But for the masses of the people who are not in the middle classes, nor college graduates, nor high school graduates, certainly not Ph.D.s, the progress has been pitifully small and slow. In some ways, to be utterly realistic, we have been on a treadmill and the masses have slipped back.

The Bureau of the Census just a few days ago issued some statistics indicating that while the number of white poor families in our cities has declined, the number of black poor has increased, and while the average income of black women who are employed seems to be catching up to the average income of white women who are employed, that of black males is lagging far, far behind.

The nation has now become aware of hunger in its stark reality, the kind of hunger which distorts and cripples and damages the child's brain in the first four years of his life and makes it extremely difficult for him to have any kind of dignified life, no matter how much enrichment is put into it later on. The kind of hunger that we thought of as existing only in India or China or Africa, we find to some extent in some parts of our own country.

We are aware of that now. The nation sees it and its eyes are open. We are aware that we have poor in our midst and the anti-poverty program has helped to bring about that awareness. So did the civil rights struggle in the dramatic decade from 1954 to 1964. Up until that time we were hardly aware of the poor in our land. We had read about them, distantly, and we knew that welfare money was going some place, so obviously it was going to some poor. But there must be something wrong with people who are poor—was the general consensus. They must be lacking somehow in incentive and/or initiative if they were unemployed and getting welfare. Such thinking takes the poor out of sight and sweeps them under the rug. We didn't see them, whether we were black or white.

The black spokesman and white spokesman alike spoke from the vantage point of the middle classes. They were the ones we saw and it was they with whom we dealt. Our transportation did not take us through the communities of the poor. The roads and streets by-passed and skirted them; elevated trains went over them and subways under them; and those who came in from the suburbs on the commuter trains scarcely looked up long enough from their *Wall Street Journal* to see the pain and misery through which they were being transported.

The poor were hardly even aware of their own existence. They went through life fighting for tomorrow's meal. But now they are bursting with a sense of their existence and have suddenly found a voice, a voice that to many of us will seem raucous, but it is their voice so long muted that is now being raised and is being heard about the nation. Because of this, something has happened to the rest of us. We are now not so sure of many of our values and of many of the myths which we have held dear, because they are being shaken. We are now questioning ourselves.

I see this as a hopeful sign. A few years ago, most of us were smug, feeling secure, not shaken, certain that where there was dissent and where there was disease, the blame must rest with the dissenters and the diseased.

That was a dangerous situation, far more dangerous than today. Now we find Americans accepting dissent. It is coming through that things are wrong, something is wrong, somewhere we have failed with the promise.

One of the myths that is being shattered, and I think that this should have been shattered long ago, is the myth that our nation has been a melting pot. It is not a melting pot. It is not homogenized.

The black man has sought to be in a melting pot and the pot would not melt, would not melt for him. It did not really melt for others. What it was was a pluralistic society. And this is grand and it is glorious; we should honor it. That is what the raucous black voices on the college campuses are saying, though oft times they may not know that that is what they are saying. We must honor that pluralistic society because the various ethnic inputs that have gone into it to make it what it is are proud and are great, and without them the total culture would not be what it is.

We must honor it in the same way Canada honors its input of ethnic varieties. When a new group comes to Canada, they do not say as we have tended to say in the past: Forget your past, forget who you are, who you were, and become somebody else; become like all of us.

They say instead, "How grand that you are different. Why not hold a festival and a parade. Wear your traditional dress and let us come and be with you. Dance your dances and let us learn them so that eventually we can dance them with you. Sing your songs that we may learn to sing them with whatever rhythm lies therein because, you, too, are a part of us. But do not forget what you are because if you lose that, then we have lost something, too." That is the pluralistic society.

We have tended to disfavor in our land the subcultures which have made up the national culture, feeling somehow that if we favored or emphasized those that we would weaken the fabric of the national culture. I believe we were wrong. I think the black man is now trying to become hyphenated. He does not seek to be unblack, to forget that he is a member of a group. We held out to him this aspiration: "Think of yourself as an individual and if as an individual you can gain a little money and education, then you will be acculturated and as an individual can be assimilated and will become in effect a white man with an invisible black skin."

This was the impossible dream that was held out. The black man quested after a kind of self-abrogation. We preached and we legislated color blindness. We would go to an employer and say, "Be color blind. Do not see the color of the job applicant or the employee. Be oblivious to it. Merely hire the best qualified person who happens to apply." It didn't work.

We went back to him two years later and said, "How many black people did you hire?" He said, "How in the world should I know? I am color blind." A visual check indicated that he had hired none. So, why did he say, "I am color blind"?

A funny thing happened in one of CORE's demonstrations a few years ago which illustrates how the law works in this regard. We had a campaign against job discrimination in the Bronx in New York in a chain of hamburger joints and we used the usual techniques. We sat in and we picketed; we marched and had garbage and other refuse thrown at us.

Finally management sat down to negotiate and they said, "We have discriminated in the past and we would like to change that. You are absolutely right. We have no black employees above the level of janitors. Now, we would like to correct that and indeed we will need fifty sales personnel within the next three months." This was their euphemism for counter people.

"However," they said, "we would like to hire blacks, but we can't do it because we get our employees through the State Employment Service and if we go to the State Employment Service and say, send us fifty black persons, they would immediately charge us with a violation of the state fair employment practices law, which says that you may not advertise for nor hire persons on the basis of race, color, creed, or national origin." This is one of the color blind laws.

Well, I called a friend of mine who worked for the State Employment Service and said, "You realize that the law is a bit archaic." He said, "Yes, it was in the color blind era. Now, we emphasize color consciousness to wipe out color inequity and discrimination."

I said, "Be that as it may, we have a problem." And I explained it to him. I said, "What do you suggest?" His answer was to have this gentleman call him and tell him of his needs and he would then call the office on 125th Street in Harlem and ask him to send fifty applicants regardless of race, color, creed, or national origin.

The attempt at color blindness was a failure. The reason it failed is that we had not taken into account the force and impact of racism in our nation's society. Not all of us are bigots, of course. That is not what the Kerner Commission report was saying. But it is now universally recognized among those who have studied the problem that all of us to some extent have been conditioned by the racism in our culture and our textbooks mirror this conditioning.

We developed a stereotyped image. Up until recent years, until the NAACP was successful in a long campaign in the fifties, the image through the entire media has been the image of a clown or a buffoon or a petty criminal or a childlike oaf whom one might love as he loves a pet and may perhaps pat on the head like a puppy dog, but could not respect, for it did not merit respect.

To some extent the black man himself has been inculcated with such an image. We have to de-program ourselves. The black youth have smashed that old image. Now they stand ten feet tall and rather than try to conceal the kinks in their hair, they honor it and applaud it by letting it grow long. When our youth ask that we introduce courses about their history, their culture, their heritage, their demands are essentially sound. I believe them to be in the best interests of the nation, not only for black youth but for white youth, too.

If the demands are excessive, then what demands are not? As an old trade union organizer, I know that one sets demands at a point from which he expects to negotiate—even when he says these demands are not negotiable. That is a part of negotiation. For example, in the case of dormitories, if any group among our students have much in common—a common past, a common present, common problems, and possibly a common future—then, naturally, they want to live together as a group. While this flies in the face of many of the values which we have accepted in the past, it is right that they should. Such a demand is not unreasonable provided the group does not force others to join it who do not wish to, and provided they do not exclude from their fellowship those who would join them, even if they are not members of the same ethnic group.

This, then, is an example of a solution that does not fly in the face of the values which we hold dear and which are important to the nation. Ultimately, then, as the black man finds his pride in his identity and his dignity for which he is so desperately searching, perhaps the polarization will be over, if we are creative and imaginative enough, because then we will not have to shout so loudly that black is beautiful, for we will know it and feel it deeply, in the marrow of our bones.

We are now shouting in order to drown out the millions of voices outside and the millions of voices inside which have been telling us the opposite. That is the way the process of de-programming and de-conditioning works.

What will the end result be? Fitting the black man into the framework of a pluralistic culture as a proud and equal partner. All of the groups in the nation which help to make it great can then accept this ethnic entity, recognize it and honor it. That is that kind of future we are looking toward.

I disagree with those of my colleagues who talk about going back to Africa. I am not going back to Africa. Neither are most black people in the country. I love Africa, mind you, but not as a place to go home to. I love Africa, rather, as the home of my ancestors. The first time I went to Africa in 1958 it was almost a religious experience. I felt like falling on my knees and kissing the earth. I had in my luggage an empty bottle which one black friend had handed me and asked me to fill with water from the river Nile and bring it home to him. I had a silver box which another had given to me and asked me to fill with soil from Mother Africa and bring it to her so she could plant a flower in it. I also had a letter from my father, an old scholar, who was not given to an outward show of emotion, saying, "Son, when you get to West Africa, look up my relatives and tell them I am doing well." Of course, he had no idea who his relatives were or where they were. As I look back on it, the feeling that I had I think was not really different from the feeling that Irish-Amercans, say, of the third generation might have going home to the Old Sod. It is a kind of search for roots, particularly poignant when the man systematically has had his roots denied to him and has been told that he had none. Africa—a search for roots, source of ancestry, pride, but not a place to go home to. My home is here as much as is anybody's; I didn't come over on the Mayflower but I met the boat. As Whitney Young has put it, we have too much sweat in this land to give it up. We are going to stay here and fight for what is ours. And we hope to build. Our problem is to work out some rapprochement where we can have a decent life for our people here. This is where the future is going to be, if there is a future. This is the destiny.

I don't envy you who are educators. I don't envy those of you who are in higher education any more than I do those who are in elementary and secondary education. Your task is enormous and you are on the firing lines and you will of course be in a crossfire as never before because now the black community recognizes that education is the key—if there is any single key.

We must recognize—and people in higher education must be as concerned with it as others—that the black child in many instances is from grade one pointed toward failure, for the tests, like the instructional materials that are used, all too often have their built-in culture bias.

The IQ tests don't yield an intelligence quotient. What they really yield is a white middle-class quotient. Now, there is nothing wrong with being either white or middle class or both. It just so happens that there are many people who are neither.

Look at the test which, for example, is given to first grade children in many schools. In one question there are pictures of three men, one man in a tuxedo; the second man in work clothes; a third man in a business suit; the children are asked which of these is a father going to work. Obviously the child who is poor or from a rural area, or whose father is a waiter or musician who goes to work in a tuxedo—such a child will fail this question unless he has had extraordinary exposure.

In Bedford-Stuyvesant, Brooklyn, 87 per cent of the kids who graduate from high school come out with a general diploma. Many of these young people, as you know, read at a third and fourth grade level after graduating from high school. Colleges around the country are wrestling with the problem. How are we going to get into our fellowship those who are so inadequately prepared?

I think the colleges and universities have a tremendous responsibility. Even if the cause lies in the home or in the community or in elementary school or in pre-school, all of us are going to have to roll up our sleeves and see if we can compensate for the damage that has been done. That means you lower your "standards" as you seek to recruit black, Puerto Rican, Mexican-American, American-Indian, white poor. What will that do to educational standards? Everyone is in favor of high educational standards, but to me that means standards at *exit* rather than entrance requirements.

Somehow we have got to take in those who would not otherwise get an education. We must be able to determine the potential of inadequately prepared applicants, select those who *have* potential and then repair the damage that has been done.

The nation cannot afford the loss. Bank Street College did some experiments several summers ago that are relevant here. They took twenty sixteen-year-old to twenty-one-year-old blacks and Puerto Ricans. Their reading skills at the beginning of the summer were zero to third grade. At the end of the summer they were all reading at least up to a sixth grade level. One youngster had zero skills at the beginning and at the end, he wrote poetry. Another with third grade skills at the beginning wrote a one-act play at the end. New vistas opened to him. In these and other ways, we have got to stop a terrible human waste; and the only way I see to bring black people into the framework of the nation is by all joining hands in this tremendous educational task.

Look at Israel to see what is possible. Their program dealing with the oriental Jews who come from disadvantaged lands can provide a lesson for us. Volunteer social workers and volunteer teachers visit parents during the months before their child is born, talking with them about the necessity for arousing the child's curiosity and learning capacities and the importance of turning play into a learning experience. They lend the parents toys which have educational value. They visit them periodically and try to repair the damage of the past so that it will not be self-perpetuating—poverty and deprivation breeding deprivation and poverty.

The problem is thus not unsolvable. We will—and must—get over the polarization. It's a transitional phase. If we can avoid the confrontation of which some speak for the next few years, as a nation we can survive. Confrontation tears up the country. No one will win. All would lose, and most of all those of us who are black. If we survive the next few years, then I think we can build sound and solid bridges. We are human and it is essential that people learn to live together. We must all live in fact on three planes—as individuals, as members of a group, and as human beings—and we live on those three planes simultaneously.

The black man had sought to ignore one of them and he cannot in a pluralistic society. Humanity transcends race, yes, but how can one love humanity unless he also loves himself? If he hates himself, it is not possible for him to love mankind.

America can become America for all its people then. In the words of Langston Hughes: "Let America be America again; America never was America for me—the home of the brave and the land of the free. The free? Who said free? Not me. Surely not me. Yes, I say it plain: America never was America for me; but by this oath, I swear, America *will* be."

~9~

RELEVANCE OF BLACK STUDIES

Charles V. Hamilton

College curricula today in relation to the black society should have a heavy component of direct experience. It is important to attempt to combine classroom studies with practical, in-field application. Many students, especially black students, are interested in "relevant" courses. To many of them, this means moving out of the ivory tower and into the community. I think this is valid. And not only to satisfy the action-oriented nature of much of the youth today, but precisely because only by redefining the classroom can we really get at much of the data. In addition, black Americans are in an urgent stage of development. This means that education, wherever possible, must be related functionally to particular needs which speak to that urgency.

This is especially important where the college or university has a relatively sizeable and growing black student body, and where, as in many places, there is an accessible black community. This would mean, for example, courses in economics which dealt

specifically with the problems and prospects of development of
producer and consumer co-ops and other business ventures in the
ghetto. It would mean courses in political science that dealt with
the problems and prospects of development of viable, independent grass roots electoral and pressure group structures: given
certain political constraints, what are the problems involved in
organizing potentially successful representative groups in low
socioeconomic black communities? The emphasis is on academe
for action, on implementation, on development. Such programs
have existed in certain fields for a number of years. For example,
I would like to call attention to the Jewish Studies program at
Roosevelt University in Chicago. It has language, literature, culture studies, and history courses, leading to a bachelor's degree.
Note the catalog statement:

> The Jewish Studies program is designed to meet the needs of
> (1) students who have careers or career-plans specifically re-
> lated to education and social service in the Jewish community;
> and (2) students who would like to secure a knowledge and
> appreciation of Jewish culture.

We must be prepared to rethink our definition of what
constitutes a "qualified" instructor. Perhaps the traditional criteria for hiring professors would have to be revised. A Ph.D. with
a list of publications behind his name might have to give way to
an indigenous activist who has knowledge of the subject not recognized by our established methods of judgment. This is not fatal.
It might threaten some of us who have spent years in the library
stacks, but modernization always challenges the old. Neither
should we be concerned especially with accreditation. I am talking about substantially *new* criteria, *different* principles for judgment of excellence, relevance, and substance. The accrediting
agencies will have to come to terms with this, lest they—like many
of us—be relegated to realms of anachronism. Moreover, we
should build into our pre-med and pre-law and other preprofes-
sional programs courses dealing with the responsibility of these
professions for helping in the development of a black society. I
might add that many young doctors, dentists, and lawyers already
are working this out on their own as they enter these professions. It is about time, I suspect, that we caught up with our
students.

We should allow for more work-study arrangements whereby students would be able to go out into the communities for a part of their school year and work and study. I urge that we think in terms of setting up storefront branches in the communities. The models are already there in agricultural extension work, and some colleges and universities do this in other fields. I am not advocating some glamorous, dramatic "Let's go to the people" kind of idolatry of the poor. If what I am suggesting is seen as gimmickry to serve as a substitute for the dull, 10–10:50, MWF format, then I am not being understood. I am not interested in making our curricula more exciting for the sheer sake of excitement, but more relevant for the sake of a more meaningful education.

It is important to incorporate more material on black Americans into our lower-level introductory courses: history, economics, political science, psychology, sociology, literature. Obviously, much could be done here by simply breaking out from the reading lists professors hand out year after year. Those lists (and our lecture notes) must be revised now. In a real sense, many of us must re-tool—almost in front of our students. But we must recognize that a substantial portion of lecture material in those innumerable introductory courses is lacking of meaningful reference to black people.

At the same time, we can develop specialized courses on black history, black literature, black politics, black psychology, and so forth, at the upper, advanced levels. Clearly, there is enough material to justify individual courses in many of these fields. I suggest that we take care and not move hastily here, precisely because there is indeed a lot to learn. If the college cannot get a qualified person to teach these advanced courses, I would be opposed to some of the makeshift efforts I see taking place around the country; many professors are literally throwing together highly technical courses with virtually no knowledge of the material. Some places have tried to solve the problem by bringing in guest lecturers during the course of the semester. Perhaps this is an answer for the time.

We should not overlook the fact that many of our own advanced courses must come under scrutiny themselves. Some professors do not like the idea of tampering with their pet courses. Thus, they would prefer the department create a separate course dealing with a black subject. But this is intellectually dishonest. I spoke recently with a professor in a Missouri college who indicated that in his advanced courses on international economic development, it never occurred to him to deal with the economic involvement of private American investments in South Africa—and what that means politically and economically. Indeed, most of our curricula around the country are woefully lacking of any reference to America and her lack of significant economic aid to Africa. Anyone who regards himself as a seeker after knowledge has an obligation to raise these kinds of questions in his courses.

Curricular changes are necessary not only where there is a black student body or an adjacent black community; in that all-white, surburban-locked college, the need is equally great. These places must have courses that reinterpret the impact of slavery and oppression on both white and black Americans. White students need to know the history of black Americans as much as black students. White students need to know the poetry of Langston Hughes and Countee Cullen as well as that of Walt Whitman and Carl Sandburg. Those students need to know the sociopolitical studies of W. E. B. DuBois and Charles Johnson as well as those of Max Weber and V. O. Key. They need to examine and understand the impact of Marcus Garvey as well as that of William Jennings Bryan. Unless these all-white—and realistically speaking, likely to remain all-white for some time—colleges begin to revise their curricula, they will cotinue to graduate students into middle-class mediocrity. They will be mediocre precisely because they will be incomplete in their knowledge of this heterogeneous world and puzzled by the pluralistic forces beginning to make their voices heard everywhere. While my central theme is the curricular changes to meet the needs of a black society, I want to stress that those needs cannot be met if we focus only on the black society. That society cannot be understood or helped in a vacuum. Indeed, I would go further and suggest that many of the problems in the black society begin without question with the ignorance and insensitivity in the white society.

Finally, I propose that each college and university in this country establish immediately a mechanism for curricular evaluation. Yes, another faculty committee! Such a group would conduct penetrating research, in-depth examination of the courses offered on their campuses. The goal would be to advise professors and departments about ways to make relevant changes. We cannot of course dictate to individual professors what each should teach. I am talking about advising them. Understandably, many of the professors need such substantive advice (the example earlier of the international economics course is pertinent here), precisely because they are products themselves of relatively insensitive graduate departments that have shortchanged them in their education. We must be careful to guard against the situation whereby a black studies department is set up and then no further attention is paid to the rest of the curriculum.

The committee could be composed of knowledgeable black students, faculty in the field, and black consultants in particular fields of expertise. Their findings would be advisory—not mandatory—but if my professor-colleagues are the rational, open-minded people they claim to be, this could open up a fruitful area of intellectual discourse.

As we work out solutions, let us recognize that there is more to be gained from charting the future than from apologizing for the past. There is more to be gained from challenging our minds than from blowing our minds. There is more to be gained from moving fearlessly ahead than from trying to hang on to entrenched established interests.

OPPORTUNITY FOR THE "CULTURALLY DISTINCT" STUDENT

James M. Godard

We are increasingly conscious of the necessity for colleges and universities to recruit students whose backgrounds would not have stimulated them to apply for admission to college—indeed, whose performance levels on the traditional criteria for admission would have been barriers to their acceptance. Recently, however, we have realized that goodwill and open doors are not enough to change the situation and that educational and ethical implications penetrate deeply into decisions involving new policies regarding recruitment and admission of these students.

If it is true that some form of education beyond high school is necessary for a large proportion of the population if they are to realize the opportunities now open, and if it is true that such factors as poverty, neighborhood environment, and ethnic background prevent many people from continuing their education, then colleges and universities must reexamine not only policies and practices regarding recruiting students but also their financial resources for providing aid to those students.

Another forward step was taken when we became aware that remedial programs in reading and other basic tool skills did not meet the needs of "culturally distinct students." Many colleges and universities have long accepted a number of students who fall below cutoff points on entrance examinations and have often provided remedial work for them. This type of special training has met with remarkable success when deficiencies in reading, composition, and mathematics were the direct causes of the difficulty. But the special needs of culturally distinct groups, and particularly of black students being admitted to predominantly white institutions, involve such dimensions as alienation and search for identity, deficient resources in counseling, and a curriculum typically based on the history and achievements of European culture.

The distance from desegregation to integration is a long one. Integration is a happening; it is something that happens to individuals in situations where communication and shared experiences across cultural barriers become a reality. The steps taken to provide desegregation on a campus are not the same steps that may create a setting for the happening we call integration. The decision to recruit and admit "culturally distinct" students whose performance records may not meet conventional standards deserves not only the undergirding of goodwill and guided studies programs but also new concepts of counseling resources and of student life on the campus.

Still another step in our thinking may have to be taken before we can expand the role of the college in the education of culturally distinct students. We must see why these students should be a part of the campus *for the sake of all students*. We must recognize that we have entered a critical point in history where intercultural understanding is necessary for survival; our age demands the presence on the campus of people, both students and faculty, of diverse cultural backgrounds, and a curriculum based on intercultural concepts in all branches of learning. Our students' search for identity will not arrive at maturity until they see themselves both in relation to their own culture *and* in relation to other cultures. Pierre Teilhard de Chardin has most force-fully expressed the urgency of moving out of a narrow academic provincialism in his concept of the convergence of man upon him-self.[1] The period of the dispersal of man around the planet and the formation of semi-isolated cultures is over. Man is inevitably converging upon himself. As a consequence, intellectual or cul-tural "apartheid" will be disastrous. Convergence requires effec-tive communication and understanding among diverse social groups. It is just as important for advantaged students as for the disadvantaged on a college campus that the disadvantaged be there.

An open-door policy that admits culturally disadvantaged students without providing for resources to meet their needs is disastrous. This point has particular significance when the admis-sion includes students who will constitute a racial or cultural minority on a campus. We have learned that desegregation does not necessarily result in integration, that in a mixed student body alienation may be keenly experienced. We have learned that the needs of so-called disadvantaged students extend far beyond the traditional remedial programs in reading and mathematics and English grammar.

Some of the resources required by an open-door policy are the following:

1. Recruiting: New student recruiting procedures—and at least one new staff member who will know how to communicate with potential candidates, with high school counselors and Up-ward Bound staff, and with community people who may provide information on motivation and aspiration factors.

2. Counseling: The services provided for disadvantaged students must cover a broader spectrum than those normally pro-vided, as these students often have not had the advantage of family or neighborhood counseling suited to the type of planning they must now do or to the kind of problems they must now face of personal identification in a new social milieu.

3. Instruction: The traditional patterns of courses in read-ing and basic tool subjects alone will not meet the requirements for compensatory learning. To some extent these learning experi-ences must be provided through instructional methods included in regular courses, which will necessitate special training for some

[1] *Phenomenon of Man* (New York: Harper, 1959).

faculty members. Much experimentation and research are still needed in this field.

4. Courses of study: The inclusion of material in the field of black culture becomes very important, particularly in relation to the identity growth of black students. In addition, the planning of majors appropriate to the aspirations of these students must be reviewed. In other words, the curriculum must be examined in terms of its relevance to the changes in the student body.

5. Campus ethos: When a college takes steps to diversify the composition of its student body in terms of socioeconomic and ethnic backgrounds, there should be a clear awareness that changes will occur in the campus ethos and in community life. Many tragic events and destructive polarizations may be prevented, or at least alleviated, by thoughtful advance planning. To lay a base for such planning, student and faculty leaders should participate both in the decision-making to alter the admissions practices and in the formulation of new educational and social resources on campus to meet the needs of the modified student body. One might hope that assistance might be secured from the faculty in the behavioral sciences and from the professional staff in the student personnel services, but the final responsibility involves the total resources of the campus.

6. Fiscal responsibility: The previous discussion should make it obvious that the new policies concerning recruitment and admission must be undergirded by budgetary appropriations to support the new dimensions of educational programs and of other campus resources which will be required. Fortunately there have been enough institutional ventures into this field to provide fiscal data appropriate to program requirements.

We must face the realities of contemporary social change and their implications for higher education. We have not really done so, and when we do, we shall discover that some of our most cherished traditions will have to be modified. The issues of our time will not even be confronted if we approach the task of expanding educational opportunity in the manner of dilettantes or even in the spirit of an expanding charity. We face instead the responsibility of redefining the mission of every institution of higher learning, and perhaps we shall have to invent some new forms of education beyond the secondary school.

~⟨ 11 ⟩~

ARCHITECTURE FOR THE URBAN CAMPUS

Warren Rovetch

The main force of American higher education is physically and psychologically oriented to the America that was born in the country. It is not surprising, then, to find, as officials at the Educational Facilities Laboratories (EFL) have pointed out, that there has not yet been produced an effective physical plan to meet the realities of institutional life in today's cities. "Nowhere," states an EFL report, "have we created the new, organic urban campus and, at the moment, nowhere has a college or university made a firm commitment to do so."

Perhaps the reason is that we have looked at the central city as something apart from the reality of a metropolitan area. Perhaps if all institutions in metropolitan areas focused accurately on their own urban condition, the resulting sensitivity and general understanding would produce more meaningful specific applications.

Of first importance is understanding the college and its residents as a community, a special kind of company town that is contiguous with or surrounded by another city or town. The college community is diverse in age, maturity, sex, marital status, and academic and personal interests. It has students, faculty, professionals, administrators, and service workers. It has classes and programs, and all the people in it live somewhere and spend money. Some of the learning, living, and spending takes place on campus and much of it spills over into contiguous areas, ordinarily called off-campus.

This relationship with the environment needs to be enhanced. The traffic of an urban campus is both in and out, both as to student movement and the involvement of the community. Equally fundamental are the ways in which the campus and the community around it reflect the patterns, the needs, and the commerce of urban man. The old notion of one student union, one place to eat, one place for coffee, one place to shop is stilted and monastic.

These two principles—in-and-out traffic and a more natural flow of commerce—translate into basic planning concepts, which in turn produce significant opportunities for the campus that opts for urban relevance. One planning concept is the extended perimeter: getting away from the notion of the neat circular or rectangular plot of land, and instead extending fingers into the surrounding city wherever possible; getting the maximum front footage to maximize contact between the "campus" and its surrounding area. This avoids the fortress campus, enlarges the development or redevelopment opportunities for the campus environment, improves the tax base of campus-related land, and permits a flexible pattern of campus growth.

A second planning concept is the multinucleated subcenter plan: making it possible for people to drink coffee or read books or study or talk or eat or attend classes or whatever in a number of medium and small subcenters rather than in one large formal center. The campus, however designed, does not function as a neat, logical organism with a library at the center. It should be people in a variety of clusters and groups with different styles and patterns of activity.

The third concept is the mixed use of land through the horizontal zoning of buildings, based on velocity of circulation. High velocity uses are, for instance, convenience-commercial and classrooms; they belong on street levels or, for classrooms, on walk-up floors. Medium velocity uses, such as faculty offices, research laboratories, and conference rooms, can be on walk-up and low elevator floors. Low velocity uses, such as business offices or living quarters, can be on top floors or in towers. Not including housing, medium and low velocity areas will ordinarily represent one-third to one-half of total campus square footage. Mixed use permits high-density utilization of land without crowding. Can you visualize a building that has snack bars and a browsing bookstore at courtyard level, and classrooms and offices above?

Another consideration of special concern to the campus in the large city is the separation of pedestrian and vehicle circulation. An interlocking system of pedestrian streets on the ground and in buildings bridging the streets permits living with the reality of urban automobile traffic without subjugating the university to the tyranny of it. It permits use of valuable air space over streets, provides for protected circulation on winter days, and enlarges the opportunities for campus interaction, while avoiding the lack of human scale and the disadvantages of the massive megastructure.

Whether it intends it or not, a college or university exerts a powerful economic force. Translating a full-time equivalent student (FTE) into a unit of measure that also includes faculty and staff and their families and the families of married students, our studies show, on the average, that one daytime FTE represents an expenditure of $5,000 per year apart from education and housing costs and apart from buying by the college. Thus for example, an FTE of 11,000 will mean $55 million in personal buying. This includes items that range from $600,000 for newspapers, magazines, and paperbacks to $4 million on meals, snacks, and beverages.

That spending is going to be done; the questions confronting the college are: how much of it will be done on campus, how much near the campus, how much elsewhere? The college does not have to try to make a profit from that spending; but it does have to recognize buying power as one of the potentially explosive developmental forces and facts of life that shape the campus and its environment.

The second major area in which campus and community mix is in housing. Few campuses today house all single or many married resident students. Nor do many students, juniors and above in particular, want to live in the stilted campus dormitory —even with visiting privileges. At so-called commuting institutions we have found at least half the students living away from home. Where do they live? Wherever they can—which accounts for the long life of ancient slums and the instant creation of new slums for new campuses.

It is time for colleges and universities to become joint venturers with their host cities and with the private sector in capturing the massive thrust of spending and housing to create a positive—which does not mean dull—campus environment and to be an invigorating force for the renewal of the neighborhood. In many college towns the word *community* could substitute for *neighborhood*.

The sense of neighborhood is of tremendous importance for the vital campus that recognizes the urban reality of its students and itself. The college or university can affect the entire city; a major university will affect the nation and the world. But mostly and firstly, a campus will affect its neighborhood; and success as a vital institution will be measured in the first instance by what effect it has on its neighborhood, and, of course, by what effect the neighborhood has on it.

Meaningful answers are to be found in a merging of campus and town planning. The academic planner must not only know that his planning will affect the city—he must embrace this as an opportunity and control the thrust of this influence. There is no need to fog the borders, so that one cannot tell where the campus ends and the city begins; but there is great and clamoring need to make the fit between campus and community close and active. The sooner educators adopt this concept, the sooner we will reach the still evasive goal of urban reality in campus design and development.

SAN FRANCISCO STATE: URBAN CAMPUS PROTOTYPE

Mervin B. Freedman

I am a member of the San Francisco State College faculty.[1] Along with several dozen faculty members and students, I stand at a fifth-floor window and watch a noontime rally of strikers and their supporters. After an hour or so of speeches, the crowd displays a certain agitation. Police begin to appear on the scene. They march and countermarch in squads and platoons. Eventually skirmishing and some open fighting develop. Several dozen strikers and bystanders are clubbed and hauled off in paddy wagons. Some policemen are injured, mostly by rocks and other missiles. The warfare lasts for about an hour. An uneasy calm then settles on the campus, and at noon the next day almost the same scene is repeated, like a regularly scheduled public spectacle.

[1] A version of this essay appeared in *The Nation*, January 13, 1969.

As I watch these terrifying events, various images come to mind—the Hapsburgs or Romanovs looking down from the palace windows through the snows of Vienna and St. Petersburg at the calvary clashing with students and workers. From time to time the military quality of the scene below suggests that I have assumed the vantage point of some nineteenth-century general, Napoleon at Austerlitz, perhaps, surveying a battle from a hill through a spyglass. Since I was raised in Ocean Hill in Brooklyn and served in World War II for three and one-half years as an enlisted man, before I was commissioned a second lieutenant, identifications with emperors and generals are not particularly congenial. The most apposite image to come to mind is Oswald Spengler's—the Roman soldier grimly going about his business (in my case teaching my classes off-campus) while his world crumbles. But I am not a very good Roman soldier, either. I have too many doubts. So I go about in a whirl, torn by contradictory impulses.

Only the theater of the absurd can do justice to some of the scenes at ground level. I stand in a crowd of strikers who are about to hold a rally. The crowd is San Francisco—pretty blondes dressed like Sacagawea, chic black girls with natural hair, assorted Oriental and brown-skinned young people, conservatively dressed, and dignified black adults, goateed black young men, bearded and long-haired white young men, clergymen with clerical collars, gray-haired white adults. I recognize some people—students, faculty members, prominent San Francisco politicians. Who are the others—strikers, supporters, onlookers, townspeople, police spies? Who knows? Suddenly a voice booms out from loudspeakers: "This is Acting President Hayakawa." He is standing on the roof of the Administration Building one hundred yards away. A great chorus of boos goes up from the crowd. President Hayakawa proceeds to pontificate over the loudspeakers in donnish tones. (The remoteness of leader from public and the elevation of the speaker remind me of Mussolini haranguing his vassals from the balcony of the Palazzo Venezia.) Meanwhile the crowd at the strike rally takes up a chant, "Fuck Hayakawa" (although most of the older adults do not join in). The President terminates his remarks by wishing his audience a Merry Christmas. The crowd responds to this seasonal civility with hoots of derision and paroxysms of laughter. My companion throughout this scene, a young assistant professor, Yale A.B. and Stanford Ph.D., has been rendered almost catatonic. Finally he blurts out, "This is too much."

The situation of San Francisco State College baffles description and analysis. The Black Students Union and the Third World Liberation Front (composed of other minorities; for example, Orientals and Mexican-Americans) have called for a strike. Their demands, centered on more support and autonomy for black and other nonwhite students, faculty, and programs, range from stipulations that most students, administrators, and faculty consider reasonable to those that seem extreme and very difficult to meet—the demand, for example, that the college admit *all* nonwhite students who apply for the fall semester of 1969–70. Spokesmen for the Black Students Union and the Third World Liberation Front state that they will not compromise their demands. Certain activities disruptive of academic procedures have been carried out. Classrooms have been invaded, bomb threats have been phoned in, small explosive devices have been set off, fires have been started, and so on. Serious injuries have been few and damage relatively slight, but it is certain that the climate is troubled and alarmed. Many classes now meet off-campus in dormitories, homes, churches, and the like. A union of faculty members, an affiliate of the American Federation of Teachers, is attempting to obtain wider union support for a faculty strike. The split between faculty members and the board of trustees of the state colleges has been growing for a long time; now one of the faculty demands is that the trustees, who have been as adamant as the striking students in their refusal to negotiate, enter into discussion with strikers, both faculty and student.

At dinner parties I am harassed by the question, "What is the solution?" By now I have a reply ready. There is, I say, no solution in the present focus. The problem of San Francisco State College is the problem of all urban campuses, and it is the basic problem of American urban society generally. Can whites, blacks, browns, reds, yellows, adults, youth, hippies, straights, revolutionaries, conservatives live together in sufficient harmony to maintain some orderly processes of society? The answer is not yet final, but the data at hand are not encouraging. Some years back I used to make predictions about complex social events, but I lack such confidence now. I offer the reader three alternatives:

1. The disorders on campuses are but transitory phenomena which will end soon.

2. During the next decade the San Francisco State situation will become the norm for urban college campuses and for cities generally. Disorder, explosions, fires, guerrilla warfare, strikes will be common events. At the end of this time a more just, humane, and peaceable society will emerge.

3. Out of recurrent tension and disorder will issue a Fascist state. College campuses and society generally will increasingly resemble South Africa.

San Francisco State is unique in some respects. It has suffered in recent years from an absence of leadership because of rapid turnover of presidents. The California state college bureaucracy is rigid and cumbersome. Militants in San Francisco are very militant, and conservatives in California, followers of Ronald Reagan or Max Rafferty, are very primitive. But the problems of San Francisco State are basically the problems of any urban campus, and the future of American higher education is increasingly the large, urban, commuter campus. No simple procedures are available for avoiding repetitions of the calamities at San Francisco State all over the country. The close interplay now seen in every big city between society at large and the urban campus is evident in the San Francisco State scene. The governor of California, the mayor of San Francisco, various state assemblymen and senators, clergymen, leaders of the black, Oriental and Mexican-American communities, and the San Francisco Labor Council have all entered the fight. Von Clausewitz's dictum may be applied to the student strike—it is simply a more militant form of political action.

The urban campus reflects the conflicts of urban society— nonwhite or non-Anglo militancy, alienated middle-class youth, repressive public opinion and public officials, heavy-handed police procedures, drugs, and the like. And as with society at large the system of academic government is not adequate to the task. Jeffersonian-style democracy and checks and balances cannot cope with the pace and the complexity of mass technological society. The traditional campus community also belongs to another age, the nineteenth century. In static times a system can carry an inadequate leader. When traditional procedures break down, the

qualities of the leader assume crucial importance. The United
States could accommodate Calvin Coolidge in the 1920s; Columbia University could do likewise with Nicholas Murray Butler.
Such indulgences are no longer possible. The president of an
urban college must grasp, make evident, and somehow cope with
a bewildering variety of issues, for many or for most of which there
are no precedents. He is thus sailing stormy and uncharted waters.

The president of an urban campus must attempt to fashion
a viable institution out of a student body that is a very mixed bag.
The interests of student groups are diverse and often conflicting
—jocks versus radicals, upper-middle-class students with educational goals centered on personal development versus lower-mid-
dle-class students who are concerned with rising out of their
parents' occupational status, minority groups versus more established groups, and sometimes one minority group against another.
The administration of most private universities and colleges,
where the student body is relatively homogeneous, is a far easier
task.

The traditional concept of a campus community is based
on the premise that people know one another and share many experiences and concerns. On a fragmented, urban, commuter campus this is hardly the case. The president frequently finds himself
discussing an explosive issue with a group of students whom he
has not met before. For all he knows, some of these young people
may not be students. Should an ex-student be considered a member of the campus community? How about a resident of the local
community who has never been enrolled in the college? Should
the president refuse to talk to a young man or woman if it de-
velops that he or she is an "outside agitator"?

Needless to say, public opinion is a force with which college
presidents must reckon. In California Ronald Reagan, Max Rafferty, and such figures stalk the land, ever alert for signs of sexual
immorality, pornography, drugs, and radical or unpatriotic senti-
ments and behavior on campuses. Public support for their views
is considerable. In the California gubernatorial election of 1966,
Ronald Reagan campaigned very successfully against radicals and
hippies on the Berkeley campus of the University of California.
I should estimate that the citizenry of California oppose the strike
at San Francisco State by a margin well above three to one. In
response to this public opinion the trustees of the state college

system and the regents of the university system have infringed upon certain faculty prerogatives—for example, in the Eldridge Cleaver case. In a time of George Wallaces and Max Raffertys it may seem ludicrous to suggest that college presidents must educate public officials and citizens at large on the basic issues of intellectual and academic freedom. But they must nevertheless try.

Students and trustees, legislators and public opinion are by no means the limit of the president's concern. When a campus is in turmoil one hears comparatively little about the faculty. This is a serious oversight, as any president knows. A faculty can immobilize a campus as effectively as any other group. One hundred students can bring in the police and cancel classes. Fifteen faculty members can block almost any program by talking it to death.

For the past year, I have been studying faculty attitudes toward student militancy and campus unrest. It may be said that faculty members are like other Americans at this time. They are somewhat demoralized, weary of conflict, and they are shifting perceptibly to the right in the face of radical challenge. Most campuses have a small group of faculty whose views resemble Hearst editorials circa 1938 and another minority that supports student dissidence. The majority of faculty members on an urban campus are liberals. Robert Kennedy and Eugene McCarthy were their candidates. They want a fast compromise solution to Vietnam. They want justice along with law and order. But at the gut level of daily action things are not so easy. Respectable professional men bristle when confronted by obscene language, outlandish dress, and bad manners. Black militants may frighten them. Differences in personal style can obscure areas of agreement and avenues of potentially profitable exploration.

Faculty members are lords of small empires and masters of orderly schedules. A teacher meets classes on Monday, Wednesday, and Friday, researches and writes on Tuesday and Thursday. Forty-two lectures on the United States, 1865–1914, are to be delivered in the spring semester. The symphony orchestra will give a concert on December 1, 2, 3, and the Drama Department's performance of *Heartbreak House* takes place on November 10 and 11. Interruptions are resented. One faculty member said to me: "If the college wants to schedule a convocation on Vietnam, let them do it nights or weekends. The convocation took two days out of my teaching. I can't afford to miss two days, considering all the material I have to cover." Roger Heyns, chancellor of the University of California at Berkeley, has made the point that the faculty presumes a college campus to be an institution that almost by definition is to be free of tension. A president must make the faculty see the unreality of such a view in these turbulent times.

The president's domestic complexities are not confined to students, faculty, or academic administrators. He must give heed to campus police, secretaries, dormitory residents, business officers, and other nonacademic staff. They are an important and neglected element of the community. When three black students meet, a campus police officer suspects that they are up to no good. Secretaries may quake when approached by a black man whose appearance is not respectably middle class. Hippy garb and grooming can be comparable sources of difficulty. These nonacademic contacts can contribute considerably to campus tension.

The financing of higher education for lower-class blacks and other American minority groups is receiving considerable attention at this time. An even more critical issue than finances is the question of what to do with such students once they arrive on campus. College presidents might begin to educate their constituencies concerning some of the implications of black studies. Militant blacks and their allies have thrown light on the hypocritical underpinnings of the "Land of the free and the home of the brave" —the slaughter of Indians, the unjust wars, slavery. They have helped to arrest the march of technology and scientism that a decade ago seemed destined to kill the humanistic spirit. They have greatly contributed to the realization that white, middle-class America does not necessarily walk hand in hand with God. And now they are taking on meritocracy, as exemplified by grades and degrees. They demand that colleges contribute to the development of students rather than that students be tailored to the abstract demands of professions, industry, and the like.

Such fundamental issues must be explained and placed within a framework of rational discussion. It may be that the conflicts besetting the urban campus cannot be solved by reason, but the president must live by the faith that rational debate is still useful. These are revolutionary times, and most middle-aged liberals are ten or fifteen years behind the times. They would have made good college presidents in 1955. They are of the alcohol rather than the drug generation.

In order to talk to dissident students today a president must know where "they are at." He must grasp their sense of outrage and their spirit of anarchy, and recognize the grounds on which they justify confrontation and violence. He must appreciate the appeal of anti-thought. He must be able to talk to students in a language that is not dead. The manners, style, and language of rebellion are powerfully evocative. The worst of sins among dissident youth is not to feel. And tired old liberal rhetoric can smother feeling like a blanket. See what it did to Hubert Humphrey's standing with radical youth.

None of this is to suggest that presidents abandon faith in democracy and the meliorative possibilities of the college. They must attempt to draw dissident students into that framework. But the tragic view is in order. They may not be successful in so influencing their students, and it may be that reform of the American system of higher education demands confrontation, that meliorative procedures will not work.

At all events the time for playing it cool is past. I suggest that presidents eschew the role of behind-the-scenes diplomat and administrator and return to the nineteenth-century concept of president as teacher and orator. Heaven knows, their constituencies have much to learn. They might begin by pointing out to rebellious students that while a revolution evokes an extraordinary sense of freedom and possibility, evocation of a mood is not a political end in itself. History indicates that revolutions cannot be expected to conform to plan, but some coherent vision of the post-revolutionary scene is nevertheless necessary. French students took over the Sorbonne and then did not know what to do with it. They thereby lost much support from the French citizenry. Exegesis of the true state of affairs in the administration of colleges and universities is badly needed. Abuse of the trustees is often misplaced. To be sure, trustees can wield power in tyrannical fashion. More often, however, policy is determined by the faculty. The view of Columbia University as a medieval fief ruled by President Kirk and the trustees is myopic. Rather, President Kirk and his trustees maintained a very loose hegemony over a series of duchies and baronies, the various departments, schools, and colleges, most of which enjoyed considerable independence. Above all, a president must find suitable ways for students to participate in the operation of the institution. Only then will students assume true responsibility. Given the nature of campus government, which has grown by accretion, this is no easy task.

A president must hold up to his faculty and his nonacademic staff the picture of rigidity and intolerance in which all of us share. The times are too perilous to afford these luxuries. This is not to suggest that faculty members should abandon standards, but some openness and humility are in order. The president might remind a faculty member who is disturbed by disruptions of his class that in five years most of his students are not likely to remember his name, much less what they learned in the laboratory of Botany 1A on April 17. Above all, a president must exhort his faculty and staff to function in their professional environment as any mature citizen must live in our turbulent society—that is, tolerating much confusion and ambiguity. The faculty can ill afford short fuses and snap judgments. Some faculty members are quick to label almost all student protest and dissent an SDS plot to revolutionize American society. Such facile judgments needlessly polarize factions.

These days the chances are that the president who abandons the role of playing it cool and stands forth to exert moral force will be punished. The president of a complex urban institution faces an almost impossible task under the best of circumstances, and statistics show that they do not last long in their jobs. Like baseball managers they come and go, but unlike baseball managers their reasons for going are rarely publicized. A president who is fired for publicly standing by principle, whose firing therefore means something, is infinitely to be preferred to the president who goes out with a whimper, because he cannot do the near impossible—that is, hold the urban campus together. Certain elements of the public may enjoy the spectacle of a Socrates receiving his just rewards. A president, however, may inspire, and unite his own constituency, his students and his faculty, by a display of moral leadership, a commodity which is usually in short supply and which appears to be critically lacking in the United States at this time. Perhaps some foundation could assume the burden of aiding financially those true teachers among college presidents who lose their jobs by taking unambiguous stands on matters of intellectual and academic principle. Foundations have been known to do less rewarding things with their moneys.

⌐𝒜 13 ⌐

SAN FRANCISCO
STATE EXPERIENCE

Robert Smith

On May 30, 1968, I assumed the presidency of San Francisco State College rather unexpectedly on President John Summerskill's departure for Ethiopia. Ours is a campus of some 20,-000 people, ninety-four acres, with a program beginning at 8:00 o'clock in the morning and ending at 10:00 o'clock in the eve-ing. It is heavily upper division and graduate, with a student body whose median age is twenty-four-plus years. The usual teaching load is twelve semester units; the plant is used at the rate of about 130 per cent of capacity. We have been viewed as the "jewel" of the eighteen-campus California State College System. We have been quick to admit that ours is a distinguished faculty, confident of its capacity to govern the institution if given reasonable freedom, and largely convinced that the trustees and chancellor have prevented it from doing so.

Since November 6, 1968, when the student strike involving the B.S.U. and Third World Liberation Front began, the campus schedule has been temporarily suspended four times because of disorder—twice by me and twice by Acting President Hayakawa, who succeeded me on November 26, 1968. There have been some six hundred arrests on campus and class attendance probably dropped as low as 25–30 per cent during the last weeks of the semester. Since January 6, 1969, the American Federation of Teachers has been on strike partly in sympathy with the students' fifteen "non-negotiable" demands and largely in behalf of improved working conditions and increased control over campus affairs. As I write, three probable candidates for the California Governorship in 1970 are locked in a public battle over whether or not the trustee-administrative-AFT agreement to end the strike has any standing. The student strike continues. A recent strike bulletin avows the intent to continue the strike by "any means necessary" until all fifteen of the "non-negotiable" demands have been met. A recent carefully drawn sample of student opinion reported that just over half of the student body supported the student strike and just under half supported the faculty strike. A January poll of full-time faculty showed 64 per cent opposed the strike. The strikes have drawn support from the Associated Students Governing body, the SDS, other white radical student groups on the campus, about one-third of the faculty, and most but not all of the black faculty and administrators on campus.

Since November 6, a number of potentially lethal bombs were discovered and defused, others detonated on campus. There have been three major instances of arson: one an administrator's office; another an administrator's home. On one day fifty small fires were set, and all toilets were stopped up except the president's. While there have been beatings on campus both by strikers and by police, no one has been critically injured—at least physically. The campus continues in a state of emergency with all rallies and large meetings restricted and with uniformed police at all access points and on most floors of some twenty buildings. Police and related costs are hard to come by. I estimate them to be in the neighborhood of a million dollars since November 6, 1968.[1]

We have had three presidents within the past year and six in the past eight years, if acting presidents are counted. Our fac-

[1] As this volume goes to print, all is quiet on the campus. Both student and faculty strikes ended during the spring semester.—*Ed.*

ulty just recently voted 416–167 to uphold the action taken by the statewide Academic Senate in May, 1968, to express no confidence in Chancellor Glenn Dumke and to ask him to resign. This compared with a 65 per cent vote of "no confidence" throughout the system's seventeen reporting colleges.

A colleague of mine who has studied some thirty college and community upheavals during the past five years, is convinced that ours is the most complex, many-faceted struggle of them all. Perhaps it is too early to say with confidence what can be learned from San Francisco State College's struggles. Perhaps my generation cannot learn what must be learned if urban higher education is to adapt itself successfully to the social and cultural revolution of which it is now clearly a part. It is important, though, to try. What follow are some perceptions I have gleaned from our experiences at San Francisco State.

Under pressure of continuing campus disorder, the latent cleavages and hostilities among individuals and groups within the institution became severe problems in efforts to maintain an intelligible, coherent response to the crisis and the resolution of the conflicts within the institutions. Ideological-attitudinal cleavages pose the greatest hazards to those attempting to work toward conciliatory solutions. The substantial breakdown of faculty government during late November and December was one major result of such cleavages and differences.

The business-as-usual pattern of student, faculty, and administrative government were not adequate to the pressures for change and could not be quickly superseded by a sufficiently mobile decision-making process in a climate of continuing tension marked by checkmating activities at several levels. The traditional dispersal of responsibility, prerogatives, and power within the academic community became an albatross in a multiple conflict situation. This, coupled with centralized control of the system of colleges at the chancellor-trustee level, seriously hampered the executive functions at the campus level. S. I. Hayakawa resolved this problem temporarily by casting his lot with the chancellor and trustees and the predominant pressure of public opinion.

In the face of student-sponsored challenges, confrontations, and disruptions, the crisis efforts of the administration and faculty leadership to contain the disorder and moderate the issues blurred the institution's policies and positions. This provided the seedbed

for major faculty and staff defections—some in behalf of dissident students, others in behalf of "law and order," and still others
in a search for outside assistance (from the mayor, the governor,
or sympathetic trustees and trustee staff members). Some faculty
groups, such as the American Federation of Teachers and the Faculty Renaissance (a moderate to conservative faculty group), have
moved strongly to consolidate their power during the extended
period of disorder. The AFT struck and the Renaissance spokesman, S. I. Hayakawa, became Acting President. The potential for
resolution of major campus issues may have thus been thrust beyond the reach of the campus.

Large-scale "convocations," involving the suspension of the
instructional schedule and called as a crisis tactic during campus
disorders, proved a precarious enterprise. The activists seized upon
it as another possibility for confrontation with the establishment
and a vehicle for radicalizing students and faculty. Most faculty
and administrators supporting it saw it as a means of exploring
issues and informing themselves and others. On the other hand,
many faculty and students viewed a convocation as appeasement
and a waste of time, or worse. The majority of trustees and the
chancellor reacted negatively along the same lines. I agreed to
the convocation in the hope that growing polarization between
faculty groups and student groups might be reduced. Successful
efforts of activist students and faculty in turning the planning and
conduct of the convocation to confrontation probably deepened
campus polarization—especially among faculty. It moved the
trustees toward massive police action as the basic approach to
campus disorder. Too hasty planning for a massive operation contributed to the random elements, despite intensive efforts of the
planning group.

The continuing campus power struggle at San Francisco
State during the past fifteen months involves racial and ethnic
asspirations translated into action. That aspect of the conflict appears to have destroyed the role effectiveness of most of the more
recently employed faculty and administrators from minority
groups within the college. This problem began to worry me about
a year ago during my work with a campus committee of interracial
composition. Despite special efforts through the summer and fall,
we lost ground on this problem steadily before I left the presidency. Since the beginning of December, most have openly joined

the militants in support of the strike and against the official stance of the college. This may prove to be one of the most costly outcomes of our disorders.

The official or institutional communication pattern within the college has been grossly inadequate in the face of cross-campus movements. This includes communications efforts of the faculty and the administration. They are largely directed to administrators and faculty rather than students and staff. They have been stylized, rational, and circumspect, largely written and telephonic communications. They have been outflanked by multimedia approaches used by student and faculty activists. These have included mass meetings, underground press, throwaway bulletins, wall posters, "truth squads," bull horns, sound trucks, agitprop theater, seminars, teach-ins, and other experimental techniques.

Traditional notions of slow institutional due process related to faculty and student personnel matters, including disciplinary codes and proceedings, have become grossly inadequate on a large campus convulsed by disorder in which large numbers of students and faculty participate. Further, attempts at reestablishing them in ways relevant to the situation in a period of conflict and tension have proved fruitless. Hence the resort to administrative edict, declaration of campus emergency, and actions akin to summary court procedures on ours and other campuses. This results in the too-quick further resort to massive police force, mass arrests, and the transfer of problems of campus social control to off-campus police jurisdictions and the transfer of student and faculty disciplinary procedures to the courts. The student demands for general amnesty as a condition of peace on campus compounds the resolution of disruptive conflict on campus, especially as the potential criminal penalties mount.

As the campus disruptions endure (four months on our campus), resolution becomes more improbable and a period of severe attrition becomes the prospect. Adamant public positions crystallize. The locus of solution escalates (ours is at the level of the governor's office and the legislature, if not beyond). Off-campus forces joining the fray multiply. They have included radical groups of the right, the left, and the racial and ethnic minorities. Political candidates, professional organizations, disturbed persons bent on destruction, blue-ribbon civic groups, nationally recognized mediators, incognito state legislators, special investigators from the governor's office, the state attorney general's office, the FBI, task forces from the chancellor's office, and mass media people from as far away as Los Angeles and Hong Kong. This changes the nature of college administration. They add to the overload of the administrative staff and the public information office. The intruders become random elements in the processes of conflict resolution as well as the propaganda and psychological battles which are a major aspect of campus crisis. Proposals for simple and pat solutions become a dime a dozen and are projected outward from the campus, returning through other channels to haunt the hard-pressed campus leaders. Much preplanning for housing, briefing, coordinating, and controlling these off-campus personnel can delimit their consequences in escalation of the problems.

Relationships between the campuses and external law enforcement agencies present an underdeveloped, precarious problem infused with dilemmas. In large urban institutions campus police and security resources need complete overhaul. As John Searles has noted, a determined, imaginative minority can almost assuredly provoke the calling of police onto a campus, and provoke them to direct counteraction to protect persons and property. The alternative is to close a campus at the drop of a hat—raising a major problem of how to get it reopened under more favorable circumstances. Once police move onto campus, the police captain or the sheriff becomes in fact the acting president—but the president retains the ensuing responsibilities. Reportedly, at least one president, grasping this fact fully, took naps during the height of noonday disturbances, thereby remaining fresh for afternoon press conferences.

The patterns of campus disruption associated with our student strike, "flea attacks" and adapted versions of guerrilla warfare, are sufficiently novel, experimental, and disruptive to require major revision of procedures for campus control during a period of well-planned campus disorder. Campuses are built for heavy, rapid movement of people in and out of buildings with many doors and stairways and much glass. Buildings are very difficult to secure and protect. Offices and staff personnel are scattered and exposed.

Patterns of college-community relationships have always been extensive and far-flung at San Francisco State. They largely relate to campus training program involvement, individual faculty community commitments, student-sponsored community service programs, cultural events, and extension programs. They include a low-pressure, somewhat neglected local Advisory Board, and special advisory groups for some programs. Efforts to establish continuing relationships with emerging minority group leadership and other groups which might have moderated campus tensions were sporadic and less than effective. The patterns of college-community relationships must be reordered.

Relationships with the chancellor's staff and trustees, with few exceptions, were totally ineffective in gaining assistance during my term of office. They consumed great chunks of precious time and were counterproductive in escalating the problems on campus and in eroding the authority of the president and administrative staff on campus. They became the vehicle for massive political involvement in the attempted resolution of difficulties.

As campus disorder persists, multiple polarizations develop and harden, and sharp ideological conflicts emerge to dominate the behavior of contending groups. Leadership moves to the most militant. Governance of the college is changed by the struggle of radical groups of the right, the left, and the racial and ethnic groups. They all attack the Western liberal traditions which tend to guide the governance of colleges in what we assume are benign, bureaucratic patterns supportive of intellectual and humane values.

During the past two years, San Francisco State and the University of California, Berkeley, have become battlegrounds in the struggle of each of these groups against the liberal, pluralistic theses of the two institutions. Further, institutional operations at the college have been disrupted by the struggle among the radical groups themselves as the radical right has gained adherents under the banner of law and order, and as the radical white left and the black and other ethnic power groups demand complete control over programs such as black and ethnic studies, backed by planned disruption within the institution and beyond. Polarization has grown rapidly; each radical group has significant constituencies within the faculty, the student body, the Bay Area community, and the state who are all committed to the struggles on the campus.

Liberals in college administration seeking reform, such as former president John Summerskill and myself, and many of the faculty and administrative leaders on campus, come under attack from the radicals of all ideological orientations. Moderates and conservatives fare little better. The *Wall Street Journal* referred to this phenomenon as "a withering crossfire."

The energetic, disciplined minorities who bluntly subscribe to any means to gain their ends have clearly had an initial advantage in jarring the patterns of institutional response. At the same time, the liberal-moderate-conservative constituency, wedded to the conventional wisdom of American higher education, while large in number, is dispersed and individualistic in response to campus crisis. They are "undisciplined."

The college and university, under such attack, is fragile. It is a superb target for radical tactics, hoisted on its own petard of dialogue and leisurely due process.

Three questions of grave importance must be asked here. Will the most fanatical of the several extremes be checked by positive and decisive leadership from those of the majority caught in the middle? Will the freedom and wide range of choices now enjoyed by the affluent and highly educated be extended to and shared with those in our society who are driven by a sense of powerlessness, exclusion, and alienation? Can we set ourselves against the growing tides of aggression and retaliation now building in our colleges and the communities they serve? Prospects for an open society, I believe, hang in the balance.

Underlying the campus disturbances at San Francisco State College are the rising aspirations of students for experientially oriented college programs, the surge of minority efforts to gain wide access to higher education, the drive for black and other ethnic studies, and a serious thrust for student power. Faculty alienation and disappointment with what I see as the deteriorating conditions of California higher education and with the increasing interference of the board of trustees provided a seedbed for faculty rebellion. The growing disparity between the norms of expectation and behaviors on a vital urban campus and an increasingly conservative ideological climate in California provide an explosive potential that threatens the future of the college and the stability of the state.

Yet, beneath the public posturing, the displays of intransigent hostilities "on camera," the actors are poignantly human, and many are thinking with an intensity never before experienced. A small sign over a secretary's desk struck my fancy the other day. It said: "The end of the world has been postponed for ninety days due to a shortage of trumpeters." I was tempted to suggest that we substitute bullhorns and get it over with. But I decided to hold off a bit because, despite the above problems and others, we are really deeply engaged in efforts to guide or moderate the urban and cultural revolution of our time. Where else should one be?

PART TWO

Aspects of
Campus Cultures

Section IV

Students

Sex, drugs, and unrest among students are topics that have already created a voluminous literature. But most of what appears in print on these subjects is useful primarily to the student of contemporary mythology or to the scholar studying trends in public opinion. The three essays of Section IV, however, are research-based, scholarly pieces.

The first essay, by Frederic Wood, presents a complex, tri-dimensional analysis of five attitudes toward sex now prevalent among an overwhelming number of college youth. They are seeking to understand the relationship between the body and their sense of personhood; they look upon sexual intercourse as an act of self-realization; they are taking individual responsibility for decision-making in the sexual (as in the socio-ethical) sphere; they have contempt for the double standard that has dominated the adult world; they are attempting to reinterpret the meaning of marriage in order to avoid "trivializing" it as so many of their parents have done.

Helen Nowlis' essay on marihuana systematically covers two subtopics of importance to educators: marihuana as a "drug," and the status of current laws about marihuana. On the second question, Nowlis favors a change in the laws, if only to allow the problem to rise to the surface where it can be studied and treated. Under present conditions, Nowlis contends, "we cannot do good research, we cannot do good education, we cannot do effective counseling, we cannot provide treatment early enough. . . ."

In the essay that closes Section IV, George Stern presents a brief analysis of campus climate and student unrest at San Francisco State College, based on data he collected on that campus in 1967, a few months after the inauguration of John Summerskill as president. These data puzzle Stern, as they appear to contradict his other findings. Readers of this volume may be able to resolve the problem by adding to Stern's analysis the insights of Freedman (pp. 83–90), Smith (pp. 91–99), and Mayhew (pp. 149–150).

The bulk of Stern's essay is devoted to demonstrating his major conclusion, namely, that manifestations of student unrest are fewer "at institutions that stress opportunities for personal growth," and that "severe sources of tension ordinarily arise in places that . . . maintain an excessive degree of control over student impulse life." Many observers of higher education have of course long been convinced on this point. It will be important to them to have the hard data Stern presents in his essay in support of their view.

JOSEPH AXELROD

~14~

NEW SEXUAL
ATTITUDES

Frederic C. Wood, Jr.

We need to begin by defining precisely what we mean by new sexual attitudes. It may be helpful to divide these between attitudes toward sexuality itself and attitudes toward sexual decision-making. Those two realms are not totally separable, and are functionally interdependent as sexual behavior changes, but they are useful for purposes of analysis. One other caveat regarding new attitudes needs to be entered. The word *new* is used with reservations. Most that appears new in this realm is new only in the relative sense that it challenges established stereotypes or mores. None of the attitudes I shall identify is new in the sense that it has not appeared before in the history of Western thought.

With regard to new attitudes toward human sexuality (or sexuality as a dimension of humanness), two are easily identifiable. One is a changing attitude toward the human body. In very broad terms, we appear to be moving in the direction of attitudes. which are generally affirmative of the human body. These may be contrasted with attitudes in the Christian heritage which were contemptuous of the body, and with more recent secular responses to that heritage, which treated the body as a neuter entity. According to the first line of thinking (which is still very much with us in religious practice and jargon), the body is at best a moral encumbrance to man's more pure soul. It is slightly tainted and tempts him away from higher things. The instincts of the flesh are evil, and man's most appropriate response is to suppress them. This is why St. Paul can say in good conscience that it is better to marry than to burn, but better still not to indulge at all. And it is why we still have certain cultic attitudes of veneration toward virginity.

One response to this line of thinking is to suggest that the body is essentially neutral, an object manipulated by the self or soul and only good or bad depending on how it is used. This is appealing to some who consider themselves emancipated from earlier Christian negativism regarding the body. It is an apparently free-thinking attitude, fostered by crusading journals which have declared war on the fetters which bind young America to a repressed sexual past.

But this is not yet what I mean by a new sexual attitude. What seems to be developing in our time is a still more affirmative view of the body. This is proclaimed by those who recognize on both psychological and theological grounds the intimate relationship between body and self-soul. This view asserts, with Old Testament writers and holistic psychology, that one does not *have* a body. One *is* his body. Therefore, bodily acts (including sexual acts) are personal acts, expressions of who you are. If you are affirmative about yourself, you can also be affirmative about your body, and celebrate its joys and capacities for giving joy.

Along with this thinking goes a recognition of the relationship between one's body (particularly its sexual differentiation) and one's identity—his sense of who he is. And that leads to a relatively "new" belief that in acting sexually, I am expressing and realizing who I am. I am affirming myself and the self of another.

Finally, along with this affirmative attitude toward the body goes a greater social acceptance of nudity or other forms of display of the body. This is particularly evident in the arts today. It has had a remarkable impact on journalism. And it is reflected in a rather radical change in the squeamishness of movie censors over the past two decades.

A second discernible new attitude toward sexuality has to do with the meaning of the sexual act, particularly (although not exclusively) heterosexual intercourse. As over against earlier attitudes which interpreted the act primarily in sacramental terms, as an outward sign of the marriage bond, or as a means to reproduction or tension release, we see emerging an attitude which interprets sexual intercourse in terms of self-fulfillment and self-realization. The act is seen primarily as expressing a particular state of relationship, attraction, compatibility, and mutual joy between two people. And this state is defined in subjective phenomenological terms, not in objective terms like marriage or the exchange of identifiable vows and commitments. According to such thinking, the sexual act becomes naturally "personal," involving at its best mutual consent, but not really touching on the vested interests of the social order. In brief, with a new individualized meaning, sex becomes, as our students are quick to remind us, a "private matter."

At the same time that these attitudes toward sexuality have been changing, we have been undergoing a mild revolution in our attitudes toward responsible decision-making, particularly in the sexual sphere. Variously characterized as *the new morality, contextual ethics, conscience ethics,* or *situation ethics,* this attitude is marked by a radical individualism with regard to questions of ultimate right and wrong. In the sexual realm, it finds us moving from a rule-centered morality, in which right and wrong forms of behavior are intrinsically defined regardless of context, to a conscience-centered morality, in which the individual must determine what is right or wrong by relating his ideals to his situation. Such a new morality usually places a high value on individual freedom from social constraint, although, when it is theologically grounded, it calls for freedom *in responsibility* to some ultimate ideal (not rule). Outside the sexual realm, the same moral attitude becomes the rationale for civil disobedience, in which there is usually some appeal to conscience over against the rules. It also justifies selective objection to selective service in selected wars.

This new morality is, however, not the only dimension of our changing attitudes toward sexual decision-making. We are also experiencing, particularly on our rapidly vanishing women's campuses, a full-scale rejection of the sexual double standard. This is a moral question because the double standard served for years, especially for the unmarried but sexually eligible woman, as a moral bugaboo. Through its various subtle expressions from the cult of the virgin to the dormitory closing hours on her campus, it taught her that she was both more responsible and more guilty for her sexual behavior than her partner. Now it is fading under a frontal assault from the new feminists, to say nothing of their eager but sometimes confused boyfriends, and we are witnessing the emergence of a new sexual equality which has implications for decision-making.

A third change in our moral attitudes is a function of a modern reinterpretation of the meaning of marriage. In general, the tendency, in theological as well as nontheological circles, is to interpret marriage in terms which do not highlight the sexual dimension as its essential condition. While it is still true that marriages which are not consummated may be ecclesiastically and legally annulled, marriage seems to denote for increasing numbers of people a particular mode of relationship, of which sexual union is only a part. This has brought a renewed emphasis on the social context and intention of marital vows, and other factors which distinguish a marital relationship from other relationships regardless of the degree of sexual involvement. This has already begun to dissolve the indissoluble tie which many once held between marriage and the sexual act. And it promises to redefine our concept of responsible sexual decision-making, within marriage as well as outside and before marriage. To the extent that marriage itself becomes less of a license for intercourse, we may expect corresponding changes in the ethical assumptions of people who are not married, and in the sense of sexual responsibility to one another held by those who are married. This has implications not only for questions of fidelity, but also for the sexual access of marital partners to one another. So-called conjugal rights may be becoming an outmoded concept, in terms of both exclusiveness and demand.

Having identified these five "new" sexual attitudes, with what problems do they present us? I must now be candid and confess that the promises of these new attitudes seem greater than the problems. The problems of the new attitudes, in any case, are vastly preferable to the problems evoked by the attitudes from which we are emerging.

With that reservation, let me identify five problems, each related to an area of change.

First, a more affirmative attitude toward the human body, along with greater acceptability of exposing the body, can lead to focusing our sexual identity in our genitals. This means an emphasis on genitality as a possible surrogate for full bodily sexuality. The new exposure of the body in the movies, for example, seems at times unduly focused on genital parts of the body. That is understandable since genitals were most concealed by those who were ashamed of their bodies. But bodies are more than genital paraphernalia, and when two people meet sexually they usually meet in more than purely genital ways. The equation of genitality with sexuality can lead to a preoccupation with genital organs which we counselors sometimes see as dysfunctional and nonfulfilling for the individual. It can block out other levels of sexual self-realization. Of course, this is not new since former attitudes toward the body also encouraged genital preoccupation. Perhaps we are still simply caught in the throes of our reaction, and not fully emancipated.

Second, our new emphasis on the meaning of the sexual act in terms of self-realization can be problematic insofar as it leads to a naive or callous neglect of the social context in which sexual behavior takes place. Right now many colleges are battling through the issue of parietals, agonizing over the freedom and responsibility of students to entertain members of the opposite sex in their "private" dormitory rooms. Although the concern of college administrators in such matters is often public relations and not morality, a neglected dimension of the debate is the extent to which dormitories are private. And however emancipated many of our young people may be, one encounters few who publicize their lovemaking in the act or who find it comfortable to be an audio or visual witness to the lovemaking of others. In other words, how are we going to keep what is private, private? At what levels does our sexual behavior entail responsibilities to and for others? When does it affect others? These are questions of responsibility which could be neglected under a highly individualist sexual ethic.

Third, the appeal to individual conscience of the new

morality can easily become a facade for rationalizing self-interest, with little regard for social responsibility in sex or even for the needs of one's sexual partner. Of course, the old rule-centered sexual morality provided no inherent safeguards against the human capacity to rationalize self-interest. But those of us who proclaim a situational ethic should acknowledge that there is a great deal of room in it for self-deception and for defining love in almost any way that suits the situation. Insofar as people can then be exploited, this is a problem. But we have yet to devise a morality which allows us to be fully human without this dangerous freedom.

Fourth, although it is hard to imagine that the collapse of the double standard could be anything but an unmitigated good, one must ask if there is any valid dimension of human experience to which the double standard points. There still are differences between men and women, biologically and physiologically, and perhaps emotionally. Whatever advances we have made, we have not eliminated the fact that only women get pregnant, bear babies, and nurse them. In rejecting the moral distinction with which the double standard burdens the feminine gender, can we lose sight of what may be an important dimension of our humanity— the complementarity of the sexes? Is it a problem if we ignore the basic intrusive and receptive modes of relating which characterize men and women?

Fifth, can we redefine marriage in a way which no longer includes sexual fidelity? Granting that our sexually exclusive expectations of the marital relationship are socially conditioned, and that polygamy and polyandry are not intrinsically problematic, the context in which sexual decisions are made (in this country at least) still includes some rather clearly defined expectations of sexual exclusivism. Interestingly, these have been carried over even into our newer sexual attitudes. Even the emerging cult of group marriage is exclusive and usually includes a covenant of fidelity to the group. And those who enter avowedly temporary marriages or "premarital" marriages (such as proposed by Margaret Mead) still appear to expect at least temporary fidelity. Will the contemporary reinterpretation of marriage which separates it from a primary association with sexual activity change this? And would that be a problem? Of course, one could easily counter that earlier understandings of marriage did very little to discourage infidelity. They simply forced it underground.

The promises of the new sexual attitudes parallel the changes and the problems. As already noted, they seem to outweigh the problems.

First, an affirmative attitude toward one's body finally means affirmation of oneself, particularly as a sexual being. This includes affirmation of the essential wholesomeness of sexual instincts, and could lead to sex with less fear and less intrinsic guilt (not situational guilt, for example, where one recognizes that he is exploiting another). Most counselors see the reduction of intrinsic guilt as a promising development. Where sexual activity is viewed as intrinsically tainted, the resulting guilt can lead to either paralysis of fulfilling sexual activity or to meaningless and often destructive hyperactivity. A case in point is the promiscuity of some students who are trying to demonstrate their emancipation from the old taboos and actually demonstrate continued bondage. In brief, less phony sexual guilt may free us to recognize real guilt in this area and become more responsible sexual decision-makers.

Second, to individualize and humanize the meaning of the sexual act is a step toward reclaiming human sex from the mechanical realm. A primary concern with biological processes and physiological consequences has mechanized sex to the point where it is common for two people to meet more as interlocking equipment than as persons. Newer attitudes which focus on the meaning of sexual activity as an expression of interpersonal relationship promise more authentic sexual involvement for a society which (judging from its advertising) seems to be starved for it. Such a starved society is also one which is journalistically saturated with phony and vicarious sex. To relieve the famine is also probably to reduce the saturation, and ultimately to lead to a society less sexually sick.

Third, individualism and idealism in sexual decision-making could lead to a rediscovery of the meaning of being inner-directed in all areas of our decision-making. At a time when social conformity and submission to the power of groups and impersonal institutions like the state seems to some to be threatening the fabric of this society, this could be a healthy sign. It is no accident that newer sexual attitudes have been associated with the use of certain drugs, particularly marijuana, where young people are refusing to have their private behavior legislated by the group. This is part of resisting moral or legal culpability where there is no discernible victim. In a society which has demonstrated its capacity to commit inhuman acts in the name of the law, the new morality's attack on rule-centered ethics is both appropriate and promising.

Fourth, like the legal double standard used for so long to subjugate blacks to white domination, the moral double standard requires rejection to right the injustice of a long history of masculine domination. The related emergence of a new "woman power" promises to bring an eventual end to the "genderism" which has divided our society and confused our sexual mores. Specifically, the fall of the double standard holds promise for the reform of our primitive abortion laws, and for more ready availability of birth control devices to unmarried women. In a time of considerable concern over our population problem, both these developments are promising.

Fifth, to reinterpret the meaning of marriage and deemphasize its identification with sex may be to recover the biblical meaning of marriage, as well as the meaning of what we intuitively recognize as "good" marriages today. This includes a covenant between two individuals which is lifelong in intention, in which each accepts the other "for better or for worse," and each grows in the relationship with that understanding. Although it usually includes sexual exclusiveness, such an understanding is unrelated to premarital behavior. And it does not trivialize marriage as a license to engage in sexual activity, or as simply a temporary social convenience. In a time when soaring divorce statistics indicate that marriage has been seriously trivialized and compromised in its meaning, this could be a promising development indeed.

~ 15 ~

MARIHUANA

Helen H. Nowlis

M arihuana is a drug only by virtue of its being so labeled in the Marihuana Tax Act of 1937 and subsequent legislation. Marihuana is one of several names for a plant, *Cannabis sativa*. It is no more a drug than tea leaves or coffee beans are drugs. All do, however, contain varying amounts of substances which are drugs. In the case of marihuana, that substance is generally accepted to be tetrahydrocannabinol, an isomerically and complex substance found primarily in the resin exuded by the female plant but also present in varying amounts in other parts of the plant. The potency of any preparation of the plant is a function of the amount of tetrahydrocannabinol present. This varies from large amounts in the resin carefully harvested just before flowering from the tops of female plants carefully cultivated in the high plateaus of India to only traces in the dried leaves and flowering tops of plants which grow wild in the northern areas of the U.S.

Much misunderstanding and controversy could be avoided if it were possible to eliminate the term *marihuana* from our considerations. We would not find ourselves in ridiculous situations such as that which occurred recently. THC[9], a recently synthesized

form of what is currently considered to be the active component
of tetrahydrocannabinol, was the center of heated controversy.
Was it an Investigational New Drug to be controlled under the
Drug Abuse Control Amendments of 1965 or was it Marihuana
to be controlled under narcotic control regulations? Like the terms
addiction and *narcotic,* which have lost any concise meaning and
only confuse issues, *marihuana* complicates discussions of everything from the effects of the substance to legalization of the substance. For the purposes of this discussion we bow to the inevitable
and consider "Marihuana: its place among drugs and moves for
its legalization."

Its place among drugs. From one point of view marihuana
is not different from any other drug. It is a substance which by
its chemical nature affects the structure and function of the living
organism. It acts according to the same principles that every drug
acts, only more so. Its effects are a function of dosage (amount of
the active ingredient), route of administration, pattern and circumstances of use, physiological and psychological characteristics,
and current state of the individual, the reasons why he takes it,
and what he expects it will do. "The subjective effects are ex-
quisitely dependent, not only on the personality of the user but
also on the dose, the route of administration, and the specific circumstances in which the drug is used." [1] As is true of virtually all
drugs, its use may result in adverse effects at some dosage level
in some people under some circumstances, some patterns of use or
reasons for use. We should note in passing that "adverse effects"
are clearly value judgments. Like beauty, they lie in the eye of
the beholder.

From another point of view it is different from most other
drugs, but not because of its pharmacological properties or the
factors governing its action. First, it belongs to a group of drugs
which the medical profession as an institution in Western society
has declared to have no accepted role in the treatment and pre-
vention of disease or the relief of pain. Second, and not unrelated
to the first, it has been declared an illicit drug and its illegal status
has been protected and nurtured by labeling it inherently evil

[1] J. Jaffe, "Drug Addiction and Drug Abuse," in Goodman and Gil-
man (Eds.), *The Pharmacological Basis of Therapeutics,* Third Edition (New
York: Macmillan, 1965), p. 300.

and by associating it with heroin and, in most states, actually labeling it a narcotic.

Despite the fact that cannabis, in one form or another, has been used for thousands of years in many parts of the world, we have amazingly little scientific knowledge about it. Several thousand articles and treatises have been written about it but only a very small number of these are of scientific calibre. Marihuana is one substance about which everyone seems to have an opinion or a belief and about which all kinds of people have written, often with more passion than knowledge.

Most scientists who take scientific method, sampling, modern knowledge about drugs and drug action, and the influence of non-drug factors on response to a drug seriously, generally agree, sometimes reluctantly, that there is no good evidence that the relatively low-potency marihuana normally available in this country is physically or psychologically harmful for most people when smoked occasionally or even fairly regularly over a relatively short period of months or even several years. On the other hand, there is no good evidence that chronic use of such relatively low-potency marihuana over long periods is not harmful. That research simply has not been done. Almost the last remaining alleged effect of occasional use of the marihuana in wide use in this country is the charge that smoking marihuana causes young people to lose interest in schoolwork, neglect the niceties of dress and grooming, and become more passive and less ambitious. A hypothesis at least worth testing might be that young people who lose interest in schoolwork, neglect dress and grooming, and become passive go on to smoke marihuana.

On the other hand, single doses of THC[9] equivalent to the actual amount of active substance in six to ten high quality joints well-smoked have been shown to produce marked distortion of perception, depersonalization, pseudo-hallucinations, and many LSD-like effects. But nobody could or would smoke that many joints that thoroughly even in an hour. Since marihuana is effective usually within fifteen minutes after inhaling, experienced marihuana users titrate the amount used, smoke only enough to attain whatever level of high they seek, and cannot be persuaded to take more. It is not like various alcoholic concoctions sometimes deliberately designed to encourage one to drink more than he realizes or intends. On the other hand, anyone who, for reasons

of his own, wants to get really stoned can do it with marihuana—
or with any of a number of other substances, including alcohol.

Testimony presented before the Senate Subcommittee on
Juvenile Delinquency in March, 1968, by Stanley F. Yolles, Director of the National Institute of Mental Health, represents the
worst one can honestly say about marihuana.

> With regard to the hazards of marihuana, the evidence
> is less clear. Clinicians (as well as the LaGuardia Report) have
> reported occasional panic reactions resulting from marihuana
> usage (especially in the novice). The frequency of these epi-
> sodes has not been determined in this country but is believed
> to be rare. . . . While there have been no reports of radio-
> mimetic effects secondary to cannabis, some investigators in
> Scandinavia are currently investigating the possibility that
> tetrahydrocannabinol, the active principle of marihuana, may
> induce similar chromosomal abnormalities that have been de-
> scribed with LSD.[2]
>
> With regard to long-term hazards of marihuana, ac-
> cepted scientific evidence is minimal. . . . In general, most
> investigators in the United States have agreed with the findings
> of the so-called LaGuardia Report which failed to find evi-
> dence to support charges of severe personality change resulting
> from marihuana usage. Additionally, the argument that mari-
> huana usage leads over time to heroin usage has been seriously
> questioned by Dr. Halbach of the World Health Organization
> who notes no pharmacological link between cannabis and opi-
> ates. His hypothesis has been supported by The President's
> Crime Commission Task Force on Drugs and other groups.[3]

Perhaps more important and more relevant for our discussion is his statement:

> Mr. Chairman, I think that it is critical to point out that in
> trying to understand scientifically the problem of drug abuse,
> one must look beyond the specific problems of such agents as
> LSD, marihuana, amphetamines, and barbiturates to some of

    [2] S. F. Yolles, Testimony before the Subcommittee to Investigate
Juvenile Delinquency of the Committee on the Judiciary, United States Senate, Ninetieth Congress, Second Session. Part 19: "LSD and Marihuana Abuse
among Young People" (Washington: Government Printing Office, 1968), pp.
4666–4667.
    [3] Ibid., p. 4667.

the underlying causes of widespread drug use and abuse. . . .
I think that if we are to get to the root of this problem of
drug abuse, we must be prepared to investigate and identify
the underlying problems which lead people to choose to dis-
tort or ward off reality with drugs.[4]

Virtually all drugs can produce mental confusion, halluci-
nations, delirium, impairment of motor coordination, and a wide
variety of abnormal physiological responses in a few susceptible
individuals at any dose or in many individuals at high dosage
levels. These include prescription drugs, over-the-counter drugs,
illicit drugs, as well as drugs we prefer to call beverages. In all of
these, the real question is for what benefit at what risk. In many
instances the "cure" may be worse than the "disease" and, in the
last analysis, this is a matter of value judgment, not of scientific
fact. It is a problem of people who make value judgments about
drugs and drug effects, about people who use drugs and their reasons for using drugs. In the case of marihuana, as well as other
drugs, a current mode is to search for evidence, even to do research, which will support one's preconceived judgments. The role
of a drug in influencing behavior is so complex and so little understood that "drug research" in and of itself will not solve our
"drug problem." But no solution which is not consistent with
modern scientific knowledge about drugs and how they act will be
successful.

This level of knowledge about a drug and the possible
effects of its use is hardly a rational basis for a system of criminal
penalties which make the possession of this substance one of the
most harshly punished crimes in our society.

Its legal status: at what cost? Aside from the basic question
of the propriety of the use of criminal sanctions to control behavior of the individual which is not clearly of danger to other
members of society, a question that has been with us since John
Stuart Mill and before, there are a number of other questions
which deserve careful consideration as we assess the current legal
status of marihuana and possible changes in this status. How
effective are current laws in accomplishing their stated purpose?
What costs are involved in attempting to enforce them? Is it worth
the price?

[4] *Ibid.,* p. 4660.

If the criterion for effectiveness of current marihuana laws is reduction in the use of marihuana, the answer must be a resounding No. Estimates of use vary from two million to twenty million. No one really knows, chiefly because it is impossible to get accurate information about anything which involves admitting to the commission of a felony. There is little question, however, that there has been a sharp and dramatic increase within the past two to three years. Marihuana possession is the most common felony in the state of California. There were over 35,000 marihuana arrests in that state in 1967. There is every indication that 1968 figures will be higher. State after state, community after community reports two- to sixfold increases. This has occurred in the face of penalties in many cases more harsh than those for crimes of violence.

Is the answer more effective enforcement? It is probably no more possible to enforce laws against the possession and use of marihuana than it was to enforce such laws in the case of alcohol. Detection of such behavior as the possession of marihuana can be only fractional at best. Because it does not involve public behavior it must be detected by chance in the course of other enforcement or through the use of informers and undercover agents. How many agents would be necessary to detect even a small portion of two million users? Could and should such law enforcement efforts be better used elsewhere?

From a completely different point of view, can penalties against the possession of specific substances control or reduce drug use? Most knowledgeable and serious students of the current drug scene are convinced that drug use is merely a symptom, that for the serious drug user the drug used is more a function of its availability than any property of the drug. Drug use can be understood only in terms of the meaning and function of such use to the individual and of the total social and political context in which it occurs. Punishing symptoms seldom cures the disease and may in fact aggravate it.

At what cost are we unsuccessfully attempting to enforce laws which are based on uncertain if not actually erroneous assumptions? In our emotion and zeal concerning one area of behavior we seldom take time to think through the implications of our actions for other, perhaps more important, areas of concern. We do not consciously analyze the impact of action in one area on other areas. This is true not only for decisions related to drug use but also for other decisions. Kingman Brewster has recently pointed out that at least one of the impacts of the draft laws is that they keep students captive in college. "This sense of captivity created by the draft is directly related to the tensions and rebellion of students who feel they are prisoners on their own campus." [5] Seymour Halleck adds another dimension: "Faced with an imminent and drastic decision, many students are justifiably frantic. Some are driven to lash back at a society that has put them into this painful position." [6]

Some of the costs of our current attitudes and practices are apparent; others are more subtle. The sheer financial cost of detecting, arresting, charging, trying, sentencing, and carrying out the sentence has been documented for one major city by a UCLA Law Review project.[7] But, as pointed out in the Foreword by John Kaplan, there are serious costs not directly associated with enforcement.

> Thus, who can compute the social cost of a law which turns approximately 30 per cent of the population of the state between the ages of sixteen and twenty-five into serious criminals: Nor can we find any calculus of the alienation from societal values that occurs when young people who, rightly or wrongly, feel that marihuana is no more dangerous than alcohol, are told that their vice is a felony while that of their elders is at most an indiscretion.[8]

An increasing number of people who are deeply concerned with optimal growth and development of young people are deeply disturbed by the impact of these particular laws on the attitude of many young people toward the law in general. If I were asked to designate the greater evil, current use of marihuana or the impact of the drug laws on the attitude of young people toward law, I would without hesitation name the latter. Once having broken a major law and, whether apprehended or not, having been

---

[5] Kingman Brewster, Address to Yale Alumni Day Luncheon, February 22, 1969. Reported in *The New York Times*, February 24, 1969.

[6] Seymour Halleck, "The Road to Chaos," *Psychiatry and Social Science Review*, 1968, 2(7), 2–5.

[7] "Marihuana Laws: An Empirical Study of Enforcement and Administration in Los Angeles," *UCLA Law Review*, 1968, 15(5), 1499–1567.

[8] *Ibid.*, p. 1502.

labeled a criminal, it is less difficult to break other laws when another issue arises. The wheeling and dealing that goes on when, as is the case in some states, the laws are so absurd that no attorney wants to prosecute, no jury wants to convict and no judge wants to sentence, particularly when sentences are mandatory, creates more disrespect for the law than can be tolerated if we are to be a society governed by law. One might also note the effect on the respect with which legislators who pass such laws are viewed.

Drug laws and enforcement practices associated with them have implications for other social institutions as well as the law, not the least of which is education. They strain every aspect of the educational institution's relationship to its students and to society. If we attempt to justify the current (and I might add, proposed) laws we lose our credibility and our ability to deal with a variety of other problems which, in the long run seem to us, at least, more important. When lack of knowledge, less than honesty, or hypocrisy are demonstrated in any area, credibility and effectiveness in all areas suffer. If we do not support current beliefs, we may preserve our ability to work with and teach students, but we run the risk of being accused of encouraging the commission of a felony or of losing our job. The threat to institutions is greater even than that to individuals. Refusal to apply law enforcement methods in the university community, in the honest belief that they both hinder efforts to deal with the problem and that they destroy the very atmosphere which is essential to true education and freedom of inquiry, can and has provided the opportunity for some to attack the whole system of higher education and for non-educators to attempt to dictate the organization, the function, and the personnel of the institution.

There are other unintended consequences of drug legislation and drug law enforcement, but these are perhaps the most relevant for us as educators. Each of you can order the values at stake. To many of us the current situation has deprived us of all of the tools with which we habitually attack a problem. Because of the criminal penalties on possession of a growing list of substances, we cannot do good research, we cannot do good education, we cannot do effective counseling, we cannot provide treatment early enough when treatment is necessary. It is impossible to cope with any problem that is driven underground. Using our methods, we almost certainly will not be able to eliminate use of marihuana

by students, but we believe that we can reduce the abuse of marihuana.

Does this mean the legalization of marihuana? Our increasing tendency to assume that if something is not good its opposite
is by definition good is very disturbing. Should we assume that if
the laws making the drug illegal are not good, then the answer is
to make it legal? Although I personally believe that society neither
can nor should legislate health and happpiness and believe very
strongly that efforts to do so will cost more than they are worth,
I have tried desperately during the almost three years in which
"the drug problem" has been my major concern to recognize that
my particular cost-benefit analysis is that of a psychologist and
an educator. I am not naive enough to expect that people with
other training, background, experience, and personal and professional investment will arrive at the same answer. My plea is that
they look beyond the immediate problem, at least do their own
cost-benefit analysis, and be aware that what they do in this area
has effects in many areas.

An increasing number of scientists and educators are questioning the assumptions on which our drug laws are based and
the impact of enforcement of these laws. The President's Commission on Law Enforcement and the Administration of Justice [9]
concluded that there was sufficient evidence to make a reexamina-
tion necessary. An international symposium of scientists held last
September in Quebec [10] officially recommended that "The penalties under the present laws for the offence of simple possession
of cannabis in the natural forms are inequitable in view of the
current state of scientific knowledge and appear to be a contributory factor to the social problem." [11] A majority of the conference
recommended that existing laws and international covenants
should be reviewed and stated that any law which permits a first
offender guilty of simple possession of small amounts of cannabis
to be incarcerated is improper.

Even some of the most passionate opponents of legalization

[9] *The Challenge of Crime in a Free Society.* Report of the President's
Commission on Law Enforcement and the Administration of Justice (Washington: Government Printing Office, 1967).

[10] "Recommendations," First International Symposium on Psychodysleptics and Pharmacopsychoses, Université Laval, Quebec, Canada, September 16–19, 1968.

[11] *Ibid.*

of marihuana feel that the current possession laws are improper. Louria has stated:

> Clearly, the possession of marihuana or other cannabis prep-
> arations, even in amounts large enough to make twenty-five to
> fifty cigarettes, should be construed as a relatively minor crime.
> . . . For at least the first two offenses, conviction on posses-
> sion charges should carry a constructive sentence, as for in-
> stance, assignment to a local anti-poverty program for an
> appropriate period of time. Additionally, it should be provided
> that upon completion of that sentence the conviction be ex-
> punged from the record, so as not to affect the individual's
> future deleteriously.[12]

Despite personal reservations as to the propriety of applying criminal sanctions, given the complexity of defining *drug* and
drug use, and recognizing our basic lack of reliable information
about the effects on the individual and on society of long-term
use of low-potency levels of marihuana, I have taken the position
that a minimum action would be to remove criminal penalties
from possession. In my cost-benefit analysis they are far too costly
and are actually aggravating all aspects of the problem. If the
issue is to be decided on the "effects" of marihuana rather than
on philosophical grounds we must get the information needed to
make a rational decision. This is impossible as long as it is criminal to possess.

I might add that my tally sheet is beginning to get over-
balanced on the cost side as I interact with more and more students, parents, teachers, and administrators in schools and colleges
across the country. Not the least increasingly apparent cost is the
completely unknown quality and potency of all of the drugs available only on the black market which young people are using despite our punitive laws. To this we should add the increasing
emotionality, polarization, and panic created in all segments of
the public by attempts to mobilize public opinion in support of
current laws and law enforcement, a panic which is making it
almost impossible to discuss, to communicate, to educate. "Narcotic addiction" has not spread from the ghetto to middle-class
American youth. But this is not to say that all is well with middle-
class American youth.

[12] D. B. Louria, *The Drug Scene* (New York: McGraw-Hill, 1968),
pp. 195–196.

~ 16 ~

CAMPUS ENVIRONMENTS AND STUDENT UNREST

George G. Stern

Taxes, race riots, and anti-war demonstrations are sure to arouse the passions of a good many Americans. Outrage is often tempered, however, by the realization that there is something, not much perhaps, but something to be said for the other side. Not so on campus disturbances. There are no second thoughts to moderate the righteous indignation directed at college trouble-makers. President Nixon unquestionably spoke what was in the minds of many people when he applauded Father Hesburgh's get-tough policy at Notre Dame and condemned the "impatience with democratic processes, and intolerance of legitimately consti-tuted authority" of "a small irresponsible minority."

There can be no doubt that the Berkeley demonstrations in 1964 brought the universities to the attention of the American public in a new and unpleasant way. Political protests were not unknown here before, but they were rare events compared with the popular image of Latin American campus events. Student disorders in the United States were ordinarily dismissed as harmless outbursts of male adolescent energy. The extent of organized student protest since Berkeley has been so surprising to many Americans that they find it easier to believe that the troubles are due to a small group of outside agitators rather than consider the possible problems of the universities themselves. It is equally significant that a determined stand like Hayakawa's at San Francisco State should receive much favorable attention, despite the fact that the school has been unable to operate openly since last Thanksgiving, whereas the effective mediation of the Brandeis or Chicago administrations in dealing with their crises has been largely ignored. Aggressive action to curb violence, countermeasures of approved violence, have a wider and more dramatic appeal in the United States than efforts at understanding or resolving conflict.

I shall attempt in the next few minutes to examine the issues over which campus disorders have occurred in the United States, and relate aspects of these disturbances to characteristics of American colleges and their student bodies. The purpose of this analysis is to clarify some of the mechanisms at work, hopefully to increase our capacity to respond meaningfully to these symptoms of social disturbance. I am cynical about this effort but, like the minister whose daughter arrived home from a dance at daybreak bearing a Gideon bible, my cynicism is mixed with hope.

There were at least 221 demonstrations on 101 American campuses in the spring of 1968, not counting Columbia, according to a survey by the U.S. National Student Association. Nearly 40,000 students took part in them. NSA found black power to be the leading issue, accounting for 44 per cent of the disturbances. Student demands for authority to regulate their own lives were involved in 23 per cent, anti-war demonstrations in 18 per cent, 6 per cent were over individual professors or administrators, and the remainder were for miscellaneous reasons.

A survey by Peterson covering 859 institutions throughout the whole of the 1967–68 academic year found Vietnam and dormitory regulations to be the two most prevalent protest issues, reported respectively by over a third of the schools in the study. These two were not only the most frequent but also the most common, taking place in all types of institutions. Other bases for student demonstrations were more selective, occurring among large numbers of universities, both public and private, but relatively infrequently among any other kind of school. Between one-third and two-thirds of the universities reported demonstrations protesting racial discrimination on campus and in the surrounding community, student exclusion from the university decision-making process, the draft, and recruitment by the military and the war industries.[1]

Peterson's data indicate that this protest pattern was not related to either size as such or to the proportion of resident students, but was associated with the proportion of faculty holding doctorates and of the student body belonging to leftist organizations. It might be added here that it must also be a function of the proportion of graduate students, since Peterson did not find the independent liberal arts colleges sharing much of this protest pattern, yet their faculty Ph.D. rates and leftist student organizations are comparable with the universities.

There may be other factors equally implicit among universities contributing to what might properly be called the University Protest Movement. Graduate departments require graduate faculties, and these tend to be a very select group even among the total population of faculty Ph.D.s. They have been recruited for the past twenty years on the basis of their potential for research, publication, and program building. Having been screened even earlier for such qualities by their own graduate instructors, they are unquestionably the most aggressive, ambitious, energetic, counteractive, pragmatic, and intellectually independent of all graduate school products, and committed both vocationally and by personal conviction to the development of others like themselves. It is in this sense that the graduate disciplines in the arts and sciences have come to be the determining force in education, reaching down through the colleges and high schools to the elementary grades to channel the brightest and the best motivated into the tracks that lead on specifically to the graduate schools. The second-

[1] R. E. Peterson, *The Scope of Organized Student Protest in 1967–1968* (Princeton, N. J.: Educational Testing Service, 1968).

best fall out to other careers; the best are encouraged to work toward Ph.D.s, and the very best to join in training others like them. The school system has become academia's way of reproducing itself.

What I am trying to suggest is that the graduate schools are a source of people, both students and faculty, who are: (1) independent of life outside the university community, and therefore more detached in their view of that world, (2) articulate and analytical, and therefore more likely to formulate a critical position on social issues, (3) engaged in a struggle paralleling that of the surgeons earlier in this century, for control of the institution that has become more and more specifically adapted (like the hospitals) to meet their particular professional needs, and (4) contributing inadvertently to a growing reservoir of frustration and ill-will among the enormously large numbers of students, graduate and undergraduate, who have neither the inclination nor the capacity to be included among the select few but who are nevertheless required to go through the same curriculum. It is after all not only the best curriculum, since it was designed to prepare people for graduate school, but also the only one.

Keniston and Astin have both argued that student activists are themselves an important source of protest since they are a unique group of individuals, suited by temperament and background to playing a radical role.[2] There is some question as to whether they alone can be held responsible for campus disturbances, however. Although it has been shown that student radicals share comparable personality characteristics, it has not been demonstrated that such people are to be found only at the universities. On the contrary, I have myself presented considerable evidence that these types are even more prevalent among independent liberal arts colleges than in any other kind of school, constituting in fact the predominant personality type at the most selective of the elite schools.[3] Yet we have seen from Peterson that these insti-

[2] Kenneth Keniston, *Young Radicals* (New York: Harcourt, 1968); Alexander Astin, "Personal and Environmental Determinants of Student Activism," Paper read at the American Psychological Association Convention, San Francisco, September, 1968.

[3] George G. Stern, "Characteristics of the Intellectual Climate in College Environments," *Harvard Educational Review*, 1963, *33*, 5–41; "Student Ecology and the College Environment," *Journal of Medical Education*, 1965, *40*, 132–154; and *People in Context* (New York: Wiley, 1969).

tutions are not representative of the University Protest Movement.

What we should most like to know is whether there are some universities that are more likely than others to erupt in violent demonstrations, or whether the causes lie instead in something endemic to the universities as a class. Can any university expect to find itself in the position of Berkeley, Columbia, or San Francisco State, or are there factors peculiar to some schools that may be likely to aggravate tensions perhaps present in all of them but ending in bold confrontation in just these few? If the latter is the case, perhaps we shall discover something of relevance to conflict resolution in other types of schools as well.

In the absence of material from a substantial number of universities, no direct answer to this question is possible. However, I do have data from the American Association for the Higher Education Campus Governance Study on problems perceived by students, faculty, and administrators at nineteen schools, and these can be related to measures of student personality and of the institutional environment to tell us something of the impact of the college on student perceptions.

The *Pre-Interview Questionnaire* (PIQ) measures the extent to which six different types of problems are perceived at an institution. These are themselves subsumed under two broader categories as follows:

Area I. Personal Growth

Factor 2. Student Autonomy .86 (Student Participation .90, Student Regulations .86, Academic Freedom .65).

Factor 5. Academic Learning Experience .76 (Teaching —.73, Requirements —.69, Counseling —.60, Student Dignity —.55, Class Load and Size —.54, Problems for Institutional Change —.41, Student Government —.38).

Factor 4. Faculty Autonomy .64 (Faculty Participation —.79, Administrative Tone —.79, Respect for Individuals —.66, Procedures for Institutional Change —.53).

Area II. Institutional Resources

Factor 1. Plant and Facilities .90 (Space .87, Services .74, Finances .69, Teaching Equipment .68, Research Facilities .62, Laboratories .51, Buildings and Grounds .47).[4]

Factor 6. Faculty Quality .86 (Publications and Records .72, Professional Relationships .67, Faculty Interaction .64, Student and Faculty Quality .48).

Factor 3. Student Leisure Resources .54 (Recreational Space .84, Student Activities Space .70, Student Involvement .54, Cultural Facilities .51, Library .42).

The *College Characteristics Index* (CCI) is a measure of psychological dimensions differentiating colleges and universities from one another. Eleven factors have been extracted from a variety of commonplace events that go on from day to day at an institution. The factors reflect such things as the quality of the academic climate, motivational systems, student dignity, group life, and so on.

Two broad, independent dimensions underlie the eleven, based on the tendency of these institutional processes to contribute toward either the personal growth of the participants or the maintenance of the institution itself. Forces for self-actualization and for institutional stability are not peculiar to higher education; studies with related environment instruments have revealed the same two general processes at work in high schools, training programs, and vocational settings in industry. The specific nuances of each type of organization are reflected in the various first-order components, but these two emerge repeatedly as the higher-order integration of the others.

There is some evidence among the colleges for a third higher-order dimension, wholly unique to them. It is based on a high level of student constraint coupled with maximal administrative organization or control. The extreme Puritanical character of this rare environmental dimension is such as to suggest that it be called Impulse Control.

---

[4] The items in parentheses represent first-order factors based on 120 individual items in the PIQ. The six "factors" listed above are second-order variates, and the two "areas" were obtained in turn from a third-order analysis of them. The value following each first- and second-order factor represents its loading on the next higher order factors. The analyses involved principle axis components and equamax rotation.

TABLE 1

RELATIONS BETWEEN PROBLEMS REPORTED BY STUDENTS AND
CHARACTERISTICS OF THE COLLEGE ENVIRONMENT AND CULTURE
(N = 35 programs)

	I	II	I Personal Growth			II Institutional Resources		
			2	5	4	1	6	3
Environment (CCI)								
Personal Growth I	−54***	−24	−52***	−46**	−40*	−47**	−26	11
Organizational Stability II	34*	−08	34*	35*	15	20	−08	−34*
Impulse Control III	37*	45**	17	36*	37*	37*	42**	40*
Culture (AI × CCI)								
Intellectual −I	−44**	−10	−43**	−36*	−33*	−37*	−10	+22
Protective −II	+29	+10	+21	+30	+19	+18	+08	−00

*** < .001
** < .01
* < .05

Table 1 shows the relationships between these three environmental characteristics and the types of problems reported by students. Schools organized in ways that contribute to high levels of personal growth are not likely to have problems in this area. Significantly fewer problems are reported in connection with either student autonomy, the academic learning experience, or faculty autonomy. Such schools tend also to have fewer complaints regarding plant or facilities. Students at these places are more satisfied than those at any other kind of school, even though it is clear that institutional resources as such are not necessarily outstanding with respect to either faculty quality or student leisure resources. We know from other data that a strong climate for personal growth is uniquely associated with small independent elite liberal arts colleges [5] which throws some further light on what would appear to be an unexpected limitation in these otherwise ideal institutions. They are not particularly distinguished for their faculty or their recreational facilities, yet students find more fulfillment in this type of environment than elsewhere.

High organizational stability—reflected in environments with extensive student services, group life, academic organization,

[5] Stern, *op. cit.*

vocationalism, and play—generate problems in personal growth. Students in such environments raise issues involving student autonomy as well as the academic learning experience. The structure is evidently somewhat oppressive, and academically trivial. Student leisure resources are more likely to be satisfactory at these schools, however.

The largest number of problems of all types are reported from schools with rigid, highly controlled environments. Complaints in every area are positively correlated with Impulse Control, with the single exception of student autonomy. The relationship in this case is still positive but substantially lower than the other coefficients. It is due to two large state universities that reverse the trend of the other schools in the Governance sample by presenting their students with an environment that is low in control but still characterized by many problems. There is a high degree of play and very little academic organization at these two schools, the students are treated with little dignity or respect, and they are very dissatisfied.

The implications seem clear enough. Institutions that stress opportunities for personal growth have far fewer problems than those that do not. But the most severe sources of tension ordinarily arise in those places that are administratively over-organized and severely restrictive of student play—that attempt, in other words, to maintain an excessive degree of control over student impulse life.

To what extent are these findings attributable to organizational climate rather than to the students? Since student types are distributed differentially among different kinds of schools, could these results be due to the students recruited to these environments rather than to the environments themselves? A partial answer to this question is given in the bottom two rows of the table. The interaction between student personality, as measured by the *Activities Index* (AI), and the environmental press (CCI) gives rise to five joint factors reflecting five basic cultural types among American colleges and universities.

Most schools tend to be somewhat vocational and collegiate in their orientation, with students reflecting appropriate qualities of conventionality and play. A separate and distinct group of them stresses expressiveness and intellectuality, both in environmental organization and in the qualities of their student bodies.

These are the elite liberal arts colleges again. Still another distinct group lies along the protective axis, representing schools which offer a high degree of support to students who are dependent and in need of structure. These are the denominational colleges, and least like institutions with either a collegiate culture or an expressive one.

The measure of intellectuality in Table 1 combines environmental qualities supporting personal growth with student characteristics most frequently associated with such environments: intellectuality and autonomy. There is no change, however, in the pattern of correlations with problems reported for the environment alone. Protective cultures, on the other hand, have none of the problems associated with either organizationally stable environments or impulse controlling ones, despite the fact that the denominational college environments have elements in common with both of these. The presence of students with compatible dependency needs has made the difference. To the extent that their personalities are conjunctive with their school environments, they report few problems despite the restrictiveness of the school.

There are significant differences between the types of men attending each of the five kinds of liberal arts college as distinguished by CCI results. The independent males have needs which contribute to the maintenance of a college culture that is intellectual and noncollegiate. They differ then from denominational men, who are oriented towards protectiveness and nonexpressive needs, and from the university men, who reveal no single strong need (reflecting the greater diversity of the university student body).

The press at the independent colleges is congruent with the needs of the male student body in both the intellectual and the collegiate areas, from which we may then infer that the independent liberal arts colleges have strongly cohesive cultures, supported both institutionally and by their male students, reflecting a preoccupation with scholarship and intellectuality and an absence of conventional student play. However, there are two areas in which student needs and school press are disjunctive. These schools are strongly nonvocational, although their male students are more conventional in this area, and the schools are also highly expressive despite the fact that the men appear to take bright academically-oriented achieving students with somewhat conventional goals and attempt to shake them loose from their prior value systems, reshaping them in a more flexible and expressive mold.

Neither the denominational nor the university-affiliated liberal arts colleges attempt anything nearly so ambitious with their student bodies. The church-affiliated schools are slightly more expressive than their students, but on the whole, the correspondence between need and press at these schools is quite remarkable. If congruence between need and press is associated with satisfaction, the students at these schools should be extremely content. The universities, on the other hand, underplay their male students in both Expressiveness and Intellectuality, and there is good reason to believe from these data that there would be expressions of student discontent at these schools and attempts to reform them in ways that more nearly resemble the independent liberal arts colleges.

The implication of these data is that faculty at independent liberal arts colleges share values not unlike those of the men attending the large universities. The common interest actually lies in the development of an emerging expressive culture, however, rather than in intellectuality as such. In the long run, then, these are only partially converging interests. Although both the independent and the denominational colleges are attempting to encourage more expressiveness, the universities are the only institutions likely to develop a relevant culture since they are the only places that have the students to sustain it. The irony is that what the other types of schools are trying to do in spite of their students, the university students are attempting in spite of their schools.

The same data for women show there is very little difference here from the situation for the men. The congruence between need and press is again greatest at the denominational colleges, and the discrepancies between the two involve higher expectations at the independent colleges and a serious underestimation of student potential at the universities.

Engineering and teacher-training programs also show a good deal of congruence between need and press, although there is some suggestion that the teacher-training institutions consistently underrate their students. The most interesting by far, however, is the relationship shown for the business administration programs. The students show extreme scores on four of the five cultures. In order of magnitude these students are highly Vocational, Collegiate, Expressive, and Non-Intellectual. The school press matches their absence of intellectuality, but attempts to dampen them in the other three areas. The cultural pattern most consistently sustained by students and schools alike in the area of business administration would appear then to be anti-intellectual.

In general it would seem that differences between the five cultures are associated with particular combinations of students and environments, and the same thing may be said of the degree and character of the congruence between student needs and environmental press. Denominational colleges are the most congruent, showing very little discrepancy between school and student patterns. The greatest divergence is shown by the independent liberal arts colleges and the business administration programs, the former setting standards of overachievement for their students, the latter attempting to hold back some of the least academically relevant interests of theirs. The large universities also provide an environment context that is inconsistent with the needs of their students, in their case underestimating student capacities for Intellectuality and Expressiveness.

We are brought back once again then to the special problems of the universities. The answer would seem simple enough now. Open the undergraduate curriculum to new all-university programs freed from the restrictions of graduate school preparation. Let it lead to a different undergraduate degree, a Bachelor of Philosophy (Ph.B.) degree, for example, to avoid issues involving presumed differences in standards. The new program can still be rigorous, though ungraded, and perhaps even more scholarly than the conventional curriculum since there is no need to begin technical overspecialization. Students in such programs would be able to spend more time in the arts, or in the community, or in many other unexpected places where significant personal growth may nevertheless take place in ways entirely consistent with the purposes and traditions of the university and fully utilizing its exceptional resources. Should some of these new graduates later wish to return to more conventional pursuits and apply for admission to graduate school there are diagnostic tests to establish their areas of deficiency and specific preparatory work that might then be required.

There are massive organizational changes required to implement such a program, but it could be brought about in time at any university. I wish that I could end on such a happy note. But the facts of life are far more depressing than the projections of social science. There is a school on record which attempted to develop in directions very close to those I have suggested here. Despite an enrollment of over eighteen thousand and graduate degree programs in forty fields, a number of genuinely innovative undergraduate programs were adopted. Perhaps the most unusual of these was its Experimental College, a collection of degree-credit courses designed by students, taught by regular faculty or students or both, and budgeted out of student government money. A very favorable two-page spread in the December 21, 1966, *Chronicle* quotes the school administration as follows:

> Responsibility is the key word here, and they are responsible kids. They have complaints about the way they are being taught and want some courses overhauled. The students are questioning the very nature of teaching, and it may be a good thing.
> Here, we have hundreds of students concerned with education. I can't think of a better thing for them to be concerned about. Not everything they do is profound, but compared with a lot of things that students do, this is well-organized and well-thought-out.

Our data clearly support everything that had been said for this school. Although it was a public university, its environment measures could not be distinguished from those for an elite independent liberal arts college. The climate was strongly oriented toward "personal growth," in the special sense I have been using those words here. Students reported an exceptionally low number of complaints and there were no signs of tension or distress.

The data were gathered in the fall and winter of 1967. The school was San Francisco State.

The critical problem stemmed from issues not yet apparent to many at the time, and not so easily resolved even by a well-intentioned administration. Admissions standards had been raised, in part because of the need to maintain enrollments at the level established by the governor's financial cuts in funds for higher education. Black enrollment at San Francisco State dropped from 11 per cent, possibly the highest in the country, to 3.6 per cent. The entirely understandable bitterness of the black intellectual community exploded into violence with the intemperate response of the trustees to a statement attributed to a black faculty member by the press. The trustees dismissed him despite the objections of the college administration and faculty.

Continued interference by the trustees (a statewide group appointed by the governor) in the internal affairs of the college contributed to the resignation of several presidents and the present acting president was appointed by the trustees without consultation, and accepted in violation of a pledge to avoid just such a situation. The events since last November are too well known to need repeating here.

The lesson seems clear enough. San Francisco State illustrates the massive opposition to change in higher education that exists outside the system. There is every reason to believe that major changes are under way in American colleges and universities. If my own institution, Syracuse, is any example, there are a number of schools that have been quietly beginning to involve students in the decision-making process at all levels. New study programs are announced every day. Given the opportunity to respond without the pressure of outside political interests, there is some reason to believe that most schools will profit from the university protest movement.

To disregard the student revolt, to dismiss it as the work of a tiny fringe of agitators manipulating issues that are entirely beyond the control of the educational enterprise, is to risk politicization of the university—to lose the ideal of an independent intellectual community, not regain it. A university kept open at bayonet point is neither a "university" nor "open." The continuance of the university as a citadel of understanding depends on the capacity of all its members to find, and respond to, those internal contradictions that are sources of misunderstanding and conflict.

Section V

Governance

In the opening essay of Section V, Harold Hodgkinson analyzes the whole of a college or university as a kind of hydraulic system; a pressure entering the system at point A does not typically create a disturbance at point A but at point M or T. Hodgkinson argues that governance structures must follow from functions, and he shows how the situation, at present, is almost everywhere reversed.

Lewis Mayhew's essay constitutes a detailed commentary on the meaning of a crucial term in discussions of governance today—"shared responsibility." He sees the solution to governance problems in a creative tension between faculty and administration. As for students, they are—in Mayhew's conception of the ideal governance structure—peripheral. He believes they have no more right to a role in campus governance than a patient has in the governance of a hospital. On this point, Mayhew quite clearly stands (to use his own words) for "a conservative doctrine, far from participatory democracy."

In the third essay of Section V, John Livingston describes the impact of current campus pressures on the governance structure. They "intensify the adversary character of relations between academic senates and trustees . . . ," he asserts, and as tensions increase between them, administrators will be "hopelessly caught in the middle." The final result, Livingston argues, is "to accelerate a trend toward collective bargaining." He does not believe this

137

trend will serve the basic goals of American higher education, but he sees no other alternative at this time.

Howard Bowen, in the final essay of Section V, also sees governance functioning primarily as a means to achieve the educational goals of the university: "The only acceptable system of governance is one that will . . . enable the university to become educationally forward looking." (Hence the title of the essay: "Governance and Educational Reform.") Among his suggestions for achieving academic reform, Bowen calls for a coalition of students and administrators "to push the faculty into action."

Bowen presents a detailed plan for a new system of governance to replace the structure that is now becoming common on many campuses (namely, a legislature-type structure with five "houses": the governing board, administrative officials, the faculty senate, student body officials, and nonacademic staff representatives); Bowen's plan, on the other hand, envisages final authority and accountability in the president, who then works cooperatively with a joint council that does not represent the goals of special interest groups but the interests of the university as a whole.

JOSEPH AXELROD

~17~

WHO DECIDES
WHO DECIDES?

Harold L. Hodgkinson

Governance is very hard to study, for some of the same reasons that sexual behavior is hard to study. In our culture, both are considered private acts, not to be performed in public to be observed and commented upon by others. Warren Bennis relates the incident in which a university president asked a group of his most prestigious professors to make a list of the most pressing problems facing the nation. After several weeks of working, the professors came up with a list of about ten—heading the list was the topic, university organization. Then the president asked the group to rank order the list in terms of those problems which the university should *actually work on*. University organization came in last.[1]

[1] On the problems of functional analysis, see H. Hodgkinson, "Functionalism," a chapter in *Education, Interaction, and Social Change* (Englewood Cliffs, N. J.: Prentice-Hall, 1967).

There are many reasons for this difficulty. Perhaps most important is the *perceptual* problem—what do we see when we think of a university? Some see a legal system, others a city, some a production-distribution system, some a communication network, some a certifying agency awarding brownie points for the meritocracy which it serves. But as long as we differ in terms of the nature of the thing to be governed, we will differ in our approach to governance as well. One can visualize the campus as a series of interlocking hollow pipes filled with fluid, in other words, a hydraulic system. If one puts a piston into any pipe and increases the hydraulic pressure, the consequences can be felt throughout the system. It is for this reason that events often have unanticipated consequences for other parts of the system, why an attempt to create a new freshman curriculum may not succeed but may result in a new structure for advising. To say that the curriculum effort "failed" is to miss the point as to how second-level consequences come about. In California, the hydraulic system exists at the state level, and the unintended consequences of certain events for other parts of the system are extremely vital. An example of unintended consequences can be found in the student demonstration the day before election day which contributed to the defeat of a $200 million bond issue for higher education. Left-wing activities bring right-wing responses. There are currently seventy-two bills under study by the California legislature to bring an end to campus violence, and most of them contain more violent provisions than the thing they are designed to prevent.

Many of my own notions about "good" governance have been shaken as a consequence of our research. For example, while I know that the evidence suggests there is no difference between democratic and autocratic teaching styles, I had the notion that "tall" rigid hierarchical forms of governance were inferior to flat, flexible, participatory organizations. But this judgment is not supported by the data. On several campuses which are governed by rigid hierarchies, there is also widespread excitement and interest in participating in governance, and this participation is encouraged. There are also campuses where, even though the structure looks loose and free-wheeling, there is a great deal of suppression, intimidation, and paranoia. So if governance is to release as much of the energy as possible within a system toward activities from which the system benefits (and that is a pretty fair

version of what governance should do) then the people who occupy the positions are much more important than the positions
themselves. In any structure, some trust is necessary.

Higher education is fast becoming the major industry in
the nation, and the efforts to control it are understandably on the
increase. The sections of hydraulic pipe often lead far off campus,
and into some pretty strange places. Someone can apply pressure
to the system in Sacramento or Washington, and a pipe can break
at San Francisco State. The model makes it difficult to conceive
of decision-making as solely an on-campus phenomenon, yet we
persist in the myth of institutional uniqueness, in which we all
assume that our college or university is different from all others,
and therefore what happens to others has no relevance for our
campus. For example, the Trustee Study reveals that trustees believe that attending college is a right, but attending *their* college
is a privilege. In any system at any level, there are two functions
operating—one is reciprocity of the part with the whole, the other
is autonomy of the part as an entity. We tend to look at autonomy
for ourselves, expecting everybody else to believe in reciprocity.
Probably the most pathetic cry of the human creature is "Why
don't those people cooperate?"

Systems of organizations seem to be moving toward more
encompassing levels all the time. Kenneth Boulding has envisaged
an entity of all social organization on the planet which he calls
the sociosphere (directly below the troposphere), and there is now
a school of sociology called global sociology. We are seldom aware
of these new organizational patterns until they affect us directly.
The New England power failure revealed a level of system integration which was virtually unknown before—we could not
perceive it until it failed and we found out where the limits of
the system were. Similarly, the phenomenon of the megalopolis
now exists, even though we have no plans for trying to govern it.

That was a long way round to my central thesis, but perhaps a necessary one. Different levels of system integration call
for different systems of governance. We know nothing about how
to govern a megalopolis. There is little consensus as to how to
govern a statewide system of higher education, perhaps the educational equivalent. Our present metaphor seems to be that of the
individual campus writ large—campuses have presidents, boards
of trustees, faculty senates, and so statewide organizations of higher

education have presidents, boards of trustees, and faculty senates. I would like to suggest that what we have created at the statewide level may be a very different breed of beast, which demands new roles and structures very different from those of the single campus.

My own conclusion is that faith in symbolic representation as a mode of governance is declining. Many feel that the president no longer represents the institution, the board does not represent the people, the faculty senate does not represent the faculty, and student government does not represent the students. Direct participation of all members of all factions seems to be the order of the day. But in adversary negotiations, everyone gets drawn into the fight; there are few if any outsiders. To refer to our title, if the faculty votes no on student participation in academic decisions, the students vote yes, the president of the institution votes yes, the board votes no, the state department of education votes yes while the governor votes no, then who decides who decides? That seems to me one of the crucial questions of this generation—how, and who, reallocates power and influence in changing governance patterns?

There seem to me to be two tendencies occurring simultaneously. The first is a deeply felt move toward decentralization on campus and in national government—to give control back to the people. But this move will not make the super-system melt away. A university of thirty separate, autonomous campuses is still a university—there must be linkages across the campuses, reciprocity as well as autonomy. My own view is that governance structures must follow from governance functions. But at the moment, we often limit our view of what needs to be done to that which the established structure allows. Functions should be served by structures, not the other way around. I am particularly impressed by the relationship of reciprocity and autonomy which characterizes the State University of New York Buffalo plan for thirty colleges, each with its own special identity. They are not out to obliterate academic departments, but to provide meaningful options to departmental ways of doing things. This same reciprocity happens at Berkeley, although in an unplanned way. Departmentalism is rife, but ringing the campus is a series of over fifty "centers"—centers for research, development, or centers for the study of something—which provide in an unobtrusive way the interdisciplinary, the synthetic, the relational perspectives. But they do not benefit students much.

The model toward which we must move is describable in terms of an analogy to the problem of class size. Classes of thirty to forty are the worst—they do not provide the meaningful exchange of the seminar of fifteen, and are inefficient in supplying information to large masses of students. Classes should either be very large or very small, depending on the function of the class. The same can be said of systems of governance. The ideal to shoot for would be a system in which decisions affecting individuals' lives and commitments would be made in the smallest possible units, while matters of logistics and support services should be made in the largest context available, tapping into the national network. People, from registrars to full professors, will have to begin to shift their attitudes (and perhaps even values) as they plug into different networks. People may have to get used to working closely with others in an ad hoc organization to solve a problem, then to disbanding the structure when the problem is solved, to pulling out friendship linkages, and to going on to other tasks. The pyramid model of organization seems to suggest that the same structure can work for all problems. There is a new awareness that different problems require different structures for their solution. To solve student discontent with a structure which by its very nature suggests that students are subservient beings, to do what they are told, is a mistake of the first magnitude. In fact, C. West Churchman, one of the founders of operations research, has now taken the position that the quality of an organization should not be ascertained by the decisions made, but by the quality of participation in the decision-making process.[2] Looked at in another way, a typical cafeteria line pushes people through a one-way closed system, passing them by a lot of stuff they may not want. Actually more efficient is the scramble access cafeteria system which has no lines, only stations, and people are free to range from station to station (each station has only a limited range of food) until they have what they want. To a newcomer, it looks like chaos, as people move around with no discernible pattern, but it is actually a system based on maximum flexibility and access.

[2] Personal conversation. See also his *Challenge to Reason* (New York: McGraw-Hill, 1968).

The urgent task remaining involves the delineating of different functions for different levels of system integration. We also must look carefully at nonsystematic elements which are a part of the human condition also—there is signal and there is noise, there is logic and there is soul. (Love, for example, is simply not a closed-loop feedback circuit, and any husband who conceives it in those terms deserves to be hit by his loving spouse with the proverbial frying pan.) We conceive of organization as rational only, but we clearly need ways of communicating affect to each other as much as we need that paragon of bureaucratic procedures, the inter-office memo. To say that we should start writing memos in the form of poems would not be totally absurd.

For adults who have devoted their lives to maintaining the structures they dominate, structures have become ends in themselves, rather than means to ends. That is one reason why we should listen to students—not that they are always right, but because they have not developed the trained incapacity of believing that the structure must be served at any cost. Structures can be modified to serve humane and human purposes, but before we modify, we must be able to state what the purposes are at various levels of integration of the hydraulic system, all the way from Mr. Finch's office in Washington to the newly arrived freshman at Colorado College. If the academic community cannot revise its own structures, the larger society will do it anyway. The bull-dozer is its own architect and planner. At least in California, the people, who apparently support the Reagan-Hayakawa position, are having their say. For academics to simply watch the passing scene doing their "job," is a tragic error; as Auden once described it, it is like lecturing on navigation while the ship is going down.

~ 18 ~

FACULTY IN CAMPUS GOVERNANCE

Lewis B. Mayhew

There is one supportable theme that the contemporary college or university cannot govern nor restructure itself so as to be responsive to rapidly changing conditions. Irving Kristal has ". . . the gravest doubts that, out of all the current agitation for a 'restructuring' of the university, very much substance will come." The faculty controls educational functions and defines educational purposes but ". . . professors are a class with a vested interest in, and an ideological commitment to, the *status quo* broadly defined . . ." hence reform must be imposed on it as on any other group. "Nor is the administration going to 'restructure' the university. It couldn't do it if it tried. University administration in the United States today combines relative powerlessness with near absolute mindlessness on the subject of education." And boards of trustees ". . . represent a kind of 'stand-by' authority, ready to take over if the executive officers lead the organization into a scandalous mess." [1]

However, there is a different thesis, which holds that existing agencies and forces within the university do hold the potential for effective governance and restructuring when necessary, if only they can be brought into proper alignment or juxtaposition. This assumes that the modern college or university can eventually deserve the high esteem which it has gained since the end of World War II but which by 1969 had become seriously imperiled.

Such a faith, for that is what for the moment it is, rests on several assumptions. The first of these is that essentially the college or university is an institution created and maintained to provide certain classes of professional services to people who wish or need them. A profession is here defined as a group of people possessing esoteric knowledge, developed and transmitted through training, which enables them to perform definite acts and services for others (a laying on of hands) and whose right to do so is generally recognized. The delivery of these services is regulated by a system of ethics and standards of conduct, relevant to the services offered, and self-created by the members of the profession.

Now it is true that much of the professional service which colleges and universities have provided has not been of a particularly high nor effective order. Teaching has not been spectacularly successful nor have curricula been designed to conform with the needs of the client, that is, the student. But these failures do not negate the underlying principle that professional services are needed and that institutions could provide them through improving the strategies and instruments available to them.

The second assumption is that of the several styles of organizing and governing colleges and universities, the adversary style, best illustrated by the collective bargaining stance of unions and union-like behavior of such one-time professional organizations as the National Education Association, is antithetical to the professional mission and conduct of institutions of higher education. The unionist stand maintains that faculty are employees whose interests (especially economic ones) are generally so at odds with those of central administration, boards of trustees and, indeed, of the institution itself, that the essential functions of faculty

[1] Irving Kristal, "A Different Way to Restructure the University," *New York Times Magazine,* December 8, 1968.

organizations should be protective of individual faculty members. Myron Lieberman argues that ". . . the function of faculty representation should not be [the] administration of an institution," that is, not administration of professional services, but rather ". . . to incorporate equitable and efficient administrative procedures in a contractual agreement between the faculty and the governing board" with the settling of grievances the fundamental concern.[2]

Faculties must be organized, just as any other group of people interested in achieving a complex goal must be organized, but the purposes of organization should be how best to render professional services through optimum utilization of the differing skills of members of the institution. The union emphasizes in effect that presidents, deans, department heads are not professional persons and are really seeking to exploit the faculty members, who are. The contrasting position is that the institution tries to deliver professional services through the efforts of its members whether they be professor, registrar, or president. How best to do this is what this analysis seeks to uncover. And the conviction that there must exist shared responsibility or total corporate responsibility, properly structured, forms the central thesis.

The third assumption is that the conditions which once assigned to the college president almost complete authority to govern an institution and to deploy its resources as he saw fit no longer obtain. The American college president's central position grew out of the historical facts of frontier conditions—he was frequently the only person present to create institutions, obtain funds, construct buildings, recruit and instruct students; and sufficiently large cadres of highly trained faculties were lacking—tutors were not presumed to have the necessary professional expertise nor to fit the prototype of the single pastor ministering to his congregation as he saw fit.

Now, however, institutions are so complex that one individual cannot even oversee necessary activities, much less seek to perform them or control them. But more importantly, there is now available a large body of highly trained faculty members with the abilities and the sense of responsibility to participate in the

[2] Myron Lieberman, "Faculty Senates: A Dissenting View," paper delivered at the twenty-fourth National Conference on Higher Education, March 4, 1969.

direction of an institution and who have a distinct professional stake in how well it fares. Frontier conditions mandated a president-centered style of governance while contemporary conditions mandate a shared responsibility style. The problem is how to bring this about. And this is no easy task, as a catalog of recent examples of institutional malfunctioning reveals. Actually American higher education is searching for appropriate styles of governance. Some guidance in that search may be obtained through examining some of those failures or malfunctionings.

When faculties have gained full hegemony over an institution without the balancing force of a strong administration, the institution has tended to stagnate and become more concerned with the welfare and prerogatives of faculty members than with the needs of students, parents, or the larger society. This is well illustrated by one Midwest college that, although its president was, for the better part of a decade, on leave of absence in Washington, refused to appoint even an acting president. During that time such innovations as a carefully established program of general education were allowed to fall into disuse because power to initiate curricular change reverted by default to faculty committees whose members found preoccupation with their own subjects and affairs more comfortable than making the effort to keep courses current with changing student needs. Syndicalism crept into the faculty as departments assumed power to search for and make appointments sympathetic to departmentalism but unconcerned about total institutional needs. Without a president constantly tempering faculty concerns with other criteria, departments tended to recruit and accord tenure to those who place disciplinary and departmental loyalty above all else. When the long interregnum ended the next president lasted less than two years, for in restoring a proper balance between administrative leadership and faculty interests, he simply made too many enemies to allow him to be effective over a longer creative effort. It is almost axiomatic that the several presidents who follow rampant growth of faculty hegemony are likely to have short and violent regimes —unless, of course, they tolerate continued faculty control, in which case the institution will likely atrophy and probably die.

A second type of malfunctioning involves not a weak or absent president, but rather a strong president preoccupied with limited interests, who, for the sake of fund-raising, construction of new facilities, or a harmonious board of trustees, allows faculty members to pursue their private activities so long as they do not cause disturbances or bother administrative tranquility. Columbia University illustrates this well, as the Cox report reveals. It had inherited from the days of Nicholas Murray Butler a strong tradition of executive responsibility reflected in autocratic decisions made after consultation only with trustees, important alumni, donors, or on occasion important city officials. Faculty members were left free for scholarship and such instruction as they chose to provide but were not encouraged to involve themselves in institutional affairs. Strong local autonomy developed in schools and departments and was allowed to operate unchecked so long as the baronies did not attempt to influence total institutional stances or activities. There was no formal senate or other faculty organization which could ponder the university as a whole and the aggregate of all faculties was so large as to be precluded from doing other than ceremonial university business. This bifurcated style of governance created a wide and unbridged gulf between the faculty and administration. The faculty became more and more remote from the problems of student life and this unconcern became all too evident to the students themselves. And the central administration was even unwilling to create a staff large enough to maintain some semblance of institutional character or coherence.[3]

A different sort of malfunctioning characterizes San Francisco State College. There, power and prerogatives necessary for central campus administration to function effectively were allowed to drift down to departments on the one hand (once a staff line was assigned to a department it would never let it go), and drawn upward to the office of the chancellor for the system on the other (only he had the power to reallocate funds from one activity to another). Robert Smith, in his essay appearing in this volume, presents the following analysis: "The business-as-usual pattern of student, faculty, and administrative government were not adequate to the pressures for change and could not be quickly superseded by a sufficiently mobile decision-making process in a climate of continuing tension marked by checkmating activities at several levels. The traditional dispersal of responsibility prerogatives and

---

[3] *Crisis at Columbia* (New York: Vintage, 1968), pp. 33–35.

power within the academic community (power lodged in departments) became an albatross in a multiple conflict situation. This
coupled with centralized control of the system of colleges at the
chancellor-trustee level, seriously hampered the executive functions at the campus level. S. I. Hayakawa resolved this problem
temporarily by casting his lot with the chancellor and trustees
and the predominant pressure of public opinion."

But undue concentration of power in the hands of central
administration also is lethal, as the experience of Parsons College
suggests. Parsons, even more than most colleges, existed as the
extended shadow of its president. President Roberts welded the
instincts of the jungle of the corporate world, the platform appeal
of an evangelist, an enormous capacity for work and food, and a
facile charm into a leadership role which allowed little room for
middle-ground response. Hear President Roberts express his ideas:
"We had problems in convincing professors that our program had
merit. Cutting the curriculum, for example, took many of their
pet courses out of the catalog. To win their support we dangled
incentives in front and pushed from behind. We raised salaries
and encouraged professors to go back to school—at full salary—
for advanced degrees. Some didn't want to go, rejecting the opportunity to assume new responsibilities. This was not a happy
situation, for we began with the idea that Parsons was to be a place
for people to grow—and that included faculty and staff as well
as students. Some holdouts are no longer with us." People regarded him with awe and respect, or saw him as a gauche charlatan
who converted an idea into reality just by thinking it is so. He
was trained in history at Chicago and theology at Yale and could
use the language of those callings. Or, he could shift and use the
vernacular of the neighborhood tough whose bite and bark both
hurt. His board of trustees was composed of men of business who
supported his desire to make Parsons a successful bastion of the
free enterprise system. Board members prized a deficit-free operation and approved using tax-free profits for new buildings and
such perquisites of top management as an executive pilot and
plane. They also supported the president's insistence that faculty
not be allowed to control the curriculum for fear that its profitable
leanness could become larded.

President Roberts believed he had solved the financial
problems of higher education and that education was a simple

thing not unlike a factory operation. There were prospective students around who could afford to pay the price to be processed through to the bachelor's degree. His admissions program was a hard sell and naturally the responsibility of the chief business officer of the college. In many respects, he proved his points. The college seemed solvent; students attended and graduated, and innovations appeared to do as they were intended to do. Or, as the president remarked, "The success of the so-called Parsons Plan is based on five interlocking programs that have been alternatingly discussed and shelved by educators for over fifty years: a reduction of courses, a trimester system for year-round operations, team teaching, an ungraded curriculum, and construction of buildings for economy and efficiency."

But President Roberts was at odds with the rest of the higher education establishment. He implied regularly in the four hundred speeches he delivered each year that most of higher education was archaic and probably dishonest. He said, "We don't take any more flunk-outs than anybody else. We did say we would which is, I suppose, heresy." "The average college . . . first . . . puts up some buildings, as impressive as possible, with the hope that the parents will see the buildings and students will go to that institution." Other presidents were seen as being jealous because he could steal their faculty members and could attract paying students. When the North Central Association of Secondary Schools and Colleges placed Parsons on public probation, he charged conspiracy to destroy a threateningly successful venture. Further, he cultivated the public rather than the dynasts of the establishment. An appearance on the Art Linkletter Show took precedence over a conference of educators. His response to the opinion of some college presidents that he operated a degree mill and kept any student around as long as he could pay his bills was that they were all doing the same thing or would have liked to. He honestly believed that Parsons was the salvation of Iowa and the townspeople of Fairfield certainly were grateful for the thriving new industry. A large Cadillac was one evidence of their esteem. But what irritated the profession was that he argued any college could do as well if it would but follow the Roberts system. And he was not above addressing board members, through the medium of his public speeches, over the heads of their presidents.

In some respects the University of Pittsburgh also exempli-

fied too great concentration of power in the hands of an overly
vigorous administration. President Litchfield had a vision of excellence, convinced his board that he could achieve it in one administrative generation and began his effort with an overly elaborate
system of administrative subordinates responsible and responsive
to him but out of touch with slower reacting faculty. Thus such
schemes as a trimester system, heavy investment in a star system
of recruiting of faculty from the president's office, and application
of new management techniques were all quickly put into effect
before the institution was ready or before the reality testing of
faculty debate had a chance to discover flaws in grand designs.
The nineteen million dollar deficit and the eventual affiliation
with the state system were part of the price of this failure to combine administrative dynamic with faculty wisdom. And this need
not have happened for even such an Olympian as Robert M.
Hutchins could remark that the short life of some of his reforms
at the University of Chicago was due in part to the fact that he
had moved too quickly and without adequate consultation with
his faculty. Thus the counterrevolution began the moment his
train left the Chicago station for his move to California.

Overbureaucratized faculty power, coupled with unclear
domains of faculty and administrative responsibility, is another
type of malfunctioning. The University of California is illustra-
tive; the effect is well established by the fact that the word *Berkeley* is a new and potent concept in the English language. "The
confusion created by this web of dependencies was accurately described in the Report of the Byrne Committee:

> In some areas the Senate is a legislative body making basic pol-
> icy, which the administration then carries out. In other areas,
> the administration makes basic policy, and the responsibility
> for implementing it is left to faculty committees, either ap-
> pointed by the administration, appointed by the administra-
> tion with the advice of the Senate, or appointed by the Senate
> itself. In still other areas, the administration makes policy and
> also attends to the problems of implementing it. There appears
> to be some variation between campuses as to which areas fall
> into which category. There has been no consensus, either
> among administrators or faculty, about the extent to which an
> administrator should follow advice from faculty committees
> when he does not personally agree with it. Nor has there been

any consensus as to the extent to which faculty opinion should be weighed by the Regents in making policy. Where consensus has not existed there has been a tendency to "play it by ear" and avoid any clear statements of policy. (pp. 25–26)

"The phrase 'faculty self-government' thus tends to cloud an accurate understanding of the faculty's role in the governance of the campus. The power of the faculty is considerable, but it is exercised within a milieu of confusion and uncertainty as to the precise jurisdiction of the Senate or the extent of its autonomy. Thus, the paradox: the faculty is powerful but lacks self-government." [4]

Other examples could be added. There is board of trustees' direct use of power in purely academic matters, as when the Board of Control for Florida senior institutions required presidential certification that text materials fell within the pale of prevailing respectability. There are innumerable examples of presidential failure to expand the administrative structure to keep pace with increased enrollment, physical plant, and budget. There is governance through secrecy said to characterize Lehigh with the administrative attitude prevailing that what central administration does is not the business or concern of faculty members. There is the almost capricious display of faculty or departmental power at Southern Methodist, brought about when the institution gave faculty members too much simply to recruit a research-oriented faculty, and used to jeopardize concern for the needs of students or of the supporting constituency of the Dallas area. But enough has been cited to establish the point that some generally accepted, better system of governance is needed.

The idea of shared responsibility is an appealing one, and has been praised in the literature of higher education for decades. However, in practice it has as frequently not been achieved partly because the nature of the various factors of the campus equation has not been understood and partly because the relationships among those factors have not been specified. Shared responsibility as urged here assumes that with respect to educational and institutional matters college and university faculties are by nature conservative. No major educational innovation has come from the

[4] Caleb Foote, Henry Mayer, and Associates, *The Culture of the University: Governance and Education*, San Francisco: Jossey-Bass, 1968.

faculty and the chief hurdle for an innovation to overcome is faculty reluctance to change. The faculty member who has been against all the many changes he has seen in forty years of teaching is representative of his class, and this is understandable. Faculty members are inclined to be solitary individuals who drifted into college teaching because that role allowed them to study, culti- vate, and preserve a subject which they found interesting. Gen- erally people do not plan to become college teachers as others plan to be doctors, lawyers, or even elementary schoolteachers. Rather, they were bright children who early began finding greater satisfaction from reading, stamp collecting, or building a telescope than they found in group activities. In college they found oppor- tunity to deepen their interest in something, and eventually, well after the bachelor's degree, they found in college teaching a career which let them do what they wanted to do. And the departmental system with its powerful defenses for preservation of individual interests provided the citadel within which to cultivate one's own concerns.

Such conservatism is not bad. It does serve as a balance to counter the effects of an overly aggressive central administration, which in the American tradition is the dynamic force on cam- puses. As a complete aside, if the more thoughtful of militant youth who are honestly seeking for university reform could but realize it, their natural enemy is the faculty and their natural ally is the administration which also seeks reform and change. It is central administration which sees the broader purposes of an institution and seeks to move it in that direction. It is central ad- ministration which suggests innovation, which encourages self- studies to create a climate favorable to change, and which plants new ideas and then encourages their growth, quite willing to give a faculty member credit, who several years later makes the same suggestion.

Actually, these two forces are complementary. Institutions cannot survive an overly powerful dynamic administration which is not checked by an effective faculty exercising the instruments of restraint. In some respects the University of Pittsburgh is illus- trative. But institutions would atrophy and lose viability if faculty gained so much power that it could block the efforts of a weak or ineffectual administration. In some way or other institutions of higher education should be organized so that the forces of faculty conservatism and administrative dynamic are brought into a creative tension. This bringing together probably must be contrived, for without a reasoned plan the contrasting valences of power could either drift into a state of fibrillation or into a completely adversary posture.

Faculties should be delegated almost irrevocable power over those parts of an institution for which their collective wisdom and expertise are most germane. The phrase "almost irrevocable" is used because the American system of chartering institutions, whether it be royal or state charter, constitutional provision, or legislative enactment, makes the board of trustees the corporate entity which is the university. It is the board which ultimately must mediate between the supporting publics and the institution; hence, the board should always retain the right to act in its sovereign corporate capacity. However, except for situations which might involve stark institutional survival, certain powers should be delegated to faculties through departments, committees, senates, and finally the corporate faculty itself expected to use them.

Faculties should have power over the curriculum, that is, over what courses should be organized. They should have power over their own membership with the right to judge whether or not an individual has the scholarly skills needed in a department and whether or not he would make an effective and representative colleague. Thirdly, the faculty should have power over the conditions of student entrance and exit—subject, of course, to any general conditions imposed by a charter or legislative enactment. The California legislature mandates that junior colleges shall be open-door colleges; hence the right to modify that condition of entrance is not available to the faculty. Lastly, faculties should have broad policy-making powers over the conditions of student life. This is a somewhat more debatable matter, but is based on the assumption that the general conditions of student life on campus do have educational implications. These conditions, of course, change as society changes; hence style of student life and the degree of prescription or freedom created should change. There were educational reasons for considerable protectiveness for fifteen-year-olds in the nineteenth-century college just as there are educational reasons for single-sex institutions to become coeducational in the 1960s.

Power over these matters is made effective through deliberations within departments and committees and policy is established through votes of senates or, at times, the entire corporate faculty. Perhaps a word about committees is appropriate here for, although committees frequently seem a fearful waste of time, the committee system is the way by which consensus is reached, new administrators are prepared, and academic freedom is preserved. Generally standing committees—curriculum, faculty affairs, admissions, and the like—should recommend policy, be advisory to appropriate administrative officers, and serve as a review or appeals agency for executive actions falling within its sphere of action. Note that the committee is not charged with executive or administrative tasks. Too frequently committees attempt to administer with failure or ineffectiveness the likely result.

These powers are considerable and some argue that in view of the conservatism of faculties, granting them may insure institutional stagnation. However, this danger can be minimized by assigning administration—presidents, deans, directors, and department heads—counter powers. First among these is financial power and power over budget preparation and budget control. No president who is held responsible for the financial viability of the institution can yield ultimate authority over this matter. And he exercises it both directly and through holding administrative subordinates responsible and accountable. Secondly, administration has the power of appointment of administrative officers. It is through the appointment of a dean that a president influences the tone and direction of a professional school, and it is through the appointment of a department head that a dean can modify departmental efforts. To these two central powers are added several supportive ones—those powers, subject of course to review, of execution of policy, the power which comes from possession of information or intelligence—data generation is an administrative function—right to build agendas, certain specified veto powers and the not inconsiderable power which adheres to high administrative posts simply because of the traditions and status of the office; good scholars still accept presidencies.

These two forces are brought into cooperation through the twin structures of legislative or faculty and the executive or administrative. The faculty thus would be organized with the corporate faculty at the apex, and the members would be every professional person having a professional relationship with someone. Thus registrars, counselors, librarians, and institutional research workers would belong as well as the teaching faculty. Below that could come the senate, if size made this desirable, an executive or steering committee, and the various standing or ad hoc committees. The chairman of each commitee would be the most relevant administrative officer. On this point there can be some disagreement and it would be possible for a faculty member to chair so long as the most relevant administrative officer were a member. But so essential for a committee is the information of administrative offices, and so close to problems needing solution that a strong case can be made for an administrative officer actually serving as chairman. Other members of committees and the senate would be elected by some device to insure both popular and departmental or school voice.

On the administrative side would stand the various line officers—president, dean, director, department head—who would normally work with at least two councils. One would be a council of his immediate subordinates and the other the appropriate committee from the faculty to advise, review, and on occasion serve as an appeals board.

From these two structures should emerge an interlocking and interrelating pattern of groups of people discussing common problems to an extent that most matters which finally reached the floor of the corporate faculty would be decided almost pro-forma. A corporate faculty in a large university is really too large to conduct effective business, but it does serve the twin roles of legitimacy and safeguarding rights and opinions of minorities.

Two factors deserve especial comment, one because of its historic and present significance and the other because of emergent and still unknown character. Although some have argued that the presidency is presently an impossible office with no power to do else save mediate between antagonistic factions, this does not seem to be true. The president is the one person who can take a real overview of an institution and can help it set valid goals and purposes. "At almost all institutions . . . the president heads the list [as the most influential in directing an institution]. He is perceived as having a great deal of say in the big decisions (mean score of 4.65 on a five-point scale)." And this position of primacy holds true regardless of size or type of institution.[5] Innovations just do not happen unless a strong president wills them to happen and an institution flounders if a weak president or one unsure of his own program is in office. At this point in time no rearrangement of organization or governance should be attempted which would reduce presidents to figureheads or servants of the faculty status. In the American context syndicalism will not work, for faculty syndicalism tends to ignore the social purposes of higher education.

The second factor is, clearly, the student. There is in 1968–69 a groundswell of opinion that students properly should be voting members of committees, senates, departments, and even boards of trustees. Where this has happened and is functioning well there can be no really strong objection. Antioch College has survived quite well with such an arrangement in force. But students have no more intrinsic right to a role in governance of a college or university than does a patient in a hospital, client in a law office, or client with an architect. These are all professions in which the practitioner decides out of his own expertise which of available instruments he shall use to provide the professional service which the client seeks. It is true that college professors have frequently been unprofessional in their practice—especially in teaching. And it is also true that students have frequently had great insight for improvement of practice. But these facts do not negate the underlying concept of the collegiate institution as a professional service-providing enterprise.

Now, certainly, students have opinions which should be heard and considered. They can make evaluations of the services they receive and have grievances which should be aired. Colleges and universities have too long been insensitive to such matters. Further, to achieve some educational goals students may be encouraged to participate in deliberations, teach, counsel, or even help in admissions. But these are not rights deriving from the right to govern. They are experiences of the same order as hearing a lecture, reading a book, or taking a field trip, which some professional has selected as an appropriate educational experience.

This is conservative doctrine, far from participatory de-

[5] Edward Gross and Paul V. Grambsch, *University Goals and Academic Power* (Washington: American Council on Education, 1968), p. 113.

mocracy. A question rightly can be asked, in view of the climate of opinion in 1969, whether leaving students out of formal governance can be accomplished even if it were sound doctrine. At the risk of being accused of wild prophecy I can suggest that the student militancy of the 1960s will eventually fade just as have other generational revolts. It is true that the movement may destroy and ultimately change much in life. The student protest in Serbia in 1914 led directly to the assassination of the Archduke of Austria which, in turn, precipitated World War I. While that holocaust did change forms of government, and the balance of economic power, the student dreams of a return to a folk society and reformed domestic institutions were not realized and the protest movement subsided. Karl Follen, who in 1814 was the first student protest leader of modern times and whose efforts probably led only to the defeat of the German constitutional movement (backlash), by 1830 had become the first professor of German literature at Harvard and could remark that "The hatred . . . has changed to indifference." [6] Very likely the present spasm of student activism from whence stem demands for involvement in governance will run its course when the national issue in Vietnam is resolved.

Such a system of shared responsibility can only operate if several conditions are present and functional. The first is obvious but somewhat difficult to achieve. There must be a desire on the part of faculty and administration for shared responsibility which does mean denial of one-faction hegemony. Much contemporary campus strife seems to result from rampant elitism which, of course, is the antithesis of sharing. Secondly, there must be a willingness on the part of boards of trustees to make definite, formal grants of power and to realize that their roles as protectors of public interest can best be served by staying out of the detailed administration of a professional undertaking. Similarly, administration and faculty must each be willing to allow the other element discretion in its own sphere. Thirdly, there must be written constitutions, by-laws, and specified procedures to insure due process. In the past colleges have operated on generally accepted standards of behavior and norms of conduct made possible because slowly growing colleges and universities were not unlike primitive societies regulated by an uncodified conventional wisdom. But a

[6] Lewis S. Feuer, *The Conflict of Generations* (New York: Basic Books, 1969), p. 66.

complex and rapidly expanding culture requires greater bureaucracy and specification of appropriate behavior. Then, too, there must be greater openness on the campus and a willingness to share information and intelligence. Until quite recently colleges and universities were highly secretive about their internal affairs and would not reveal details of student admissions, salaries, or budgets. This condition has begun to change but must change much more rapidly if the ideal of shared responsibility is to be realized. A president, aware of impending deficit financing, cannot obtain the benefit of faculty wisdom unless he is willing to distribute copies of real, not spurious, budgets.

The great tradition of the university stresses the value of community, of mutual respect, and concert of effort to achieve the humane life. These can be realized only through some version of shared responsibility for a professional undertaking.

~ 19 ~

ACADEMIC SENATE UNDER FIRE

John C. Livingston

cademic senates are irretrievably caught up in the processes of revolutionary change in America. The causes, the general character, and the probable outcome of these revolutionary forces are beyond the scope of my present purpose and my insight. But, more specifically, it can I think be said that the central challenge to academic senates is rooted in the dynamics of the egalitarian ideal. The struggle to define and realize equality has entered a new phase in which this "greatest of all doctrines and the hardest to understand," as Mark Van Doren described it, has affected the campus in two central ways.

The first is the erosive effect of equality on the traditional status of higher education institutions as centers for the cultivation of the abilities of an intellectual and social elite. Clark Kerr described the problem from the traditional perspective in *The Uses of the University*. "There is," he said, "the urgent issue of how to preserve a margin for excellence in a populist setting when more and more of the money is being spent on behalf of all of the people. The great university is of necessity elitist, the elite of merit. It operates in an environment dedicated to an egalitarian philosophy. How may the contribution of the elite be made clear to the egalitarians, and how may an aristocracy of intellect justify itself to a democracy of all men? It was equality of opportunity, not equality per se, that animated the founding fathers and the progress of the American system, but the forces of populist equality have never been silent. . . ." [1] But surely the ideal of equality, as Van Doren implied, is more difficult to understand than this account allows. From another perspective, "populist" pressures on education reflect, however vaguely and imperfectly, the perception that "equality of opportunity" is an empty ideal which serves mainly to conceal and rationalize actual inequalities of real opportunity. Moreover, while the intellectual Darwinism implicit in the ideal of an "elite of merit" is clearly under attack, it is by no means clear that it has lovelier or more humane consequences than other elitist concepts or that our problem is to find ways to induce the egalitarians to accept it. From an egalitarian perspective the problem is not how to persuade the mean and jealous masses to support their intellectual superiors, but the more difficult problem of how to maintain the vision of excellence in a mass educational system. Similarly, the problem for faculty is increasingly the more difficult one of how standards of excellence are to be maintained when it is no longer possible simply to dodge the issue by building these standards into the criteria for admission. More specifically, for faculty in elitist institutions the problem is how, or whether, to justify patterns of expenditure which are inversely related to the past opportunities of students. In public systems, especially, the question is whether the masses should continue to provide greater financial support for institutions which educate the children of the wealthy than for institutions which educate their own children or the children of the disadvantaged. Even the magic and slippery formula of equal opportunity fails to justify this common inequity, an inequity which is being clearly exposed by the demands of ethnic minorities

[1] Clark Kerr, *The Uses of the University* (Cambridge: Harvard University Press, 1963).

though it seems odd that its exposure should have had to wait on those demands.

Whatever valuation we are to put on the egalitarian pressures to expand educational opportunity, they exist and they force new roles on faculty and academic senates and create new tensions between senates and other parties. Elitism (intellectual and social and economic) is firmly built into the structure of higher education. Even in the private sector, in an oligopolistic corporate economy corporate donations to elitist private colleges represent a form of compulsory "tax" support by consumers. In the public educational sector, faculty who teach in the more "populist" institutions resent the second-class status to which they are assigned by the elitist implications of resource allocation.

The second central way in which the egalitarian tide has affected the campuses is, of course, the way in which the struggle of ethnic minorities for racial equality has used the campus as a major lever of social change. Demands like those for greatly expanded minority group enrollment and for minority group "self-government" in the development of ethnic studies programs put traditional academic standards and usages to new and severe tests. So also, of course, do the verbal violence, the disorder, the threats and intimidation and occasional violence that accompany this struggle.

In ways that I hope to clarify, the pressure of these new problems on the campus seems to me likely to increase the tension among faculty organizations, to create new problems in the relationship of academic senates to the external organizations, to intensify the adversary character of relations between academic senates and trustees and administrators, and generally to accelerate a trend toward collective bargaining. My analysis draws heavily on the experience of California because I am most familiar with developments there. Its general relevance, therefore, depends in some measure on the accuracy of our chancellor's comment that "things tend to happen first" there. (This, of course, is only a methodological hypothesis; I do not wish to be understood as hoping the rest of the country will follow our example.)

Unrest on the campus promises to continue to sharpen the conflicts between faculty and trustees. As the recent Educational Testing Service survey of some five thousand trustees confirmed, the "typical" trustee is the model representative of the establishment: white, Protestant, middle-aged, wealthy, successful, and, most important, inclined to take a managerial view of his institution. He believes that trustees should select a strong executive and that the old saw that authority must be coextensive with responsibility provides an obvious and authoritarian answer to the question of campus government. The faculty role in decision-making, he believes, should be limited to "academic" matters, narrowly defined (half of the five thousand respondents did not believe faculty should have power to appoint an academic dean or grant faculty leaves; 53 per cent thought faculty should sign loyalty oaths).

In tranquil and normal times these trustee attitudes constituted no great barrier to the develoment of shared authority on the campus. What trustees did not know or were willing to overlook did not irritate them, and they were often preoccupied with enjoying the prestige of reigning over, without ruling, their institutions and debating the adequacy of the fenestration in schematic drawings for new buildings. Where they were unwilling to delegate authority to faculty and administrators, they often deferred to them in fact and rubber-stamped policies and proposals which originated on the campus. More recently, they have intervened in areas delegated to academic senates (the appointment of Eldridge Cleaver at Berkeley) and have issued directives or initiated policy changes unilaterally in areas previously reserved to local campus administrators and faculty (the firing of George Murray and the opening of the campus at San Francisco State).

Trustees are likely to move in the direction of assuming greater power and control under pressure from donors or potential donors, from the public, from parents, from alumni and, especially in public institutions or systems, from politicians. Political pressure may be direct or indirect. Direct pressure may take the form of punitive legislation, often accepted by trustees as desirable or politically necessary. Retaliatory laws may be directed against students, faculty, or administrators; almost invariably they will enjoin or mandate behavior and establish penalties with the effect of removing from the campus areas of discretion that have traditionally involved consultative processes and shared authority. Several bills, for example, have been introduced into the California legislature which would make it illegal for a college president to delegate any of his authority to or share it with faculty bodies; one bill in the current session would establish an independent commission, appointed by the governor, with power to investigate, hear, and establish penalties for all violations of campus order; the Governor's own legislation would mandate severe penalties for faculty or students found guilty of disrupting normal campus processes.

Indirect political pressures are exerted by public pronouncements by politicians on the state of the campuses, by threats to withhold funds from budgets, and by the power of appointment to the boards where this is vested in political agencies. Political pressures, whether direct or indirect, are backed by "public opinion" as reflected in correspondence to public officials and in letters to the editor in newspapers. Whatever its form, the dominant theme of public and political pressure is likely to be the familiar, nearsighted, and misleading clamor for law and order. Here as elsewhere, California leads the way in disclosing the vicious and contradictory consequences of this approach. The governor, who occupies an *ex officio* seat on the boards of both the university and the state colleges and also appoints their members, was recently reported in the press as saying that the "basic issue . . . is simple, not easy but simple. It is that the basic educational process cannot go forward under threats of force." This in a speech in which he reiterated his belief that campuses should be kept open "at the point of bayonet" if necessary! In addition to the obvious inconsistency in this approach, there is a dual blindness here: one eye is blind to the fact that the campuses have inherited the historic fruit of American racism and the bitterness of the unfulfilled promise of democratic politics; the other is blind to the terribly fragile character of the educational process. This blindness permits the governor to use the sensitivity of faculty and administrators to these realities against them. These attitudes dominate the political climate in California and even "liberal" legislators have informed faculty leaders that the academic community is politically isolated and cannot expect support from any political quarter. Insofar as these attitudes are reflected, through pressure or natural inclination, in the attitudes of trustees their relationship with faculty will take on increasingly a power-oriented, adversary character in which forms of communication other than pressure and threat will become increasingly difficult.

Adversary attitudes toward governing boards and a disposition to embrace collective bargaining will also be promoted among junior college and state college faculties by the difficulty they encounter in redressing their second- or third-class status. They are likely to be increasingly frustrated by the fact that the social and political elites are heavily representative of the elitist educational institutions, and by the fact that members of their own governing boards also occupy second-class status in comparison to the boards of more prestigious institutions and, partly for that reason, are reluctant and politically powerless to press the claims of their institutions as vigorously as the spokesmen for their more affluent neighbors. Collective negotiation, backed by effective sanctions, may come to be viewed as the only effective means of forcing trustees to act more aggressively and of putting muscle in their demands.

In these circumstances, administrators are put under extreme pressure to take a harder line in order to forestall more punitive action by trustees or politicians and to preclude their own dismissal and replacement by a more rigid and authoritarian appointee. The direction of the pressure is the abrogation of consultative processes on the campus and the assumption by the administrator of the oligarchic power of the executive in the business or military model. The failure of administrators to yield to the pressures puts their jobs in jeopardy, and few administrators indeed are able to imagine that the continuity of their own tenure is not necessarily a condition of the salvation of their institutions. But their dilemma is real: failure to dissociate themselves from faculty postions and faculty influence is calculated to give further currency to the charge that, in the words of a California state legislator, "it has become obvious that many of our present campus administrators are totally unfitted by training, by temperament and in some cases by personal ideology to deal with" force and violence on the campus.[2] Moreover, the effort to escape between the horns of this dilemma by reversing Teddy Roosevelt's dictum and speaking toughly while carrying a very small stick is likely only to further alienate both faculty and trustees or politicians. In the future, therefore, the prospect is for increased tension between faculty and governing boards, with administrators caught hopelessly in the middle.

[2] John G. Schmitz in the *Sacramento Bee,* February 12, 1969.

As academic senates are brought into more intense and direct conflict with trustees and administrators, strategies on both sides tend to sharpen the adversary character of their relationships. The ordinary tendency of faculties to exaggerate the establishment views of trustees by putting them all in the same bag is intensified, and trustees are systematically dehumanized and depersonalized by the increased popularity of the view that they can be known by their corporate or other establishment connections. On the other side, trustees increasingly play the game of "we represent the public interest and the senate represents no one." Thus, when the academic senate challenges administrative or trustee positions, its representative character is questioned or it is claimed to be a captive of one of the more militant external organizations; when it fails to support the more militant organizations, it is acclaimed as representative of the "silent majority" of faculty for whom the trustees or administrators allegedly speak.

Administrative and trustee efforts to use the academic senate against the more militant external organizations are resented by the senate as a tactic of divide and conquer. The senate resists by seeking to strengthen its ties with the external organizations while keeping an official neutrality with regard to the issues that divide them. At the same time, all of the organizations move toward greater support of some form of collective negotiation. The academic senate itself feels less sanguine about the possibilities of reasoned argument as a means to influence the administration and the board (with good reason, of course, where trustee or administrative reaction to campus turmoil takes the form of showing the faculty and students who is boss); it feels a greater obligation to conciliate or to surmount the rivalries of external organizations; it sees its own organizational power threatened by the aspirations of the external groups to bargaining status. It is likely, for all these reasons, to endorse the method of collective negotiations, loosely defined, and to propose that it serve as negotiating agent.

The impact of egalitarianism, both in broadening educational opportunity and in focusing the demands of ethnic minorities on the campus, poses new problems for academic senates and creates new tensions in their relationships with external organizations. Academic senates will be sorely tested by the necessity to deal with a variety of new and difficult issues, both substantive and procedural. How ought the problem of force and violence on

the campus be dealt with? How should the institution respond
to such demands as that for self-government by ethnic minorities
in the development of ethnic study curriculums? Under what
conditions is amnesty justified for students found guilty of vio-
lating campus rules? How should faculty react to the question of
the right of faculty and students to strike? Should faculty react
to public pressures and attacks by using a public relations approach to improving their image or by trying to persuade the
public to modify its assumptions and attitudes? While generalizations about faculty attitudes need to be recognized as describing
only broad tendencies, it seems probable that disagreements over
these issues will intensify traditional faculty cleavages. The defense of elitism will be undertaken mainly by faculty in the professional and graduate areas, attacked by liberal arts faculty with
a primary orientation toward the undergraduate curriculum. Liberal arts faculty will include most of those who take what might
be described as tolerant attitudes toward student protest and
responsive attitudes toward minority group demands; the law-
and-order approach finds more adherents in the applied and vocational areas. The cleavage runs generally along the same lines with
respect to whether faculty response to adverse public attitudes
should be image-centered or problem-centered. When these
schisms are added to long-standing faculty cleavages, it becomes
even more difficult for academic senates to act decisively and effectively or, indeed, to act at all.

    These same issues threaten to sharpen the conflicts among
external faculty organizations and to bring their latent differences into the open. The more militant organizations are not
simply more aggressive in pressing for faculty interests; they tend
also to put themselves more firmly and publicly on the side of
egalitarianism. The more cautious organizations become at the
same time more openly conservative in their attitudes toward
issues raised by egalitarianism. The result is that what had been
mainly a disagreement over tactics takes on also the character of
ideological warfare. The academic senate's task of accommodat-
ing the rival postures and working out an effective faculty position
becomes immensely more difficult.

    In some situations, for which California may be a pro-
phetic model, the academic senate may be forced into the position
of defending militant faculty groups. On campuses disrupted by

the confrontation tactics of black and brown and revolutionary white students there appears to be an increasing tendency on the part of trustees, some administrators, and some politicians to refuse to acknowledge that the problems on the campus are fundamentally social and political and to construct a conspiracy theory to explain them. Reluctant openly to challenge or accuse ethnic minorities, these forces tend to focus on "a small group of subversive faculty" as the root of the problem. In these circumstances the academic senate may be compelled to defend the rights of colleagues under attack. If the militant faculty are organized in an AFT (American Federation of Teachers) chapter or another group, one of whose objectives is collective bargaining, the senate may find itself in a trap.

So long as an academic union is too weak to threaten to be successful it may be welcomed by an academic senate as a source of pressure to move the senate into a more dynamic and aggressive posture and as a potential threat to administrators and trustees that prompts them to look more kindly on a strong senate. But if the union gets strong enough to strike or seriously to threaten to strike, the senate is put in a difficult position. It is likely to support most of the strike demands, yet the legitimacy and future of its own organizational position is seriously challenged. It may be called upon to defend the *right* of union members to strike and to take vigorous countermeasures against punitive dismissals of striking faculty without endorsing the strike itself—a clear enough posture in principle but one which in practice will have the effect of strengthening the union's demand for bargaining rights for its own members. In these conditions the senate is likely to find itself pushed into a position of endorsing collective bargaining and itself contending for the role of bargaining agent.

The record of faculty senates in dealing with questions like these leaves something to be desired, and even the most ardent supporter of faculty self-government must entertain doubts about their ability to survive the current crisis. For their survival requires that they be able to reach viable agreements on how to deal with these issues which can produce sufficient faculty support to enable the faculty collectively to contend successfully against outside pressures. It is not only a matter of the complexity and difficulty of the issues, though heaven knows they are complex and difficult enough. There is also the problem of the constitutional ineffectiveness of faculty in reaching agreement on *any* issue. However much we proclaim the supremacy of reasoned dialogue on the campus and however insistently we assume that the dialogue in which faculty are trained is a means by which reasoning men reach reasoned agreements, anyone with even a minimum of experience with faculty meetings knows better. What other group can so easily embroil itself in parliamentary impasses from which it is sometimes not even clear that adjournment can be effected? Who does not suspect that faculty resistance to student membership on senates is partially motivated by a reticence to allow students to observe what goes on? The problem is ordinarily not that faculty are too political in the sense of playing games of strategy with one another; it is, rather, that they are not political enough in the sense of skill in the arts of reaching agreement. The typical skills of faculty are, after all, not the skills of the Platonic dialogue; they are, instead, the skills by use of which a seemingly coherent reality is made to reveal its contradictions and inconsistencies. Faculty tend to be experts at making distinctions, not reaching agreement; posing problems, not offering solutions. Politically their skills are divisive (although it is true that, in Jefferson's phrase, "integrity of views" furnishes a bond of "mutual esteem"); in this sense, faculty politics is a contradiction in terms. I do not mean to exaggerate this faculty attribute (faculty still do, perhaps more than any other group, give allegiance to the ideal of reasoned dialogue as a means to decision), or to depreciate its value. I mean only to say that it complicates the faculty's task in the current crisis and perhaps makes it more likely that faculty senates will work out their responses to new and difficult problems primarily within the framework of their adversary relationships with other parties.

My analysis and my conclusions are not optimistic, and I do not pretend to have any pat or easy answers to the power struggle that seems increasingly to catch us all up and lead us to make choices of the lesser evil. Nor do I find comfort in the sophistry that the lesser evil is some kind of good, for the very essence of our predicament is that we no longer are able to judge or act on some conception of a good or goods that would bring purpose and direction to our activities. We seem destined, in short, to move increasingly toward relationships of an adversary type, characterized by confrontation and bargaining, backed by force, by threat and intimidation. I agree with a colleague of mine that "when the people of the colleges and universities abandon reason for force in an effort to effect changes, then, at that time, the purpose ceases to be improvement of the quality of the institution; and the issues, for which that sacrifice of reason was made, become empty." Bargaining is not thoughtful inquiry, and the two are not brought noticeably closer together by the reflection, however accurate, that bargaining rather than inquiry and dialogue is the common way of settling differences in the "real world" of American economic and public life. Indeed, that characteristic of the "real world" lies somewhere near the center of things that are responsible for the crisis on the campus.

Even apart from such personal valuations of the bargaining process, it is doubtful that the organization of effective faculty bargaining strength can realistically be expected to modify the negative and destructive public and political attitudes that appear to me to be at the heart of our problem. Effective faculty organization for bargaining, indeed, seems more likely to intensify those public attitudes and to disarm faculty efforts to change them.

Still, it is difficult to imagine in the present context how the trend might be reversed. And collective bargaining has, as it has always had, this to recommend it: it is preferable to warfare (even though, to borrow Clausewitz' analogy, it *is* "warfare by other means"). There is, perhaps, some hope in the willingness of academic senates to take on the bargaining role. There are dangers here as well: the possibility that a senate will come increasingly to take on the characteristics of another external organization as it organizes itself for effective bargaining, and the more serious problem of reconciling its bargaining role with its professional claims to self-government. But, on the other side, an academic senate seems to pose the best chance for defining collective negotiations in flexible ways and for keeping alive the idea that bargaining is a second-best alternative to which, unfortunately, events have forced us.

Although in principle a clear distinction can be drawn between decision based on the process of discussion, debate, and reasoned argument on the one hand and decision based on accommodation, compromise, power, and pressure on the other, in practice one process blends into the other. (The distinction in principle is clearly put in Joseph Tussman's distinction between "solving" and "getting." The decision of an academic senate, therefore, to embrace collective bargaining and to enter itself in the contest to select a bargaining agent need not be regarded by faculty or by other interested parties as anything more than a conclusion that exclusive reliance on the cogency of their reasons and arguments has proved ineffective and that the protection of the vital interests of their profession requires additional means to power. If the movement to collective bargaining is so regarded, it may not be irreversible in happier circumstances, and the process of negotiation may itself retain more of the flavor of reasoned discussion—consequences that, from my value structure at least, are devoutly to be desired.

~ 20 ~

GOVERNANCE AND EDUCATIONAL REFORM

Howard R. Bowen

The observation is frequently made that human relations in the universities are at about the same stage as were industrial relations in the 1930s. At that time, a bitter and passionate struggle for power occurred, marked by sit-down strikes, sabotage, intimidation, violence, invective, charges of Communist influence, court injunctions, and most of all by hurt feelings and wounded pride. Out of that struggle came the organization of great industrial unions, a vast body of law and custom to regulate industrial relations, numerous corps of labor negotiators and industrial relations experts, and eventually an ability to operate a large portion of the economy under collective bargaining with substantial power vested in labor unions. Possibly, in the universities today, we are in the early stages of a comparable process. I shall try to show, however, that relationships in the universities are vastly more complex than those in industry.

The question now being asked on all American campuses is: How should influence and power be distributed among the many agencies and groups who are eager to take part in directing the affairs of universities. Some of these groups are external to the institution and some internal; and the university is caught in a kind of crunch between these two sets of forces. Among the external groups are federal and state legislative bodies, federal grant-awarding agencies, state administrative officials, state coordinating boards, accrediting bodies, and foundations and other private donors. The influence of the external groups affects the autonomy or independence of the university; that of the internal groups affects the decision-making process for matters remaining within the discretion of the institution.

I shall be concerned in this essay, primarily with internal decision-making. The internal contenders for influence and power are five in number: the governing board, the administration, the faculty, the students, and the nonacademic staff. Some of these groups tend, however, to splinter into subgroups. For example, there are clear differences in outlook between senior and junior faculty. Graduate assistants do not identify fully with either faculty or students. The graduate and advanced professional students do not wholly share the interests of undergraduates. Black students and other ethnic minorities are showing signs of separatism. The nonacademic staff tends to divide into fairly distinct white-collar and blue-collar groups. The white-collar group is of special interest because of its increasing number and importance. It includes hundreds of well-educated persons, keenly interested in university affairs yet regarded neither as faculty nor administration, namely, nurses, technicians, librarians, secretaries, administrative assistants, engineers, supervisors, and so on. Each of the several subgroups organizes into councils, senates, or unions; each seeks to participate in decision-making; each seeks elaborate due process in personnel actions; and each asserts rights, privileges, and immunities for its members. Each subgroup has its activist leaders and its passive majorities. The number of separate internal groups contending for a place in university governance ranges from eight to twelve or more.

Traditionally, the underlying theory of university government has been that the president in consultation with the board is the responsible decision-maker. Strictly educational and research questions are delegated to the faculty subject to general review. On nonacademic matters, the faculty and others participate only as consultants and advisers.

This pattern of university governance is being widely criticized, and the faculty, students, nonacademic staff, and their subgroups are all clamoring for increasing influence or authority, and all are forming councils, senates, or unions to exercise the power they hope to get. The theory is widely advocated that a university is a self-contained democracy in which the people are the members of the community or some subset of these members.

Universities the world over are confronted with the issue of broadening formal participation in governance. Probably no institution anywhere has achieved a satisfactory solution which permits all parties to participate equitably and usefully, and yet enables the institution to act decisively and to have coherent policies in the public interest.

In the endless talk about governance, emphasis seems usually to be placed on the *rights* of individuals and groups rather than on the soundness and timeliness of decisions. That broadened participation would result in better decisions, in the social interest, is seldom claimed. Rather, it is implied that if only a particular group had a larger role in the decision-making process the interests of *that group* would be more fully achieved.

It would seem that rights, though important, are only one consideration. The question of governance should be considered also in relation to other goals. For example, a good system of governance would enable the university to be a progressive institution responsive to the changing needs of its members and of the society it serves. A good system would be compatible with improvements in education, research, and intellectual vigor. It would encourage rising efficiency of operation. It would foster reasonable order and discipline without infringing on free thought and expression. It would not get in the way of prompt and decisive action.

An objective observer of present trends in the governance of higher education can hardly escape the suspicion, if not the conclusion, that the system of governance of the recent past gets low marks for progressiveness, educational advancement, efficiency, order, and decisiveness. And it is not evident that current developments in governance are leading to better results. What is needed is progress toward a system of governance that harmonizes the rights of constituent individuals and groups with the social responsibilities of the organization. It is possible, I think likely, that concern for rights can be compatible with, even contributory toward, the other important needs and goals. But the formula for this happy result has not yet been found.

In some ways the current discussion of power in the university proceeds from a false assumption, namely, that the several groups have not had power, or at least great influence, in the past. Obviously, all have had substantial power whether or not formal structures for its exercise have existed. A university that has not responded to the needs and wishes of faculty has not been able to retain competent teachers and researchers; a university that has not met the needs and wishes of students has not been able to attract students or to interest them in its program; a university that has not paid attention to its administrative and nonacademic staffs has fallen into deep trouble. And, of course, the power of these groups has grown with the rising mobility of the American people, with the increasing scarcity of qualified faculty and staff, and with the intense competition for gifted students. The idea that the members of an academic community have not had power is utterly false regardless of formal organization—though institutions have doubtless differed in responsiveness.

Possible Alternatives. One can visualize several possible modes of participation. First, the several groups (students, faculty, nonacademic staff, administrative officers) might divide up the areas of decision-making among them, each being responsible for certain areas—for example, the faculty for the curriculum, the students for extracurricular programs, the nonacademic staff for working conditions and parking, and the administrative group for whatever is left over. I see little prospect that this kind of tidy division of labor will survive. The concerns of each group are much too broad for that, and properly so. Second, each element might serve as a pressure group advancing its own interests within the university. It takes little imagination to visualize, for example, the students opposing tuition increases needed to finance faculty salaries, or nonacademic staff seeking salary increases at the expense of new buildings, or teaching assistants seeking lighter loads at the expense of regular faculty, or all three groups quarreling over the allocation of parking space. The several groups surely are interest groups, though they are more than that. Third, each of the groups might be concerned with the full range of policy issues, but each would express the particular point of view of its constituency. Each would be a combined policy and pressure group. In my opinion, this is what we are heading toward—each group believing itself competent to deal with any subject, each eager to deal with a wide range of subjects, and each approaching each issue from the point of view of its particular interests.

Since the several groups will not always agree, the question remains: Who is to resolve the differences? The umpire, whoever he or they may be, must see the institution as a whole, not only in its internal dimension but also in its relation to the public interest. The role of umpire, coordinator, and link with the public inevitably falls to the president and his administrative colleagues. They, however, are also an interest group. Not only do they have their personal interests, but their interests include the advancement of the university. They are therefore not fully qualified to serve the public interest. It does not necessarily follow that whatever is good for the Claremont colleges or the University of Iowa as seen by the president is good for the country.

The function of the governing board is to be a guardian of the public interest while insulating the university from undue pressures of outside groups. The governing board must so clearly represent the public interest that it can protect the autonomy of the university from improper encroachments of legislative bodies, government agencies, donors, and other outsiders. In many instances, governing boards have identified fully with their universities, and have seen their role solely as the advancement of the institution rather than the protection of the social interest. In my opinion, this posture leaves a vacuum which outsiders are eager to try to fill—with great danger to academic freedom.

A joint council. I have described the university as though it were a legislature with five or more houses: governing board, the president and administrative officials, faculty, students, and nonacademic staff, and their subdivisions. Is it practically possible in terms of sheer time to debate every issue five or more times? Will the result of many separate debates produce better answers than one or two? One could argue, I suppose, that the resultant of numerous deliberations and of competing pressure and persuasion would result in a beneficent outcome. Perhaps something akin to Adam Smith's "invisible hand" or Galbraith's "countervailing power" is at work within organizations.

In my opinion, such multiple consultation does not necessarily produce good results, it is a frightful waste of time, it results in paralysis of action, and it threatens to undermine the sense of community which is essential in a university. A more workable participation of the five or more groups—and I see no sound basis for excluding any of them—might be achieved if all (except the governing board) were represented in a single joint council. Through the deliberations of such a body, various points of view could be communicated, differences resolved, and decisions reached which were in the interests of the entire institution. These joint decisions could then be put to the test of the public interest by independent review before the governing board.

The joint council would deal with the entire gamut of policy—academic and nonacademic. However, for obvious reasons its role in the academic area would be limited to broad, general review. The council would not necessarily replace the senates and councils of the various constituent groups, colleges, and departments. It would not necessarily supplant the various specialized university committees such as those dealing with athletics, cultural affairs, student housing, library, parking, and so on. It would receive recommendations from these groups, and it would be free to refer issues to these groups. However, it would assume broad responsibilities and perhaps take over the duties of many existing bodies. The net influence of the council would be in the direction of centralizing policy-making rather than providing merely another layer in the endless process of buck-passing, delay, and inaction represented by the present ramified and diffuse organization. It would ordinarily be the principal body to be consulted directly by the president. In that position it would have substantial influence. The joint council would be expected to consider matters from the point of view of the welfare of the institution as a whole, not from the viewpoint of any particular interest group. Its agenda would be broader than that of the governing board; it would meet more often (perhaps weekly) and consider matters in greater depth.

The advantages of a council such as I have described are

that it would avoid much duplication of effort when matters must be reviewed with representatives of several different bodies; it would be a vehicle by which differences among groups could be talked out and by which an all-university point of view could be expressed; and it would provide the president with support for decisions jointly reached.

Should such a joint council be advisory to the president or should it make final decisions on some or all matters (subject to the approval of the governing board)? By only a small step, such a joint council could assume authority over the university. It is often suggested today that the president should become a figurehead serving as chairman of an authoritative council, as master of university ceremonies, and as public relations officer— while full authority and responsibility would be assumed by the council. Some would even merge the council with the governing board. In my judgment, the council should be advisory to the president, but of course the president should take council recommendations seriously. If the decisions of the council were final, accountability would then necessarily be transferred from the president to the council. I question whether a council with many members having rotating membership is in a position to assume responsibility for the progress of an institution, or can be held as strictly accountable as can a president. There are few organizations that do not place executive responsibility squarely on one man. Those organizations that do not (certain churches and some public agencies) are seldom among the more progressive and successful organizations. A strong executive is needed to get things done. One of the most serious problems of the university is that executive authority is weak, and is becoming weaker under present tendencies. The need is for a strong executive combined with workable participation by the several groups within the university and of course with due process in all personnel actions and other adequate safeguards for academic freedom.

A strong executive, working with a lay board of distinguished citizens, is needed also to assure that decisions of the university will be related to the needs of the institution as a whole and reasonably conformable to the public interest. Each of the internal groups—faculty, students, nonacademic staff—is an interest group and seeks its own advantage, which may not be consistent with the welfare of the institution as a whole or of so-

ciety. Each sees the institution from a particular and partial point
of view. The several groups are likely often to disagree, and even
if they were to come into agreement through negotiation, coalitions, or similar means, the result would not necessarily be in the
interest of the university or the public. The invisible hand as
applied to organizations is a doubtful theory. I believe there is
need in an institution for a leadership—namely, the president and
his associates working with a lay governing board—which spe-
cializes in seeing the institution as a whole, coordinating its parts,
and relating it to the public which it serves and from which it
derives its support. I do not mean to say that the president, his
administrative colleagues, and the members of the governing
board are more perceptive, more honest, more wise, or more capable than other groups in the university. I am only saying that
their interests are more closely identified with the university as
a whole and with the broad social interest. The weakness of faculty, students, and nonacademic staff, as holders of institutional
power, is that they are, and often behave as, special interest groups
and that they are often insensitive to public responsibility as well
as to public relations. This allegation will undoubtedly be challenged and undoubtedly there are exceptions. However, I submit
that the claim is essentially correct. It is in no sense a criticism of
faculty or students or nonacademic staff as people, but only a
comment on the implications of their roles in the university.

Having said that authority should reside in the president
working in close association with a lay governing board, I hasten
to add that any worthy president will arrange for all individuals
and groups in the university to express their views, and he will
listen to these views. Moreover, he will welcome both formal and
informal channels of communication throughout the organization,
and will heed the advice received. And he will give special heed
to the advice of the faculty who are senior partners and long-term
members of the community, who have vital interests, who are
professionally involved, and who (regardless of the formal details
of organization) have great influence. However, final decisions
should be the president's subject to approval of the governing
board, and it should not become a constitutional crisis when the
advice of some group is not followed.

The proposal to eliminate the governing board by merging
it with the joint council, thus creating a single governing group

consisting of insiders and lay citizens, is also unsound in my opinion. A lay governing board composed of distinguished citizens is needed to insulate the university from improper pressures of the public, politicians, and donors, and to represent the public interest in a way that no combination of administrators, faculty, students, or employees could do. It is the broad public interest that a university should serve, not privileges for any group or combination of groups and not even glorification of the institution.

The joint council would not be attractive to those who look upon the faculty as having primacy in the governance of the university—especially to those who subscribe to the ancient aphorism that the faculty *is* the university. But once students have been admitted to the decision-making process, and once nonacademic employees, teaching assistants, and others have successfully asserted their role, it is hard to make the case that the faculty is more than one of several interest groups. Because of the long tenure of faculty members, their professional competence, their mobility, and their experience, the faculty is inevitably the most influential of the groups. Moreover, the professionals (the faculty) must be relied upon primarily for educational and research decisions. To determine the proper content of programs in Greek literature, or surgery, or nuclear engineering, or music, or to set degree requirements, or to decide what research tasks are important in these fields, or to recommend what equipment is needed or what books ought to be in the library is primarily a matter for faculty decision. No lay board, no administrators, no nonacademic staff, no students, or any combination of these would be fully qualified to make these decisions. They must be delegated in large part to the professionals with only broad review and evaluation by others. It does not follow from this that the faculty, as individuals, departments, or colleges, should be immune from regular evaluation by outsiders, or should be impervious to suggestions from the outside particularly in matters of educational philosophy, methods and costs of instruction, interdisciplinary relationships, and relevance or importance of research and public service. The mystique of professional specialization does not render outsiders totally incapable of useful evaluation and suggestion. Moreover, in carrying out their responsibilities faculties would do well to ensure broad participation among their own numbers in policy matters, to consult their peers outside the university, to listen regularly to the opinions of their students, and to call upon outside help in problems of educational philosophy and teaching methods. But in practice the decisions must largely be theirs subject only to broad review by the joint council, the president, and the board.

Outside the strictly academic area, the decisions and operations of the university are not very specialized and technical. These decisions relate to business management, fund-raising, salary scales and fringe benefits, internal allocation of operating funds, building priorities, parking, student rules, extracurricular life, student housing, and the like. In these areas, everyone is an expert—or believes he is. Faculty, students, and nonacademic staff—as well as some outside groups such as parents and alumni—all have something to say on these matters. Moreover, in the interests of good education, students should be involved because of the many opportunities for learning in connection with university affairs. Even if students could contribute nothing, we would be obliged as educators to encourage their participation.

What I have said so far presupposes that the various groups in the university will function through discussion and persuasion, not coercion. The really new feature of university governance is *coercion* in the form of demonstrations, sit-ins, collective bargaining, strikes, publicity campaigns, direct appeals to governing boards and legislative bodies, and the like. Faculty, students, and nonacademic employees have all been involved to varying degrees. The universities have been shocked, and also moved, by these tactics.

The existence of coercion reinforces my conclusions about governance. If the parties are to assert their demands by coercion in its various forms, it becomes essential that final authority rest with the president and a lay board having responsibility for the whole institution and having special concern for the public interest as distinct from the partial interests of faculty, students, and nonacademic staff. The greater the tendency to coercive tactics, the greater must be the authority of the president and board. In the absence of coercion, the institution can afford delegation, wide consultation, and participation in decision-making. But when the game is a ruthless struggle for power, the authority must be firmly in the hands of the president and the board. Otherwise, the institution will fly apart or fall into the hands of a group which

may not be responsive to the public interest. The tactics of coercion can, by the way, be employed against any of the various
groups—students, faculty, and nonacademic staff—as well as
against the administration. In fact, many believe, and I tend to
agree, that the next victim of coercion will be the faculty, and that
when this happens the faculty will need the protection of a strong
administration and governing board.

Governance and educational progress. As I stated earlier,
a good system of governance will harmonize the rights of the
constituent individuals and groups with a capacity for progressiveness, educational advancement, efficiency, and order. I have proposed a system of governance which lodges final authority and
accountability in the president subject to supervision by a board
consisting of distinguished laymen and which creates a joint council of faculty, students, nonacademic staff, and administrators to
advise the president on a wide range of issues. I have suggested
that academic decisions must largely be delegated to the faculty
but that the joint council, the president, and the governing board
might properly be concerned with matters of educational philosophy, educational methods, costs of instruction, interdisciplinary
relationships, and relevance and importance of research and public
service.

This proposed system departs from present practice in that
it clearly establishes the position of the president and governing
board, and gives a strong position in the joint council to students,
nonacademic staff, and administrators. Would this system help to
change the built-in resistance of the academic community to
change in educational methods?

The university may be a fertile source of new ideas in
chemistry or economics or literary criticism, but it is not a dynamic and venturesome place in its educational content and
methods, in its relationships to its students, or in its efforts to discover economies of operation. Higher education (along with
health care) must be one of the most backward or least progressive
parts of our whole economy. In a world of scientific and technological change and of increasing productivity, the university is
clearly a laggard.

In all candor, it is hard to identify any significant change
in educational technique since World War I. It is true that new
subjects like nuclear engineering, linguistics, and area studies have

been introduced, that many specialized courses have been added (but few dropped), that facilities have improved, that faculties are better trained, that the research effort has been intensified, and that standards have become more rigorous. It is also true that there has been constant tinkering with curricular requirements, and there has been some desultory experimentation with films, TV, computer-aided instruction, programmed learning, and independent study. But when the record is reviewed in its entirety, one can only conclude that the basic mode of instruction—courses, textbooks, lecture-discussion, close supervision, frequent class meetings, frequent tests, laboratory instruction based on "cookbook" manuals, credits, and grades—has been essentially unchanged. And in efficiency or economy of instruction, few if any gains have been made. Teaching loads have, of course, declined markedly; but this decline has had the effect of diverting faculty time to research and has not necessarily changed the mode of instruction or affected its cost. Indeed, the principal change in the university since World War I has been increasing research activity and reduced teaching loads of professors.

The record suggests either that optimal methods of instruction (as to effectiveness and cost) were discovered long ago, and no significant improvement is possible, or that the university under its present system of governance is incorrigibly conservative. Take your choice.

I am not one who believes that there are panaceas. Not all the answers lie in the use of audiovisual gadgets and not all present practices should be scrapped. I believe that part of the answer lies in helping our students become independent learners rather than in nurturing their dependency through the close supervision common to present teaching methods. I believe we can improve education, in the deepest sense, while reducing cost. Whether or not I am right in this particular opinion, it is clear that the academic world needs a more venturesome and experimental approach to education. One's conclusion about governance should, in my opinion, be based primarily on this need for a new progressiveness in educational policy. The only acceptable system of governance is one that will, among other things, enable the university to become educationally forward-looking.

It is often alleged that the university's educational conservatism exists precisely because academic policy is the area most

completely under faculty domination, and least influenced by
governing boards, administrators, or students. The primacy of the
faculty in the academic area has been generally accepted for the
reason that faculty members are professionals and others have
been hesitant to challenge the dominance of the experts. While
it is unquestionably true that faculty members are experts in the
substance of their fields, it is on the whole not true that they are
experts in pedogogy—either in the philosophy or techniques of
education. There is no reason whatever for concluding that only
faculty members can have useful opinions or recommendations on
the objectives and methods of teaching. There is a legitimate role
for administrators, students, and various specialists to assist, advise,
lead, and stimulate faculties to improve the learning of students.

Though faculty members may have been primarily responsible for inaction in educational reform, I do not wholly absolve
administrators of the blame. They have not used all their powers
in promoting reform. Their position has been weak because excellent faculty have been scarce and highly mobile. It has also
been weak because they have been preoccupied with public relations and fund-raising and have not been able to give close attention to the problem. Moreover, intent on institutional prestige,
they have aided and abetted the faculty by supporting a reward
system that strongly encourages research and scholarship but provides little incentive to educational reform.

The impetus to educational reform may come from students. They have already made an impact by instituting such
changes as the pass-fail grade, Afro-American studies, the free university movement, independent study programs, and evaluation
of courses and teachers. If the principal advisory council were
composed jointly of administration, faculty, students, and nonacademic staff, it is possible that the agenda would begin to include
educational issues, and that a coalition of administration and students would push the faculty into action. This push might be
strengthened by the coming financial pinch which will dictate
greater attention to economy.

If orderly changes in the internal balance of power will not
produce results, then I would expect either contention, disorder,
and coercion from within, or pressure from outside (including
restriction of financial support), or both. We have reached the
end of the era when it is possible to ignore or postpone educational

reform. There is obvious need for research and experimentation in methods of higher education, looking toward both improved effectiveness and lower cost. There is also need for simple and obvious changes that would produce better results and reduce costs, long before the results of any research program were known. One of the ironies of our plight is that we have been through our greatest era of growth and development but have not captured the enthusiasm of our students. We have employed thousands of faculty, raised salaries and fringe benefits, built buildings, purchased books and equipment, entered new academic fields, and organized new institutions, but we have not devised a form of education that fits the late twentieth century.

Section VI

Role of the Nonrational

Spokesmen for the younger generation often emphasize the significance of nonverbal modes of perception among today's youth, often expressing this idea together with some pity or disdain for the older intellectual who has been "hooked on thinking" (to use a phrase from the Berkeley Barb) *and now languishes as the slave to the grammar of some language. The three essays of Section VI explore facets of this important dimension in the lives of contemporary students.*

Rollo May, author of the first essay, takes as his theme the significance of myth and symbol. A civilization's myths, May asserts, carry its values; more than that, they are "the means by which the individual finds his sense of identity"; they enable him "to negotiate the crises of life." The demise of symbol and myth in our culture, May asserts, is the surest sign of disunity and trouble.

James Shiflett, in the second essay of Section VI, attempts to define three new influences in the contemporary world: "happening," "Living Theater," and "Soul." They are, in essence, new forms of communication—and necessary ones, Shiflett argues, that tell us "our society needs to be jerked (happening), questioned and defied (Living Theater), and given an experience of what it means to be a whole, feeling person (Soul)."

In the last essay of Section VI, Andrew Greeley approaches these nonrational dimensions in a quite different way. He sets himself the task of demonstrating that the psychedelic element in popular culture "represents, in part, the resurgence of man's need for the sacred." In the first part of the essay, Greeley shows the common character of the psychedelic and the sacred. They are both attempts at the ecstatic; processes that are primordial (that is, prerational or antirational); means for attaining "truth"; ceremonial processes; phenomena characterized by ritualism, communitarianism, and profound sexuality.

In the second part of the essay, Greeley moves from the role of value-free sociologist to that of judge and critic, quite explicitly shifting into a normative framework. From that vantage point, he finds that the world of psychedelia "is plagued by hang-ups of its own and does not provide much in the way of viable alternatives" to the society against which it has reacted. Greeley analyzes what he believes these "hang-ups" to be. Nonetheless, though he finds the solutions psychedelia offers unsatisfactory, the movement is still significant, Greeley states, as "a powerful critique of modern society."

JOSEPH AXELROD

⌁ 21 ⌁

REALITY BEYOND RATIONALISM

Rollo May

There are two ways man has communicated through human history. One is by way of discursive language. This is specific, empirical, objective, tends toward mathematics in science, and eventuates in logic. The important criterion of this kind of communication is that the person who is speaking the words is irrelevant to the truth or falsehood of what he says.

The other way is myth. The myth is a story which begins in history but then takes on the special character of a way of orienting oneself to reality. The myth carries the values of the society and is the means by which the individual finds his sense of identity. The myth always moves toward totality rather than specificity. It transcends the antinomies of life—such as conscious and unconscious, historical and present, individual and social—and unites these in a drama which is passed down from age to age. Whereas discursive language refers to an objective fact, the myth refers to the quintessence of human experience.

189

The myth, as Thomas Mann says, is an eternal truth in contrast to an empirical truth. It does not matter in the slightest whether a man named Adam ever actually existed or not; the myth about him presents a picture of the birth and development of human moral consciousness which is true for all people of all ages and religions. Oedipus had been an archaic Greek tale, which in the hands of Homer took on the proportions of a myth and in the pen of Sophocles became the myth of the hero who seeks his own reality. This is known in our day as the search for identity. The man who cries, "I must find out what and who I am," and then—like all of us—revolts against his own reality, stands not only for the Greeks but the everyman in his ambivalent struggle to find his identity. This myth, like most of the ancient Hebrew and Greek myths, transcends language, customs, and mores, and becomes true for people of all cultures—which is the definition of a classic. The great anthropologist Malinowski writes, "Myth expresses, enhances, and codifies belief, safeguards and enforces morality, vouches for the efficiency of ritual, and contains practical rules for the guidance of man."

We cannot derive myth from language, or language from myth; nor can we explain one in terms of the other.[1] They develop in parallel fashion in primitive man and in man in all stages of history ever since. It was the fond hope of the nineteenth-century materialists, such as Max Muller, to explain myth away by saying "myth is but part of a more general phase through which all language has at one time or other passed." But language abandons myth only at the price of the loss of the human warmth, color, personal meaning, values. For we understand each other by identifying with the subjective meaning of the language of the other person, and experiencing what his words mean to him in *his* world. Without myth we listen like a race of brain-injured people, unable to go behind the word and hear the person speaking. There can be no stronger proof of the impoverishment of our culture than the popular—though profoundly mistaken—definition of myth as falsehood.

Language and myth need each other. Discursive language expresses man's perpetual need to objectivity; myth expresses man's likewise perpetual need to exercise his creative imagina-

[1] See Ernst Cassirer, *Language and Myth* (New York: Dover, 1946), for a sound demonstration of this truth.

tion in giving meanings and values to experience. "Again and again," writes Cassirer, "myth receives new life and wealth from language, as language does from myth. And this constant interaction and interpenetration attests the unity of the mental principle [from] which both are sprung, and of which they are simply different expressions. . . ."

The myths enable us to negotiate the crises of life—the crisis of birth in the myths underlying baptism, the crisis of puberty in the myths underlying confirmation and Bar Mitzvah, and so on through marriage, profession, up to and including death itself. Funerals and the myth of immortality may seem to be mockeries to most of us, but they are the deteriorated expression of a once sound and noble effort to give meaning to death.

Freud himself was ambivalent on the subject of myth. On one side he appreciated the value and power of myth in addition to his using the Greek classic myths tellingly in his theory. In 1932 he wrote to Einstein, "It may perhaps seem to you as though our theories are a kind of mythology, and in the present case not even an agreeable one. But does not every science come in the end to a kind of mythology like this? Cannot the same be said for your own physics?"

But Freud also thought and spoke out of an alienated age. Wedded to nineteenth-century, Helmholtzian materialism, he struggled—though unsuccessfully—to formulate the motives of human behavior in physiological terms. One result of this is that he did not appreciate the positive side of myth. He saw that the myth *disguises* the truth but he did not see that the myth also *discloses* new truth. He lacked Cassirer's insight, "Man lives with objects only insofar as he lives with these *forms;* he reveals reality to himself, and himself to reality, in that he lets himself and the environment enter into this plastic medium, in which the two do not merely make contact, but fuse with each other."

Ernest Hemingway is an example of a man whose life was given meaning by the myth of potency. He lived out the tough man in hunting big game, in creative writing, and in sexual potency—which was a real problem for him. When he lost these, when he could no longer write or hunt and was sexually impotent, he acted out the myth of potency in its logical conclusion in the one act left to a man, suicide, which rounded out his existence like a Greek tragedy.

The process of myth-forming is essential to mental health. Since myth is man's way of constructing interpretations of reality which carry the values he sees in a way of life, and since it is through myth that he gets his sense of identity, a society which disparages myth is bound to be one in which mental disorientation is relatively widespread. I propose the following hypothesis: When a culture is moving toward integration and unity, it has a system of symbols and myths which give integration to the members of the society, and people then are relatively free from psychological breakdown. But when a culture is in process of disintegration, it loses first of all its myths and symbols. This loss predicts the disintegration of the culture as a whole. People then experience psychological distress and loss of identity. These are the periods when people come in large numbers to seek help in psychotherapy and other therapeutic professions.

Our own period is always hard to see clearly. Nevertheless, I cite one myth which did give values to American society for a couple of centuries, the myth of the frontier. This was a myth which emphasized self-reliance, individual strength, courage to draw one's gun at a moment's notice, capacity for hard work and effort, honesty, and so forth. The positive side of this myth is personified in the characteristics of Abraham Lincoln; some of the trailing power of this myth rubbed off on such figures as Adlai Stevenson. This myth gave meaning and dignity to Americans' lives as they participated in the westward expansion. But in the late nineteenth century this myth spawned the Horatio Alger myth —the myth that success would attend anyone's hard effort and honesty, be he farmer in Wyoming or German worker from Bavaria or Jewish merchant from Russia landing at the Statue of Liberty.

The myth of the frontier, as well as its child, the Horatio Alger myth, has now become confused and self-contradictory. Its demise was marked by Arthur Miller's play *Death of a Salesman*. At the grave where Willie Loman is being buried in this play, Arthur Miller has the younger son, as a typical expression of the myth, say, "He had a good goal, to be number one." But the older son shakes his head and answers, "He never knew who he was." This accurately describes the situation which obtains whenever the myths by which a man has lived disintegrate.

That our age is characterized by the disintegration of myths and symbols is shown on all sides. Kenneth Keniston concludes in his book, *The Uncommitted,* that one cause of the alienation of young people is the bankruptcy of the positive myths in our society. We now covertly believe in the "myth of a mythless society"—which is a counsel of despair. Jerome Bruner, also noting this fact, writes, "When the myths of a period are not adequate to man's predicament, the individual first takes refuge in mythoclasm, and then undertakes the lonely quest for inner identity."

I do not mean to make the disintegration of symbols and myths the cause of our present predicament. They are rather the critical expression of the culture, and their demise is the surest sign of disunity and trouble in the members of the society. We do not make myths or symbols; we rather experience them—mainly unconsciously as the source of the images of the charter of the culture such as the values, the goals, and the identity. By becoming conscious of the process we can, however, mold our myths and symbols. Marshall McLuhan sees the movement toward a new mythology: "We actually live mythically and integrally, but we continue to think in the old fragmented space and time pattern of the pre-electric age. . . . For myth is always a montage or transparency comprising several external spaces and times in a single image or situation."

I have argued that the myths and symbols express the meaningful unity of society, and give the society a system of values. The myths are discovered by us as our heritage as we develop individually, but each individual must take his own stand with regard to them: attacking them, affirming them, molding them, or lamenting their absence. The social and individual factors in experience come into fusion at the point of myth. It is in the myths we find our intentionality—or, as in our day, our lack of it.

~⟨ 22 ⟩~

SOUL

James A. Shiflett

There is a new genius striding the land. There is a life shouting in our canyon streets. There are people waking up at odd hours and poking heads out of windows and doors, recognizing brothers. The urban soul is stirring. For fifty years the mad scientist has been experimenting with the creation of the urban monster. He built its industrial heart and its military larynx. Suburban arms and legs appeared as if by magic. He stretched it along the waterways, across the great plains, through the swampland, until the nations of yesterday are called cities today: the United States city, the European city, the Japanese city, the Indian city. By electrical impulses the heart was caused to beat, the larynx to speak, the arms and legs to move, but there was no heart, no soul.

The scientist thought to himself, "I must build a head that can move the body and order its life." He looked out on his creation for the material to build the head, and his eye fell on the great urban bowels. They pleased him because of their uselessness and chaotic activity. Perfect for making the head. Attaching his jumper cables to the urban electrodes, he prepared to send a billion volts into the chaos, thus creating the nerve center. The switch was pulled, the current flowed. The great bank of computers began to smoke, transistors exploded, the current backed up into the laboratory, the scientist stood transfixed—quiet voices coming up from the sparks and smoke. "Hey, man, you disturb my cool, you dig?" "Señor, you knocked my house down, man." "You all crazy baby, stop this foolin' around." And the last voice: "You have a groovy place here, jack, but you're square." The scientist heard the ugly truth. The head already had life, it breathed, it thought, it felt. The head had soul. Could he turn over his body to the head? Could this head order the great complex machine that he had created? And why should he give up all of his work to a discourteous head that would not even recognize him for all of his ingenious creation?

A battle of cosmic significance began. The head and the scientist arranged their forces, the head using soul power, the scientist using mechanical power. An the battle rages today. This is the agony of the United States and the world.

You cannot talk about soul, you recognize soul. Living Theater is not reviewed, it is experienced. Happenings are not analyzed, you are involved in them. These "new directions" all seek to reach the individual, to uncover his soul, to give him his life, and the only way that this gift can be given is for the giver to know his own person, to have uncovered his own soul, to have received his own life. When we talk about the social impact of "new direction" in art, we are talking about the struggle to live. To live is to be aware that you are alive. A happening is an exercise in jerking you into awareness of your environment. It just so happens that a cellist runs into a ballerina at State and Madison at twelve o'clock noon. The cellist plays and the ballerina dances. The bus comes along. The ballerina gets on and rides away. The cellist walks into the subway. State and Madison will never be the same for those who passed by or stopped. The policeman present probably does not know whether a law has been broken, and the newsstand vendor was entertained. A new awareness was established. A person's life changes because of one awareness-giving experience.

The Living Theater is best understood when Julian Beck and his company are experienced. In this experience, you are

made to question every cliché that you have held sacred. They
wander through the audience at the beginning of *Paradise Now*,
presenting the *no* of our society, and crying in agony:

> I am not allowed to travel without a passport.
> I am not allowed to smoke in the auditorium theater.
> I am not allowed to smoke marijuana.
> I am not allowed to spend my money for peace.
> I am not allowed not to kill.
> I am not allowed to burn my draft card.
> I am not allowed to stay in the park after eleven o'clock.

Until finally, the cry:

> I am not allowed to take off my clothes——

And they take off their clothes. They cannot stand the agony of
the negatives any longer. They will meet irrationality with a corresponding irrationality. But is it so irrational? Why does our society get nervous when one taboo is challenged? Because all of
the taboos may be challenged and that would be anarchy. Anarchy
is exactly what the Living Theater movement is preaching. They
have a great evangelistic fervor. Destroy the system! The system is
dead!

The impact the Living Theater should have upon the
United States is to cause serious questioning about our life. It is
difficult to build a case for the restrictions placed upon us by the
laws and mores of our land being just for our welfare and safety.
The anarchists have a point that the taboos are more for keeping
the system alive than for keeping human beings alive. Educators
must hear the Living Theater's message, because you are a part
of the system they speak of, and you are being challenged today
as you have never been challenged before. You are on the battle
line of the revolution (or you are on the battle line of urban life
coming of age).

When you come to Soul, you come to a mystery. Here you
have the poetry of the urban life, because it names the misery and
the agony of our shared life. It comes out of the deeps of our
existence. It comes out of the dumps of the political machine's
urban plantations. If the history of our day is written with perception, it will tell how the great urban revolution became irre-

versible when it discovered the source of its soul, its life, the headwaters flowing from the polluted streets, alleys, and rotting plaster apartments of our ghettos. Bobby Bland sings "Loan a Helping Hand":

> Well, somebody, yes somebody,
> Please, somebody, before I go insane,
> Won't somebody,
> Please lend me a helpin' hand?
>
> I've got money, and I've got a place to stay
> I've got money, and I've got a place to stay
> But everybody needs a friend, both night and day.
>
> Well, I walk, talk—but all by myself
> Well, I walk, talk—but all by myself
> I'm so afraid it's gonna wear me to death.
>
> Well, somebody, yes somebody,
> Please, somebody, oh, baby,
> Please, somebody,
> Won't you lend me a helpin' hand?

This song, and the blues in general, tap into the life root of a people. When they hear, they respond: "Tell it like it is." Bobby Bland, Howlin Wolf, Redd Foxx, B. B. King, and others, are culture heroes not just of one-eighth of our society, but of the emerging urban cultures. They sing of the misery, the loneliness, the joy of a people. They sing of human beings, and the urban culture must be a culture for human beings or we have no culture at all.

But Soul is more than words. It is also body. The Soul body is the body that participates in living. If the body is not present to the life situation, no amount of words will suffice. One must put his ego in his hips, thighs, toes, shoulders, and hands. The culture-hero blues man sings with his whole body in response to words, audience, his own self. The uninitiated call his movements gyrations, but this term is false. He communicates his song with a singing body. The nonverbal is more important than the verbal because the soul's song, its believability, is lost without the body's presence to the song and the environment. Therefore, the arts are saying that our society needs to be jerked (happening), questioned and defied (Living Theater), and given an experience of what it means to be a whole, feeling person (Soul). The basic assumption of the "new direction" in art is that our society is not geared to treat human beings as whole persons, but as fragmented slivers of selves and therefore not human. If this assumption is true, then our society is immoral. If our society is immoral, then is it purposely so? If it is not purposely immoral then a jerking (happening) into a consciousness of human wholeness will be sufficient. If it is purposely immoral, then it should and must be defied (Living Theater).

Because the art world does include happenings (a passé form), Living Theater, and Soul, we must accept the fact that there are some who believe fervently that our society is immoral, that it purposely fragments and destroys human beings by "turning off" persons from their senses, feelings, and imaginations, thereby creating rational robots. This cry was voiced by the University of Chicago protesters. A spokesman of that demonstration said the university student body and faculty are too rationally inclined to actually make the demonstration a success. One of the things this spokesman meant was that the students and faculty were cut off from their bodies. There was not enough feeling feeding the rational. The demonstrators were unable to act as persons who had experienced being human beings, and they claimed the university was responsible.

Let me assume that most of my readers are not inclined to the students or the "new direction" arts action stance, but that you sympathize with their point of view. Perhaps you would deny that there is a conscious plot to dehumanize men. Consequently your position is that we need changes in our educational system to make it possible for teachers to meet the educational needs required by today's society. You define the aim of education to be the preparation of a person to participate as a full human being in our society. Traditionally being idealists, you believe that our society desires persons to participate as full human beings in its life, and that this participation will make for a strong, healthy society. You recognize that the problem in education is to keep the student open to or connected to the tools of his personhood; sight, hearing, taste, touch, and smell. His senses give him his awareness and his desire to assimilate. If a person is not aware of himself and that which is around him, he is slow to learn and he may not even learn.

The traditional awareness tools in education have been in the past the paddle and the arts. A person is discovered by fear in the paddle syndrome, and by his experience in the arts world. Indeed, one behavioral scientist refers to certain arts processes in theater, writing, and music as experiential pedagogical processes, and that these experiential processes must be placed in the hard curriculum of our educational process if our children are to learn. The social implication of the new direction in art and the experiential processes (for example, the Theater Games Workshop of Viola Spolin, the Story Workshop writing process of John Schultz, and the music experimentation of William Russo) say to us that there must be a union between the arts and the teaching of English, history, social science, mathematics, languages, and so on, if we are serious about education as a process in which the student is discovered by himself and his environment.

Therefore, those who say that they do not notice a lack of educational curiosity on the part of college students, that they seem to be able to learn and that they seem to be reasonably well-integrated human beings, must be aware of two answers to their position. First, the student revolt, if one reads between the lines of our newspapers, is saying that this attitude is a lie, and that students are interested in participating in an educational process that has as its main concern their humanization. Second, our colleges never see one half of the students from our urban society that could come to college, because the public school teachers that are being cranked out of our colleges and universities do not have the tools to teach the children of this decade. They are turning off our children; and the educational systems of our urban centers, directly connected to the Ph.Ds of our universities, are not willing to make the necessary decisions that will make real education possible in our urban centers.

At a particular public high school in Chicago, the student body numbers 2,400. If you divide 2,400 by four classes, then each class should be 600 apiece. But the graduating class numbers only 325. This means that the other classes are bigger than 600. You conclude after a series of mathematical computations that the freshman class needs to be about 800 in order to produce a 325-member graduating senior class. Is it normal for a class, during four years of high school, to decrease by close to 60 per cent? It is not. The dropout rate in our urban centers is fast approaching

50 per cent of the student population. When we reach the 50 per cent mark and pass through it, the educational system can no longer claim to be the educational system.

The dropout of the sixties is a living art form that combines the jerk of the happening and the questioning and defiance of Living Theater in regard to education. We are on the edge of anarchy in our educational system. Our only hope is the embracing of Soul, of involvement by community and student in the educational process, in the decision-making committees and boards that are presently making decisions for an educational system that will soon have no students. The curriculum must be changed to include and inaugurate the experiential tools of the arts in the hard core curriculum so that students will begin to sense their wholeness.

The cosmic battle continues. The struggle for the head of the monster rages. The voices coming out of the urban mix are aware that they are being manipulated by unfeeling forces, and they resent it. The "new direction" for the arts is both the vehicle that freights the voices into the hearing of wholly unfeeling structures, and the source for an emerging urban society to cope with what it means to be human. Urban society can be an environment for humanness or it can be the context for a new breed of urban robot. And we are the ones to make that decision.

~ 23 ~

THE PSYCHEDELIC
AND THE SACRED

Andrew M. Greeley

Harmony and understanding
Sympathy and trust abounding
No more falsehoods or derisions
Golden living dreams of visions
Mystic crystal revelation
And the mind's true liberation.

Thus do the hippies in the folk-rock opera, *Hair*, announce the age of Aquarius—the new era of peace, love, freedom, and unity which they see growing out of the psychedelic movement. Whether the age of Aquarius is about to dawn is a question that we can put aside for the moment, though some cynical observers may think that it is rather the age of Leo the Lion that is dawning. My intention here is to explore that dimension of popular and perhaps emergent high culture that we can subsume under the title "psychedelic" and to suggest that the psychedelic represents, in part, the resurgence of man's need for the sacred in the face of secularized society.[1]

It is necessary for us to spend rather more time on the definition of terms than one normally would in a presentation such as this, because both terms—*psychedelic* and *sacred*—and particularly the latter, are tricky and illusive. By *psychedelic*, I mean that collection of phenomena associated with hallucinogenic drugs, rock and roll music, beat communities, the art of dissociation—be it music, painting, or literature—and the new concern about esoteric oriental religions; psychedelia, in the strict sense, exists only among a relatively small handful of American young and not-so-young people. Fellow travelers of psychedelia, be they teen-agers listening to Jefferson Airplane, young adults going to electric circuses, or college professors wearing turtlenecked shirts and pasting flowers on their Volkswagens and talking the language of the hippy community, represent a much larger phenomenon than the hard-core psychedelics. I would also include as at least related to psychedelia, underground films, underground newspapers, and perhaps even the politics of irrational violence advocated by some political commentators and practiced by a handful of alienated white young people.

By the sacred, I mean not merely the nonrational, for if I did, my case that the psychedelic represents a quest for the sacred would already be established by definition. Nor do I oppose the sacred merely to this-worldly. The Secular City enthusiasts would have us believe that modern man has rejected the other-worldly and intends to find his life satisfactions and challenges entirely in the this-worldly. Psychedelia clearly refutes such a naive assumption because it obviously represents a frantic attempt to escape the this-worldly, to tune out in order that one might turn on. While the other-worldly does, indeed, represent an element of the sacred, I intend to convey rather more than this in my use of the word, for by *sacred* I mean not only the other-worldly, but also the ecstatic, the transcendental, that which takes man out of himself and which puts him in contact with the basic life forces of the universe. This, I argue, is the function of the sacred in any society that sociologists or anthropologists have known, and this,

---

[1] Editor's note: Another version of this essay appeared in *The Critic,* April, 1969.

I further argue, is precisely what those who have joined the psychedelic society are aiming for.

When Tom Wolfe argues in *The Electric Kool-Aid Acid Test* that Ken Kesey and his Merry Pranksters are, in fact, a total religious community, he is, in my judgment, not engaging in mere rhetoric. Kesey and his disciples were engaging in behavior on their trips (whether in a bus or on drugs) that anthropologists of another planet would almost automatically categorize as religious.

At the root of the emergence of the psychedelic is the end of scientific, democratic, secular rationalism and a return to the primordial, instinctual, ecstatic irrationalism that was permitted and even encouraged in most preindustrial societies. The culture and the social organization which has made our economic abundance possible was designed basically to meet the emotional and spiritual needs of Adam Smith's Economic Man. It has succeeded in its goals and, at least by the inhabitants of psychedelia, it has been found wanting for the service of other goals. Its rational, civil, optimistic, individualistic citizen is, from the viewpoint of psychedelia, only half a man, a man caught in the "work-war-wed bag."

I am not suggesting that the society of bourgeois economic rationalism is about to collapse, but I am suggesting that it is in serious trouble; an increasing number of its more sensitive younger members want to have no part of it, and sees the madcap irrationalities of psychedelia as a highly desirable alternative.

Let me now specify precisely what characteristics of psychedelia are, in my judgment as a sociologist, characteristics of religious behavior.

First of all, psychedelia is explicitly and consciously an attempt at the *ecstatic,* whether it be through drugs or music or a combination of the two. As one commentator on rock music puts it, rock can "move people's muscles, bodies, caught up and swaying and moving so that a phrase . . . can actually become your whole body, can sink into your soul on a more-than-cognitive level. Rock, because of the number of senses it can get to (on a dance floor, eyes, ears, nose, mouth, and tactile) and the extent to which it can pervade those senses, is really the most advanced art form we have. The acid head or the rock devotee wishes to escape, tune out, to leave behind the prosaic, dull, "uptight" world of bourgeois society and to achieve union with higher forces as rep-

resented by throbbing rock beat with a marvelous clarity of insight furnished by an acid trip. Psychedelia enables rational
industrial man and his children to pull out of himself, to back
away from and over against ordinary experience and judge it in
the quality of new insight or from the perspective of new unity.
Such have been the goals of ecstatics and mystics down through
the ages, though they have sought their ecstasy much less consciously and in most cases much less artificially than does the psychedelic ecstatic.

Psychedelia is *primordial,* that is to say, prerational when
not explicitly antirational. It seeks to put aside the hang-ups of
organized society and its conventions in order that it might get
in touch with the profound underlying natural forces in which
we are all immersed, even though the conventions of society cause
us to forget this immersion. Psychedelia strives desperately and
highly consciously to be natural (which is probably, one might
note, a self-defeating quest). The new hair styles for both black
and white represent, if in a rather mild fashion, in many instances,
an attempt, however pathetic, to achieve naturalness. As the song
in *Hair* puts it—"Long, beautiful, shining, gleaming, steaming,
flaxen, waxen, long, straight, curly, fuzzy, snaggy, shaggy, raggy,
matty, oily, greasy, fleecy, down-to-there hair." One might even
observe, in passing, that such stalwart institutions of the bourgeois
establishment as the American Association for Higher Education
are now inhabited by people whose hair is considerably longer
than it would have been back in the old days of the crew-cut
world.

Those who know about such things tell us that rock and
roll music results from a marriage of black "rhythm and blues"
music with the "gospel" tradition of black music. In our perspective this marriage was not an accident. "Rhythm and blues" is a
superb manifestation of black soul—that is to say, the casual,
primordial, sensual style which some blacks have (and which many
blacks and many whites would like to have)—a style which is a
ribald rejection of the industrial middle-class society that has first
of all rejected the blacks. Gospel music, on the other hand, represents an enthusiasm, a vibrancy in religious devotion which is
also part of the black tradition. Putting the two together, one
produces a combination of sensualism and near-hysterical enthusiasm which provides the hung-up hyper-rationalized white

man with two qualities of behavior—sensuality and enthusiasm—
that are dysfunctional in his bureaucratized, formalized, com-
puterized life.

The hippy communities, of course, are another manifestation of the highly conscious attempt to return to nature—an attempt which has been well described by Philip Gleason as a new
romanticism. Romantic it is, and unsuccessful it probably will
be, but as a judgment on realistic secular society, it is quite effective.

Psychedelia is, or at least attempts to be, *contemplative.*
By this I do not mean that it is quiet, for generally it is not, but
I do mean that it tries to break through appearances and see *truth*
"like it is." As one rock song puts it:

> *I think it's so groovy now*
> *That people are finally getting together*
> *I think it's so wonderful—and how!*
> *That people are finally getting together*
> *Reach out of the darkness, . . .*

It must be confessed that this particular mystical insight is not
terribly original and does not carry the mystical tradition much
beyond John of the Cross or Meister Eckhart, to which the psychedelics will reply that while their insight is not new, they perceive truth as not merely on the cognitive level but in the deepest
level of their personality. How deep that is perhaps remains to
be seen, but the significant point about the contemplative development in psychedelia is not that it is new, or not even that it
is very meaningful, but simply that it is.

Psychedelia is also *ceremonial.* By this I mean in the present
context that it is given to the use of exotic and esoteric symbols—
such exotic and esoteric things, that is, as beads and flowers, fancy
garments, neck jewelry for men, turtlenecked shirts, Edwardian
coats, and other such costumes, uniforms, baubles, and trinkets.
The Beatles in their nineteenth-century musical comedy clothes,
the Merry Pranksters in their American Flag suits, the flower
people with their neck amulets, and even the Hell's Angels in
their black leather jackets are, in fact, wearing *vestments.* They
have donned uniforms to set themselves off from and over against
the Brooks Brothers gray flannel suit. I note, in passing, the su-

preme irony that precisely at the time when the Roman Church
is under pressure to give up vestments and avoid ceremonies, the
world of psychedelia is creating new vestments for its ceremonies,
and that precisely at the time when bishops are under heavy pressure to yield up their beloved pectoral crosses, neck jewelry for
men has become the fashionable rage.

Psychedelia is *ritualistic*. By this I mean not that it has an
elaborate system of rubrics which specify in great detail the pro-
tocol of behavior, but rather that it achieves its effects through
the stylized repetition of sound and action which simultaneously
releases the individual from old unions and immerses him in new
unities. The rolling of the dervishes, the twisting of the Holy
Rollers, the measured cadence of the Gregorian Chant, the repeti-
tive dances of the black Africans and American Indians—are all
ritualistic. But the ritual was not ritual for its own sake, as it
used to be in the rubricized Roman liturgy, but rather ritual for
the sake of producing psychological states in which the religious
initiate was able to free himself from the controls and rigidities
of ordinary life and "break on through" (as the Doors put it)
"to the other side." While most of the denizens of psychedelia
would not think of their behavior as ritualistic, and would surely
deny that the "Go-go" dance floor was anything to the religious
ritualistic past, the similarity is unmistakable and perhaps even a
linkage can be traced through the black gospel music.

The psychedelic is *communitarian*—that is to say, it attempts to create the relationships of everyday living to some kind
of concrete and practical application of the insights of mystic
union which it has perceived during its shamanistic experiences.
Heavy emphasis is placed on being "natural," "out front," "honest," "authentic," and "spontaneous" in one's human relationships; but such honesty, authenticity, spontaneity, and frankness
are often mere self-defeating pretexts for aggression and exploita-
tion, and it is rather beside the point. Psychedelia is repulsed
about the artificiality, the phoniness, and the dishonesty of the
stylized relationships of bourgeois industrial secular society, and
tries to create communities of its own, motivated by common faith
and common love, in which true believers may relate to one
another as authentic human beings. Hardly any small religious
community in human history has failed to make the same claim.
The only thing that makes psychedelia different is that it is

equipped with the Freudian and Group Dynamics categories and insights which, while they do not necessarily facilitate one's relationships, at least provide one with the words by which one is enabled to talk intensely about human relationships.

Finally, and I am sure it will come as no surprise to anyone, psychedelia is profoundly sexual, as are most religious phenomena. Sex and religion are the two most powerful nonrational forces of the human personality. That they should be linked, and even allied in their battle to overthrow the tyranny of reason, is surprising only to the highly Jansenized Christian who has lost sight of the sexual imagery in its own faith—the intercourse symbol of the candle and the water on Holy Saturday, for example, or the pervasive comparison of the Church to marriage in both the Old and the New Testament.

A good deal of the sexual anarchy of psychedelia can be written off to plain, old-fashioned lust, which operates in the square world, too, but in a more stylized and conventional fashion. However, in addition, psychedelia is dissatisfied with what it takes to be the narrowness, frustration, and joylessness of that relationship of convenience between the sexes called "upper-middle-class marriage." The psychedelics say, "You squares are hung up on sex; you talk about it, analyze it, worry over it, read books about it, strive mightily to achieve fulfillment with it, but you're too uptight about it to be able to enjoy it. All we do, man, is enjoy it."

On the philosophical level, Norman O. Brown seems to be arguing for the same goal, and the popular novel, *The Harrad Experiment,* contends that some kind of relaxed sexual polymorphism is not only possible in the bounds of upper-middle-class society, but would make those who are trained for it far more effective in working within that society.

I have argued elsewhere that within the Christian tradition it is necessary to assert that sex must be joyous and playful and that all human relationships are profoundly sexual in origin. The sexual anarchy of the psychedelics or of *The Harrad Experiment,* for that matter, may not be an adequate response to these truths; but the sexual style of middle-class American society—even one might say especially among its more enlightened and "liberated" segments—is neither playful nor joyous nor sustaining of a wide variety of healthy human relationships. Sex and faith, sex and mystical union, sex and the primordial forces of the world, sex and ritual—these relationships have been part of the implicit wisdom of most human religions. The failure of contemporary Western religions to remember this wisdom is one of the reasons for the reappearance of the wisdom in the world of psychedelics.

I should like to point out that *ecstatic, primordial, contemplative, ceremonial, ritualistic, communitarian,* and *sexual* are words that can be predicative of almost any religious liturgy that the human race has observed. I am therefore contending not merely that psychedelia is religious, but that it is liturgical, and indeed, a judgment upon us for our own past liturgical failures.

In summary, then, psychedelia is a revolt against the superego and against everything in the bourgeois industrial culture of the Western world that smacks of the superego. The reality principle in man has, in liberal industrial society, allied itself almost entirely with the superego. The result is that the transrational, whether it be the suprarational of mysticism and contemplation or the infrarational of sensualistic orgy, are now in open revolt. Reason cannot rule over the passions and emotions of man as a tyrant, at least not for very long, without running the risk of having an open revolution on its hands. Religion has always been conscious, implicitly, that man is more than mind—that he is also *soma* and *pneuma*—that is to say, both body and spirit—and that while these two characteristics of the human personality seem to be opposed to each other in theory, in fact, they are quite closely related and frequently in alliance against prosaic, secular, everyday rationality.

The secular society and most of the religions of that society have simply failed to recognize these facts. They have insisted on treating man as though he were the sober, calculating, individualist of Adam Smith, with perhaps some Freudian sexual instincts added. Reason must govern as a constitutional executive over the passions and emotions, over the infrarational and the suprarational. The scientific world has thought otherwise and the result is psychedelia. The traditional religions were skeptical of the scientific world, but nonetheless have been so influenced by its Cartesian rationalism that they, too, have lost sight in practice of the importance of the infrarational and the suprarational. For nonliturgical religions like most of the Protestant denominations there may be some excuse for this, but psychedelia is a particularly

harsh judgment on that most liturgical of Christian denominations—the Roman Catholic Church.

While I have tried, in this presentation, to maintain a
sympathetic attitude toward psychedelia, I suppose my basic ambivalence has not been altogether repressed—an ambivalence
based, at least in part, on the fact that no matter how many times
I listen to them, I still think the Beatles are loud, uncouth, and
noisy; while I am prepared to concede to the comments of learned
musical scholars that they are important musical innovators, I
still prefer to listen to Bach.

While the world of psychedelia represents a powerful critique of modern society, it is, in my judgment, plagued by hang-
ups of its own and does not provide much in the way of viable
alternatives to that society. It is, first of all, an escape, a loss of
nerve, a despair about the Western cultural tradition. The psychedelics have given up—they are, in the fullest sense of the word,
alienated. If their alienation is a passing phase, it may be a helpful
power to the maturational experience. Alienation as a way of life
is, in fact, a form of adolescent fixation. Even if you despair of
Western culture and Western society, you are still a prisoner of
it—you still live in its context, criticize it in the name of its own
values, and define yourself almost entirely in its own terms. Alienation has never been a means of human progress in the past, and it
is unlikely to be a means in the present. Differentiation and distinction, as square as these activities may seem, are the proper
response to our ambiguous scientific rational society, since at the
present time we can neither live with it nor without it. The psychedelic replies that he does not care about human progress; he
does not care about the future; he only cares about his own particular life and the options available to him in that life. It remains
to be seen whether a man can have a satisfying or satisfactory life
if his only response to the world around him is tuning out and
turning on.

Similarly, it is not evident that the abdication of reason is
any more tolerable an alternative for human living than the
tyranny of reason from which the psychedelics are trying to escape.
It is a truism by now that the capacity for conceptual thought is
what distinguishes man from the other higher apes. Drugs, music,
rejection of the most stifling conventions may be assets to man,
the conceptualizing animal, as he struggles toward self-discovery

and self-fulfillment, but they do not make any less necessary the use of this power of conceptualization.

One might say, finally, too, that there has been a great deal of nonsense spoken in favor of psychedelia, not the least of it by learned professors. Rock music is an interesting and powerful folk cultural innovation; the hippie communities are an intriguing development of the beat generation of a decade ago; the hallucinogenic drugs are perhaps an interesting substitute for John Barleycorn; electric circuses are, one must admit, something beyond the jam sessions of an earlier period; but that there are here either great musical innovations or notable social experimentations, much less salvation, seems to me very much open to question. Benjamin DeMott's comment that the future may see "the appearance of a generation so rich in experience of merger and self-transcendence that to its mind Cromwell and Charles and early twenty-first century Harvard sophomores will seem all one" is, one presumes, not meant too seriously. The present younger generation is different from the one that preceded it, but it is not different because of psychedelia; on the contrary, one suspects that psychedelia is the result of the difference in the generations. And given the skepticism of youth about the popular culture of its predecessors, one would be much better advised to speculate that by the end of the present century the acid rock of such groups as The Doors may be as dead as the "big bands" are today. Psychedelia, then, is significant as a symptom of something wrong, rather than as a promising response.

Section VII

Research on Higher Education

Warren Martin and Dale Heckman, the authors of the first essay in Section VII, report that there are today more than three thousand individuals doing research in one form or another on higher education. There is no question that in the last decade, the amount of research done in higher education has increased enormously, but the Martin-Heckman figure may come as a surprise to some readers. (Kenneth A. Feldman and Theodore M. Newcomb, who in their Impact of College on Students *[San Francisco: Jossey-Bass, 1969] summarize all of the research that has been done on that particular subject, state that the last decade has been "characterized by a more voluminous research output, probably, than all of the preceding years taken together [p. 3]."*)

Martin and Heckman are the authors of a research inventory in higher education, a project sponsored jointly by the Carnegie Commission and the Center for Research and Development in Higher Education. Their essay describes the inventory and summarizes from that volume fifty research projects that are related to the themes of "agony" and "promise."

In reading the essay, one is inevitably reminded of the "knowledge gap," a point stressed also by James Gavin in his essay in Section VIII. In higher education, as in other fields, we often have all the knowledge we need for the solution of a given prob-

211

*lem, but that knowledge is not effectively translated or imple-
mented. "Development" does not, for a variety of reasons, keep
up with research. The essay of Martin and Heckman bears witness
to the pressing nature of that dilemma for those who are currently
involved in higher education research.*

*The second essay in Section VII is a review of the scholarly
literature in the field of higher education during the year 1968.
Richard Meeth reports that some three hundred books appeared
during the year. Two themes, he states, emerged often in the literature: student power and the future of American higher education institutions. Meeth then reviews in detail twelve pieces—a
pamphlet, an issue of a magazine, and ten books—representing in
his view the "best works of the year." Readers who might wish
to see, at a glance, which works these are will find them listed at
the close of Meeth's essay, on page 240, divided into two categories
—those that approach the subject primarily through institutional
problems and those that essentially focus on students.*

JOSEPH AXELROD

UNDERSTANDING MALADIES AND EFFECTING CURES

Warren Bryan Martin

Dale Heckman

The agony and promise of higher education concern not only legislators, parents, editors, and youth, but also many educational researchers. They hope to contribute to the relief of the agony and the fulfillment of the promise by disciplined inquiry— into the structures and functions of colleges and universities as well as into the psychological and sociological dimensions of life as experienced by members of the academic community. Information is essential to understanding, and research can help to inform.

213

Understanding is prerequisite to effective change; thus research that informs may help to persuade.

Today more than three thousand individuals are doing research in one form or another on higher education. The *Inventory of Current Research on Higher Education—1968*, a project sponsored jointly by the Carnegie Commission on the Future of Higher Education and the Center for Research and Development in Higher Education, University of California, Berkeley, listed nearly a thousand projects and had contacts with more than two thousand researchers in sixty countries.[1] Yet the inventory made only cursory probes of the research under way in university departments (with the exception of education), as compared to institutes, centers, and agencies, from which inventory listings were numerous. The inventory was not exhaustive, but it indicated the extent and direction of current activity. It showed that researchers, like politicians, gravitate toward the focal points of social concern. And today, given the power, malaise, and changes in institutions of higher education, the researchers are focusing on the institution itself—as seen from outside and from within, as a self-contained entity and as a societal structure, as a complex organization where governance is affected by sociopolitical factors and ideology, where subcultures proliferate, values differ, and change is perhaps the only constant questioned.

There are several studies under way or recently completed which concentrate on those forces external to colleges and universities that do in one way or another affect activities, goals, and programs on campus: Lanier Cox, in association with the Educational Commission of the States, has finished an inquiry, by means of conferences and interviews with state budget officers and institutional budget administrators, to determine for each state how college and university officials work with legislators and state office personnel in the development of budgets for public institutions of higher education. Cox had earlier done research on the nature and extent of the impact of "state-oriented" federal programs for higher education as compared to those that were "institutionally-oriented."

Selected legislators and executive officers in nine states are

---

[1] Dale Heckman and Warren Martin, *Inventory of Current Research on Higher Education—1968* (New York: McGraw-Hill, 1968).

being interviewed by Heinz Eulau of Stanford University to determine their opinions and attitudes toward higher education.[2] Eulau's study also includes inquiry into the legislative record for education in the same states. Resulting data should provide information on factors contributing to politicization of educational institutions.

The effects of statewide planning on individual college campuses in four states are among the research outcomes recorded by Ernest Palola and his associates at Berkeley in their recently completed project. By interviews with administrators in one hundred colleges and universities, private as well as public, and with appropriate state officials, this research illuminates issues in statewide planning for higher education, shows how they have been dealt with in California, Illinois, New York, and Florida, and indicates the ways such mechanisms facilitate or hinder the development of a differentiated system of higher education.

The American Council on Education has sponsored a related and interlocking study of statewide systems of higher education, a project directed by Robert Berdahl. By a comparative field study extending, directly or indirectly, into twenty states, an analysis was made of the evolution of the concept of coordination, of agencies performing this function, as well as the effects of the relationship of colleges and universities with the suprainstitutional coordinating bodies.

The research of Harland Bloland on the reciprocal differences and relationships between federal agencies and the national educational associations, a project completed in 1968, shows the way in which suprainstitutional value orientations can develop and may have qualitative as well as quantitative consequences for colleges and universities. Three case studies are given, two of which follow the processes of legislation related to higher education.

An example of a specific form which outside influences on institutions of higher learning may take is given in the project of Peter Libassi: a federal survey of campus racial discrimination. This government survey is being carried out by questionnaires distributed annually and is aimed at enforcing Title VI of the

[2] Data for all studies mentioned in this essay are given in a special listing at the close of the essay.

Civil Rights Act of 1964: "Armed with statistics from the government survey, federal officials will visit twenty-five colleges . . .
to gather evidence of possible racial discrimination."

Two research projects, one by M. M. Chambers, and the
other by André Bennett (a dissertation, under the sponsorship of
Richard Colvard), examine other external influences that bear
on college and university affairs. Chamber's concerns are legal,
particularly court decisions affecting colleges, 1967–70. He has
been organizing, classifying, and reporting court decisions in fifty
states, with special reference to those in the federal jurisdiction;
decisions that reveal trends and disclose future probabilities for
the legal relationship of the institution of higher education to the
courts. The Bennett and Colvard project concentrates on the relationship between colleges and universities and the major private
foundations. More specifically, this research has examined trustees
of twelve foundations against three general questions: (1) Who
are these men? (2) What do they do? and (3) What is their impact
on American higher education?

The flow of influences in the other direction, from campus
to general community, is of no less interest to researchers. Colleges
and universities, viewed historically, have always been part and
parcel of the society, and today, amid much talk of autonomy and
accountability, researchers are properly interested in chronicling
and evaluating both sides of this complex relationship.

Studies representative of the current emphasis in research
on the real or desired services of the university include a project
to develop a curriculum for the training of social workers for professional roles in community organization and planning, based on
theoretical and empirical investigation. Arnold Gurin and Arnulf
Pins, principal researchers, included in their curriculum design
direct association between students and practitioners of community organization and social planning as well as with governmental and voluntary agency administrators.

John Chase's research (a dissertation, University of Michigan's Center for the Study of Higher Education) on the contribution of education to economic growth in the state of Michigan
is representative of numerous analyses of income differentials for
various levels of education and of studies on migration patterns
for college graduates. In Chase's project, a questionnaire was

mailed to ten thousand graduates of Michigan's public colleges and universities.

Another study in the manpower "need and response" category is one directed by J. O. Nyhart, and concerns postprofessional degree education. Nyhart's emphasis is on continuing education as perceived by professional men and women whose formal education is a decade or more behind them. One unique dimension of this study is a lateral rather than a vertical design, cutting across a number of fields—management, engineering, law, and medicine.

Robert Clark's research on the international migration of talent (persons with higher degrees), from underdeveloped countries in the Far East, Africa, and the Near East to Western nations, should help to assess the economic cost of this mobility to the country of origin and the role of Western European nations as importers of high-talent manpower.

Economic factors of the university's service function in society are obviously only one dimension of the modern educational institution's social involvement. Forest Harrison has been the director of a research project dealing with another social concern. He is developing a package of assessment instruments that can be used for the evaluation of compensatory educational programs for the disadvantaged adolescent. With these instruments, educators may have mechanisms with which to determine whether the objectives of compensatory programs are being realized.

Criteria for the selection and training of teachers to work with the culturally disadvantaged is the objective of a project at Wisconsin State University, Oshkosh, directed by David Bowman and Bernice Miller. Attention in the first phase of the project centered on an exploratory comparison of academically marginal freshmen students withdrawing from college for scholastic reasons. By means of questionnaires, personal interviews, and the College Characteristics Index, information has been gathered that, hopefully, will lead to the development of an academic training program appropriate to the needs of students with special social and academic problems.

Two studies will be mentioned here which deal with the interaction of societal and campus influences on a particular campus. The Free Speech Movement at the University of California, Berkeley, has received popular and critical attention *ad nauseum,* but the ongoing research of David Gardner is unusual in that it is a historical case study using mostly unpublished sources— regents' records, administrative files, academic senate records, personal papers. Such a panorama of the antecedents to the movement, on campus and off, as well as implications from what went on during the critical months, as seen from the perspective of time and the context of a wealth of detailed information, should result in a report that will make a notable contribution to the literature.

Ludwig von Friedeburg of Johann Wolfgang-Goethe University, Frankfurt, Germany, has done a historical case study on another subject. Using standardized interviews with a random sample of 1,277 students and open-ended interviews with student leaders at the Free University of Berlin, von Friedeburg hopes to "explain the failure of the peculiar constitution of the Free University," taking into account the political education and attitudes of students, as well as the relationship between the institutional structure, prevailing community attitudes, and the participation of students in the government of this postwar university.

Mention of student participation in academic policy formulation introduces a number of current research projects dealing holistically or in part with institutional governance. Perhaps the most massive effort in this connection is the AAHE Governance Study, directed by Morris Keeton.[3] By a comparative evaluation of eighteen campuses, using questionnaires from approximately eight thousand students and four thousand others (including faculty, administrators, and trustees), Keeton and his associates proposed (1) to develop an account of critical questions that must be resolved on a well-governed campus, (2) to clarify the problems of governance implicit in attempting to provide a great number and variety of students with highly individualized services, (3) to study the effect of good communication on campus governance, (4) to explore patterns of participation and autonomy for students and faculty in governance, and (5) to consider problems of purpose and morale, "based on the idea that governance is as much informal as formal."

Roles and value presuppositions of students, faculty, and

---

[3] The chapter by Harold L. Hodgkinson in this volume presents data from the AAHE Governance Study.—*Ed.*

administrators in policy-making are the concerns of Maurice Troyer's project, involving five institutions of varying size and type. This study should provide data for comparison with those of the Hefferlin Institutional Vitality Study [4] and the already published *University Goals and Academic Power*, by Edward Gross and Paul Grambsch.

After examining faculty participation in governance at the University of California, Berkeley, T. R. McConnell and Kenneth Mortimer transferred their attention to three other selected institutions. These researchers have been concentrating on administrator-faculty relationships and the significance of these contacts for institutional governance. Faculty interest in and responses to change are also subjects of special interest here.

Research on a particular organizational arrangement, the subject-matter department, is the focus of attention for the research of Paul Dressel. Working out of the Office of Institutional Research, Michigan State University, Dressel evaluated one hundred departments in ten selected universities, studying the structure, functions, roles and administration of departments as perceived by faculty, administrators, and departmental staff personnel.

Morton Rauh has completed an exploratory survey by questionnaire of eleven thousand trustees in six hundred institutions to determine the backgrounds, attitudes, and functions of trustees.

Meanwhile, coming to the subject of governance from another perspective, or from another interest group, was Roger Rapaport's "Report on Student Power." This study included an analysis of the origins, nature, and impact of student power in American colleges and universities, plus a section, for comparative purposes, on student power in foreign institutions.

Richard Gatchel has completed a study likely to draw the attention of all interested in the governance of the institutions of higher education. It has been a documentary search and a field study involving interviews with students, faculty, administrators, and trustees at ten colleges and universities on the West Coast to identify "freedom issues in American higher education." It suggests some guidelines for the practice, protection, and promotion

[4] JB Lon Hefferlin, *Dynamics of Academic Reform* (San Francisco: Jossey-Bass, 1969).

of such freedom "as appears appropriate to the pursuit of humane learning."

By far the greatest volume of research is currently being done on student characteristics, student development or change over time, and certain "conservation" themes such as student attrition. Oddly, the *Inventory of Current Research on Higher Education* did not uncover projects on student sexuality or certain other controversial topics: consumption of tobacco, alcoholic beverages, aspirin, barbiturates, or other narcotics by students. Most institutions may hesitate to collect data on these subjects, thinking that information on LSD and other hallucinogenic drugs, or marijuana, might involve them or their students in litigation from outside agencies (such as municipal or county courts). Also, information pertinent to the drug subculture or related topics can sometimes be gleaned from questionnaire items which treat the subjects obliquely and are included in research projects on other themes.

Following are several studies on students that seem especially germane to the agony and promise of higher education, particularly in three areas: ethnic and cultural group relationships, graduate and professional students status, and student values.

Milton Yinger of Oberlin College and his associates are continuing their research on supportive interventions for higher education among students of disadvantaged backgrounds. The hypothesis is that significant motivation in the educational behavior of students is related to the amount and type of supports provided by extra-school groups.

Leslie Berger directed the *Seek Program* in New York City, a developmental project beginning with two thousand disadvantaged youth, for the purpose of showing the educability of unqualified ghetto youth for baccalaureate education as well as to demonstrate the unsuitability of regular admissions criteria for these youth. The study included the development of methods of teaching and counseling disadvantaged youth.

A comparative study of Negro and white college graduates, with Sydney Spivak and Robert Althauser as chief researchers, matched 935 Negro and white alumni of three eastern universities for the purpose of determining to what extent a college degree would underwrite comparable economic rewards and middle-class values or attitudes when the Negro degree recipients were from integrated versus predominantly Negro schools. Another interest is in tracing the occupational concerns of Negro graduates compared with the matched sample of white graduates.

Ruth Beard at the Institute of Education, University of London, is studying the difficulties of Afro-Asian students in comprehending oral and written English, particularly as found in various technical materials. Her intent is to develop remedial programs for medical students with Afro-Asian backgrounds.

The relationship between the professional, academic, and political orientations of unaffiliated graduate students and of those in a campus union called The University of California Employed Graduate Students was a special interest of Richard Brown and Martin Trow. A more comprehensive study of graduate education is being carried out by Ann Heiss. She is completing a comparative field study of the organization and administration of ten graduate institutions. The capacity for change in these programs is a special concern of this research.

The effects of college on student values, with special attention to values encouraging social responsibility, as shown by data drawn from the Haverford College classes of 1968 and 1969, have been studied by Sidney Perloe, with the hope of developing an instrument for measuring various aspects of orientations toward social responsibility. Roland Reboussin has studied student values at Beloit College, using various instruments to measure changes from freshman through senior year. Similar research interests and designs have been in use in Britain under the terms of a project directed by D. Marsland and J. Bocock; also at Plattsburgh, a college of the State University of New York (S. W. Johnson); and at Peabody College, with research there directed by L. S. Wrightsman and Frank Noble. Comparative studies of the differences in inputs and outcomes for the students in twelve church-affiliated colleges of the Central States College Association using several standardized instruments, with one hundred subjects at each college, are all part of a research project under the direction of Donald Ruthenberg and Robert Hassenger.

The interim report for a study of moral education, John Wilson and associates, Oxford University, was published in 1968 as *Introduction to Moral Education*. This study, which is continuing to 1975, concerns English children and adolescents and "all institutions that cater to them: schools, clubs, colleges. . . ."

The project's intent is to discover what conditions, contexts, and types of teaching can best assist individuals to develop a coherent, reasonable standard for moral judgments within their societies and to achieve the emotional maturity to act on them.

George Schlesser and John Finger have directed a project to construct a nonintellective measuring instrument that will predict academic achievement with as much validity as do intellective measures. This instrument—the Personal Values Inventory—would be useful in counseling and advising students who are regarded as academic risks as well as for research in personality patterns.

To advance beyond campus turmoil the various groups involved need more than stereotypes of one another. Some research on student "activism"—but by no means all—attempts to distinguish and understand several different kinds of students who do or do not become involved in protests and public causes. Smith, Block, and Haan have pursued their study of "Moral Orientations of Student Activists" with Kohlberg's moral dilemmas test, biographical information, and other means to describe the psychological antecedents of action for several types of students with several kinds of sociopolitical outlook. Flacks and Neugarten and their associates spread their nets wide to study the participants in various causes, including civil rights, anti-draft, and anti-protest. This group has even taken a careful look at the predispositions and family backgrounds of some activists (plus a control sample) through interviews with their parents living in the Chicago area.

The time may well come when any systematic interviewing and "questionnairing" of student movement people will depend on its likely usefulness to their cause. Meanwhile researchers, if not the public, are learning far more about students than about any other party to the agonies of higher education.

Efforts move on apace to establish multi-institution facilities for research, some of which include data storage and retrieval systems for data on students. The College Research Center in Poughkeepsie, New York (see inventory listing for Kenneth M. Wilson), for example, has made available to eight liberal arts colleges for women such a facility. Lewis Jones has described (in *Research in Education,* October 1967) another such consortium for institutional research among seven predominantly Negro colleges. And, of course, the data from studies of hundreds of thousands of students and hundreds of institutions by the American Council on Education (see listings for Alexander Astin et al.) mount up to an impressive collection of information for further research on students.

As of this writing, plans have gotten under way to establish an ongoing inventory of current research on higher education at George Washington University. If our one-year probe indicated correctly, such a resource could put researchers and practitioners in touch with one another before they must "bank the fires" of hot projects and proposals.

While most of the research projects reported in the inventory appear to be well designed, efficiently managed, and on relevant themes, it must be said that the emphasis in much of the current research has been on understanding more than on transforming higher education, on illuminating conditions in existing institutional structures and functions rather than lifting out by research those components appropriate for new beginnings. If research on higher education is to become a national resource, more imagination, audacity, and sophistication will need to be shown in the organization of projects and in the dissemination and development of their findings. But perhaps the basic problem is that, to date, our understanding of the maladies has been so limited that we have yet to gain the knowledge and confidence necessary for the prescription of cures. Recent research has helped to isolate and describe the problems. Perhaps soon educational research will have more to say about the solutions.

BIBLIOGRAPHY

Althauser, Robert P., and Sydney S. Spivack, *Comparative Study of Negro and White College Graduates*. Princeton, N. J.: Sociology Department, Princeton University, 1968.

Astin, Alexander W., and Robert J. Panos, *Educational and Vocational Development of American Students*. Washington: American Council on Education, 1968.

Beard, Ruth M., *Introductory Courses in London Medical Schools University Teaching Methods Research, Institute of Education, University of London, London, England; Person-to-Person*

Teaching . . . In Training Dentists and G.P.'s. London: University Teaching Methods Research, Institute of Education, University of London, 1968.

Bennett, André, and Richard Colvard, *Private Foundation Trustees and Their Academic Professional Affiliations.* Buffalo: Department of Sociology, State University of New York, 1968.

Berdahl, Robert O., *Statewide Systems of Higher Education.* San Francisco: San Francisco State College, 1968.

Berger, Leslie, *SEEK Program.* New York: City University of New York, 1968.

Block, Jeanne, Norma Haan, and M. Brewster Smith, *Moral Political-Social Orientations of Student Activists.* Berkeley: Institute of Human Development, University of California, 1968.

Bloland, Harland G., *Role of Associations in a Decentralized System of Higher Education.* Berkeley: Center for Research and Development in Higher Education, University of California, 1968.

Bocock, Jean, and D. Marsland, *Student Values and Attitudes: Change and Development During a Four-Year Course.* Brunel University, Great Britain: School of Social Sciences, 1968.

Bowman, David L., and Larry Campbell, *Selection and Training of Teachers of Culturally Disadvantaged.* Oshkosh, Wis.: School of Education, Wisconsin State University, 1968.

Brown, E. Richard, and Martin Trow, *Professional Orientations of Graduate Students and Membership in the Graduate Students Union at the University of California.* Berkeley: Survey Research Center, University of California, 1968.

Chambers, M. M., *The Colleges and the Courts, 1967–70.* Bloomington: Indiana University, 1968.

Chambers, M. M., *Higher Education in the 50 States.* Bloomington: Indiana University, 1968.

Chase, John S., *Contribution of Education to Economic Growth in the State of Michigan.* Ann Arbor: Center for the Study of Higher Education, University of Michigan, 1968.

Clark, Robert L., *Study of International Migration of Talent ("Brain Drain").* New York: Education and World Affairs, 1968.

Cox, Lanier, *Impact of Federal Programs in Higher Education on State Planning and Coordination of Higher Education.* Atlanta: Southern Regional Education Board, 1968.

Cox, Lanier, *Development of State Budgets for Higher Education.* Denver: Educational Commission of the States, 1968.

Dressel, Paul L., *The Structure, Functions, Role and Administration of the Department.* East Lansing: Office of Institutional Research, Michigan State University, 1968.

Eulau, Heinz, *Survey of Legislative Opinions and Attitudes on Higher Education*. Stanford, Calif.: Institute of Political Studies, Stanford University, 1968.

Finger, John A., and George E. Schlesser, *Measurement of Academic Motivation*. Hamilton, N. Y.: Colgate University, 1968.

Flacks, Richard, Philip Altbach, Gar Alperovitz, and Kenneth Keniston, *Student Participants in the Vietnam Summer Project*. Madison: Department of Educational Policy Studies, University of Wisconsin, 1968.

Flacks, Richard, and Bernice Neugarten, *Youth and Social Change: Study I—Student Activists and Their Parents*. Chicago: Sociology Department, University of Chicago, 1968.

Flacks, Richard, and Bernice Neugarten, *Youth and Social Change: Study II—The Anti-Rank Sit-in at Chicago*. Chicago: Sociology Department, University of Chicago, 1968.

Gardner, David P., *The California Free Speech Movement*. Santa Barbara: University of California, 1968.

Gatchel, Richard H., *A Study of Freedom in American Higher Education*. Berkeley: Center for Research and Development in Higher Education, University of California, 1968.

Grambsch, Paul V., *Academic Administrators and University Goals*.

Gross, Edward, *Academic Administrators and University Goals*. Seattle: Center for Academic Administrative Research, University of Washington, 1968.

Gurin, Arnold, and Robert Perlman, *Community Organization Curriculum Development (Social Work)*. Waltham, Mass.: Heller Graduate School, Brandeis University, 1968.

Harrison, Forest I., *The Development of an Evaluation and Assessment Package for Compensatory Educational Programs for the Culturally Disadvantaged Adolescent*. Claremont, Calif.: Claremont Graduate School, 1968.

Hassenger, Robert, and Donald B. Ruthenberg, *Student Values Study: Central States College Association*. Bloomington, Ill.: Office of Institutional Research, Illinois Wesleyan University, 1968.

Hefferlin, JB, *Origins and Development of Distinctive Institutions*. New York: Institute of Higher Education, Columbia University, 1968.

Heiss, Ann M., *Study of Graduate Education in Ten Graduate Institutions*. Berkeley: Center for Research and Development in Higher Education, University of California, 1968.

Johnson, S. W., *Progressive Changes in Students' Values, Needs, and Educational Objectives*. Plattsburgh, N. Y.: State University at Plattsburgh, 1968.

Keeton, Morris, L. Dennis, Harold Hodgkinson, and Stephen Plumer, *Campus Governance Program*. Yellow Springs, Ohio: Antioch College, 1968.

Libassi, F. Peter, *Federal Survey of Campus Racial Discrimination Office for Civil Rights*. Washington: Office for Civil Rights of the Department of Health, Education, and Welfare, 1968.

McConnell, T. R., and Kenneth P. Mortimer, *Faculty Participation in Governance at the University of California, Berkeley*. Berkeley: Center for Research and Development in Higher Education, University of California, 1968.

Miller, Bernice, Clarence H. Bagley, D. Nasca, McTaraghan, and Sachastanandan, *Four College Study of Institutional Development*.

Mortimer, Kenneth, and T. R. McConnell, *Faculty Organization and Government at Selected Institutions*. Berkeley: Center for Research and Development in Higher Education, University of California, 1968.

Noble, Frank C., and Lawrence Wrightsman, *Changes in Attitudes and Values of College Students*. Nashville, Tenn.: Peabody College, 1968.

Nyhart, J. D., *Post-Professional Degree Education*. Cambridge: The Sloan School of Management, Massachusetts Institute of Technology, 1968.

Palola, Ernest G., Timothy Lehman, and William Blischke, *Statewide Planning in Higher Education—Its Implications at the Institutional Level*. Berkeley: Center for Research and Development in Higher Education, University of California, 1968.

Perloe, Sidney, *Effects of College on Values Relevant to Social Responsibility*. Haverford, Pa.: Haverford College, 1968.

Rapaport, Roger, *Report on Student Power*. Berkeley: Carnegie Commission on the Future of Higher Education, 1968.

Rauh, Morton A., *College Trustee Project*. Yellow Springs, Ohio: Campus Governance Program, Antioch College, 1968.

Reboussin, Roland, *Changes of Norm and Value among College Students*. Beloit, Wisc.: Beloit College, 1968.

Troyer, Maurice E., *Roles and Value Presuppositions of Students, Faculty and Administration in Policy Making*. Syracuse, N. Y.: 1968.

von Friedeburg, Ludwig, *Student and University in Berlin*. Frankfurt am Main: Institute for Social Research, Goethe University, 1968.

Wilson, John, Norman Williams, and Barry Sugarman, *Moral Educa-*

tion. Oxford, England: Farmington Trust Research Unit, Oxford University, 1968.

Wilson, Kenneth M., *College Research Center, An Agency for Interinstitutional Cooperation in Educational Research.* Poughkeepsie, N. Y.: College Research Center, 1968.

Yinger, J. Milton, Kiyoshi Ikeda, Frank Laycock, and John M. Antes, *Supportive Interventions for Higher Education among Students of Disadvantaged Backgrounds.* Oberlin, Ohio: Oberlin College, 1968.

~ 25 ~

SELECTED
LITERATURE
OF 1968

L. Richard Meeth

The past year produced a bumper crop of books and articles on or related to American higher education. It was not, however, a vintage year. During 1968, over three hundred books and double that number of essays were presented to the public for reading, annotating, filing, and critical review, but no one or two books stand head and shoulders above the others or are likely to be considered classics such as *The American College* or *The Reforming of General Education*. Standing out of this mass, however, are two particular themes which are relevant, appear frequently, and bear directly upon the theme of this book. The future of American higher educational institutions and the presence and power of college students appeared often in the literature and also represent the best works of the year.

228

An overview of the mood of the present generation of college students was presented by the popular press in the January 1969 issue of *Fortune* magazine. This special issue dedicated to American youth reviews the rebellion of youth in the United States but concentrates on a contrast between non-college and college-going students, between the "square universities" and the "free form revolutionaries." Daniel Seligman, in "A Special Kind of Rebellion," reports that roughly three-fifths of the college students think of college chiefly as a path to improvement of their social and economical status. The other two-fifths are disdainful of "careerist" values and show a tendency to radical views; about half of them believe that the United States is a sick society. In a list of personalities admired by this two-fifths of American college students all three of the major presidential candidates in the 1968 election ran behind Che Guevara.

In another survey *Fortune* reveals that young adults eighteen to twenty-four now make up a smaller share of the total United States population than before World War II and not a larger share as is commonly supposed. They also point out that the higher education gap between men and women is widening not narrowing, the economic impact of growth in number of households headed by persons eighteen to twenty-four is really less than 8 per cent of all U.S. households and that the tidal wave of youth is beginning to crest. In other words, by the early 1970s the number of eighteen- to twenty-four-year-olds will be increasing at essentially the same rate as the total population.

Two articles on the university are of particular import. One entitled "The Faculty is the Heart of the Trouble" by Max Ways contrasts the student demand for involvement and relevance with the characteristic detachment of the faculty and points also to conflicts between the national loyalty to his discipline increasingly felt by the mobile professor and the local needs of the university and the community in which he teaches. "The Square Universities are Rolling Too" by Jeremy Main may give some comfort to administrators of these institutions and parents who send their offspring with some confidence they will not end up majoring in rebellion and minoring in pot. The "square universities" and colleges enroll the majority of American students but even on these relatively calm campuses students are transforming the governance of the institution and especially the regulations

affecting students' lives. The articulate students who seek responsibility on the quiet campus do not want to wreck their college
or their society since they know that in a few decades they are going to have to run them. Mr. Main has traveled widely and brings
at least the authority of a good interviewer to his argument.

The other article of particular significance is entitled "The
Jewish Role in Student Activism" by Nathan Glazer, who points
out that although only one in twenty American college students
is Jewish, among the committed identifiable radicals on the college campus probably one-third to one-half are Jews. Glazer shows
that this phenomenon is readily explainable: the tradition of
familial and nationalistic Jewish radicalism out of which the students have come has tended to push them into the movement of
the New Left.

Of the numerous work published last year on the college
student, one document which every faculty member and administrator should read is *The Student in Higher Education,* a report
published by the Hazen Foundation. The Committee responsible
for this report was chaired by Joseph Kauffman. The two major
themes of the report are these: "(1) The college is a major influence on the development of the student's personality and must
therefore assume responsibility for the quality and direction of
this development, and (2) even the college's central task of guid-
ing the intellect cannot be done well unless the school realizes
that the acquisition of knowledge takes place in the context of
emerging adulthood." Unfortunately, the report does not describe
ways by which an existing college might renovate, innovate, or
transform its present curriculum into something more viable for
the whole student. In spite of this shortcoming the volume clearly
and concisely states the priorities and commitments which to the
authors appear critical for changing the agony of present student
involvement into the promise of the future.

Joseph Katz and his associates at Stanford University last
year published a five-year study of 3,500 entering men and women
at Berkeley and Stanford University entitled *No Time For Youth.*
This book, together with two others to be mentioned in a moment, constitute in my judgment the major research underlying
the statements made by the Hazen Foundation Committee on the
Student in Higher Education. A careful reading of Katz' study,
of Paul Heist's *The Creative College Student,* and James Trent

and Leland Medsker's *Beyond High School* will provide a college faculty with the hard data which they so frequently need as the bases for curricular decisions.

Katz and his associates at the Institute for the Study of Human Problems at Stanford report that although college students do change somewhat, moving toward more liberal, open attitudes, these changes do not result from any perceivable or rational effort on the part of the university. While students become more tolerant and liberal in areas of their personal life a revolution in behavior does not appear to have taken place. Several chapters in *No Time For Youth* are especially helpful for student personnel workers who may find the case studies of particular usefulness in counseling.

The authors of this excellent companion to Nevitt Sanford's *The American College* stress, as he did, the need for a curriculum directly related to the developmental task and experiences of students rather than to the logic of specific disciplines. How to do it is again unanswered. The book concludes with a chapter outlining a new approach to curriculum building in which the individual development of the student becomes a central goal. But the recommendations stress policy and philosophy, rather than structure and relationships of power, which are more the concern of faculty these days.

The next two books need to be taken together since both are publications of the Berkeley Center for Research and Development in Higher Education and concentrate essentially upon interrelated problems of the college student. The book edited by Paul Heist, *The Creative College Student: An Unmet Challenge,* is essentially concerned with the college "push-out"; the individual who finds the system intolerable or whom the system finds intolerable. The second, *Beyond High School,* by James Trent and Leland Medsker contrasts and compares high school graduates who never enter college, those who enter but drop out, and those who enter and persist. These two works are written in a scholarly fashion and report the results of several years of study of high school graduates and college students. Although the Trent and Medsker book could be more readable—the volume presents a mass of hard data covering ten thousand students—they both present their case in very strong terms. Unfortunately, neither has been written by a Michael Harrington and, although they deal with the poverty of the American system of education in cutting off the underachiever and the creative, they will not stir the imagination of the American public, the civil servants of bureaucracy, or the state and federal legislators the way *The Other America* did. Both books are, however, extremely moving, damaging, and discouraging; and taken seriously they should cause any reader to react in anger over the present state of American higher education which allows—in fact, which fosters—conformity of the kind described in these two studies.

In *The Creative College Student* the authors challenge what they claim to be the general assumption that students who possess unusual talent or exceptional creative potential perceive and learn no differently than do most other college students. Consequently they maintain that there has been no recognized need for greater understanding, special provisions, or individualized treatment for the creative student. Far too frequently programs for the highly able or academically capable students have included the youth who have high potential for creative expression but the authors clearly substantiate the inadequacy of such arrangements. For example, the high attrition rate of creative individuals testifies to the error of assuming that the educational needs of the creative student are being met by honors programs, tutorials, and independent study courses which have been touted as particularly suitable to students of high grades and expressed interest. The primary criticism within the book is aimed at the teaching methods of the common curricula of American colleges which the authors feel are sadly inadequate to help the majority of creative students learn. For although high ability is often a characteristic of the highly creative it may not be disciplined in such a way that the ability fits a highly conforming system.

Donald MacKinnon's two articles entitled "Selecting Students With Creative Potential" and "Educating for Creativity: A Modern Myth?" are particularly enlightening. MacKinnon challenges the present system of educating creative students and questions whether or not any of the other forms of education being proposed today would succeed any better if tested. He does suggest a number of guidelines which he thinks would be useful with creative students, all of which have been proposed from time to time in the past but which have never been collectively utilized or evaluated.

The chapter entitled "Curricular Experiences for the Creative" by Paul Heist and Robert Wilson is important to those
concerned with curriculum development in our colleges. The
authors point out that the major focus of concern among creative
students apparently centers on what faculty members do or fail
to do both directly, in their interactions with students in and out
of the classrooms, and indirectly, in their roles as formulators of
policy and structure. They then proceed to analyze the problems
facing faculty in teaching creative students. Again, a person looking for specific suggestions will be disappointed, for the authors
provide only guidelines relating to the breadth and depth of the
curricular experience. The chapter suffers from a lack of illustra-
tion of the points which would spur thinking for the less creative
who are charged in every institution with building the curriculum
for the creative.

Beyond High School is a comprehensive study of a sample
of ten thousand high school graduates in sixteen communities
throughout the country. The study follows the individuals from
their senior year in high school through work, college, and sometimes marriage, analyzing the impacts of college and employment
on their values and attitudes.

Although the authors point out the variety of differences
among the three groups—those who enter the work force, those
who enter college and finish, and those who enter college but
leave before receiving a degree—they are unable to distinguish
many important differences in human experience. They do establish that there is a difference between college attenders and non-
attenders in terms of the value placed on intellectual matters but
little difference in terms of human values. The authors substantiate the notion that the home or early environment is an essential
factor in success in college and in establishing an individual's
value orientation but go no further in helping any institution interested in understanding why its students drop out. The authors
conclude that college matters, that it is, indeed, beneficial to attend college in terms of shaping of character and destiny; yet it
leaves unanswered the questions "To what extent?" "Precisely
what elements in the college do the shaping?" and "For how long
will the changes last?"

The College Student and His Culture: An Analysis, by
Kaoru Yamamoto, is an anthology of readings which should serve

as a good text for students of higher education as well as college
administrators and trustees who would take the time to read it.
Yamamoto has drawn together a number of outstanding articles,
most of which have been printed earlier in other places, and has
ordered them in such a way as to provide an excellent analysis of
the college student in the 1960s. Because the role of the student
is changing so rapidly these days, primarily because of pressure
from students themselves, this volume could find itself very soon
listed among the good histories of the student generation between
apathy and revolution.

Yamamoto's writers generally represent a position corresponding to Philip Jacob's—that values of college students change
very little. The volume contains an urgent appeal for students of
higher education to study the myths *of* the American college
student rather than the myth *about* him as a means of better understanding him and his world. I believe this book will last the
longest of any published in 1968 both because the editor has
chosen well in compiling the anthology and because the articles
themselves reflect more abiding themes and underlying issues than
do many of the more frantic, irrelevant, contemporary pleas for
urgent reform.

Time, said St. Augustine, is a three-fold present: the present as we experience it, the past as a present memory, and the
future as a present expectation. By that criterion the second major
theme of the publications in higher education in 1968, the future
of educational institutions, is already upon us. Decisions which
are made now about the way curriculum is designed, buildings
are constructed, personnel employed, and institutions structured
commit the future. The future is never a leap into the beyond,
the future is now.

Essentially this notion comprises the theme idea running
through the significant books written in 1968 concerning the
future of our present institutions of higher learning. It is an awe-
some concept, particularly in light of the agonizing complications
of the riot-torn, dissension-ridden, revolutionary-minded students
who attend them and the profession-oriented, tenure-minded faculty who teach in them. But it is also a promising concept because
the decisions made today can shape the future of American higher
education, can determine whether or not our colleges and universities will be flexible, open-ended learning centers or whether
they will continue to be monolithic citadels of conformity.

The six volumes selected for review in this discussion all look at the future of American higher education in terms of the present. They all begin with the premise that the future is now. *Campus 1980,* edited by Alvin Eurich, is an excellent collection of articles on the shape of the future of American higher education. The first article, "Agenda for the Colleges and Universities," by John Gardner, sets the tone for the concept that the future is now. Gardner argues that the first order of business for the future is to make an agenda: to propose, debate, and clarify some priorities among the myriad tasks which crowd in on the academic community. He believes that among the urgent matters needing attention are the lack of focus and meaning in undergraduate life and strengthening the role of the campus in the community.

Another excellent chapter is "The Future of Teaching," by William Arrowsmith, which was originally delivered as a keynote address at the 1966 meeting of the American Council of Education. This chapter proclaims that our university scholars are professional and technocratic but as educators they have been disqualifying themselves for more than a century. Demanding a return to the high art of teaching William Arrowsmith argues that there is no necessary link between scholarship and education or between research and culture. He stresses the need for men who embody in themselves the values they are endeavoring to instill in their students. Reorganization and revision of curriculum will not, in themselves make education relevant. The final essay, by Clark Kerr, "Conservatism, Dynamism, and the Changing University," poses the most perplexing question for the future of American higher education: "Can American higher educational institutions change themselves sufficiently to meet the challenges and demands of the society they have educated?"

Paul Woodring's *The Higher Learning In America: A Reassessment* is a book rich in the conventional wisdom of American higher education. There are virtually no new ideas here for the professional student of higher education but the volume serves as a good overview for faculty, students, and the public. The university neglect of undergraduate teaching and the faculty desertion of liberal education in favor of specialized research are the recurring themes of this volume—themes which have been worked over for the last five years.

In answer to the question, "Who ought to be admitted to college?" Woodring guesses that perhaps a third to a half of all

high school graduates can profit enough from some kind of higher
education to justify the time and expense. Already that number
are enrolled; the nation has felt that the time and expense are
justified and the likelihood that we will far surpass his conservative estimate is very strong. Woodring's expansive generalizations
make his book difficult reading for responsible students of higher
education, but nevertheless it seems to me to be one of only two
significant treatments appearing during the year for the general
public who are increasingly concerned about their institutions of
higher learning.

A more exciting but equally traditional analysis of the
present and future of American higher education is *The American University: How It Runs, Where It Is Going* by Jacques
Barzun. Iconoclastic, bombastic, and caustic but entertaining and
exciting, the book presents many good ideas for the future of the
educational enterprise. Barzun is an extremely able and colorful
writer who will be most appreciated by those who adhere to
the scholastic tradition in American higher education. One of the
central themes of his book, for example, is the notion that the
best students should go to the universities and the rest to other
colleges.

Barzun's concluding chapter, "The Choices Ahead," is most
entertaining as well as enlightening. He proposes sixty-eight
choices which he feels a university must make if it is to determine
what it fundamentally thinks it is and if it is to reflect that particular style in all its activities. Although he has, in other writings,
spelled the demise of the liberal arts college, he concludes his
essay on the American university by saying, "I do not doubt that
if circumstances send the·institution into an eclipse, the idea of
it will survive into another day." Barzun is an astute observer of
the university—in fact of the whole higher educational enterprise.
His is a well-organized exposition, brief but rich, encompassing
the agonies of today and the promises the university holds for
the future if reformed. Would that Barzun had spent his life in a
liberal arts college.

Alternative To Irrelevance by Warren Martin is the most
conservative but to me the most provocative of the four volumes
assessing the present and the future internal operation of higher
educational institutions. The strength of Martin's book does not
lie in his proposal for cluster colleges as a solution to irrelevance

in American education but in his succinct and provocative analysis of the nature of change and the professorial dichotomy that impedes it in the academic community. He conceives of current college and university unrest as an essentialist-existentialist confrontation. In spite of the fact that Nevitt Sanford writes in the foreword that it remains to be seen if such "moderate proposals are too little and too late," Professor Martin presents one of the few specific plans to be published last year for actually implementing the developmental, experiential, or existentialist philosophy of educating students in the twenty-first century.

Reading the second chapter, "Resources For Comprehensive Innovation," which concerns itself with the essentialist-existentialist conflicting philosophical assumptions, one has the feeling that Martin has hit precisely upon the underlying and perhaps even unconscious dichotomy that frustrates administrators, faculty, and students interested in genuine innovation—by which I mean radical discontinuity with the past—and at the same time frustrates faculty, administrators, and students interested simply in renovation—by which I mean an evolution or maturation of what is.

Martin defines essentialists in education as formalists who draw on Dewey, James, Hegel, Kant, Mill, Locke, Calvin, Augustine, Aquinas, and Aristotle while the existentialists in education center on the student and draw on Buber, Sartre, Camus, Kierkegaard, Rousseau, Socrates, and Job. Essentialists in education contend that there is a specific body of knowledge to be taught and learned, that human nature is the same in every epoch and that tradition, ceremony, history, and experience are worthy teachers. So subject matter, standards, prerequisites and sequences —these are essentialists' concern, as are the disciplines and the departmental style of life. Educational change for most essentialists is possible as long as continuity is not sacrificed to immediacy. Essentialists are likely to be conspicuous in making academic freedom a matter of conceptional entities—definitions, mechanisms for implementation, and penalties for violations.

Existentialists on the other hand, are more likely to see academic freedom as a relational condition obtaining among persons. They are less concerned about continuity with the past than about present and personal relevance. There is interest in historical perspective but not in historicism. Existentialists emphasize that instruction and involvement are both facets of the learning process, stressing the affective, in opposition to the essentialist pedagogy, which stresses the cognitive side of learning. The essentialist is primarily concerned about what the teacher says and the existentialist is primarily concerned about what the student hears.

Since most colleges are in the hands of essentialists, the climate of learning and the possibility of innovation are extremely limited. The essentialists must share the responsibility for the present situation in American higher education since students by and large reflect the existentialist point of view. The extensive treatment that Martin gives to this concept in his discussion of innovation and confrontation is an addition to the permanent literature of higher education.

The last two books concern themselves much more with the future of the relationship between American colleges and universities and the society in which they function. *Higher Education In Tomorrow's World,* edited by Algo Henderson, is a collection of essays by internationally known scholars which bear upon issues and problems with which the university ought to deal in the society in which it exists, namely the world. Although the essays are geared primarily to the large university and its influence upon the world community, the volume is still good reading for those in smaller liberal arts colleges as a basis of understanding their own heritage and because, if the past is any predictor of the future, the small colleges will continue, unfortunately, to imitate the larger universities.

The first essay, by Eric Ashby, entitled "A Case For Ivory Towers," posits a distinction for the university to bear in mind as it faces the future. He suggests that the university should base its future upon the understanding of the "inner logic" of the past. Ashby interprets the hereditary future of the world universities as growing out of the nature of their birth and the various historical strands which have contributed to their present concerns.

The essay by Kenneth Boulding, "The Role of the University in the Development of a World Community," and the chapter by Courvoisier, on "The Quest for Values and Choices," are particularly solid reading. The latter presses for victory over self as the essential ingredient which will make tomorrow's civilization worthy of the name *civil*-ization. He maintains that unless the university "remains in the service of man in his integrity and in his dignity, and unless it opens the way to springs where he can truly assuage his thirst," it will not be worthy of existing.

The final book on the future of higher education, the winner of the American Council on Education 1968 book award, is *The Academic Revolution* by Christopher Jencks and David Riesman; it is also the most exciting and most controversial. This book is not about the internal revolution in American higher education but concerns itself with the rise to power of the academic profession in this country and its effect on the rest of the society. The authors refer to Michael Young's *Rise of the Meritocracy*, which seems to me to be essentially the theme of the whole volume and the nature of the revolution. The academic profession, according to Riesman and Jencks, has established an achievement-oriented society, which tends to substitute knowledge for wisdom, research for scholarship, and teaching for learning.

The volume is well written, penetrating in its analyses and insightful in its projections for the future. In the introduction, the authors carefully disavow all faults which the book may contain and charge off any failures in perception or scholarship to lack of time and breadth of the subject. In spite of their lengthy admission of the possibility of shortsightedness, the authors plunge ahead with their generalizations in support of their theses. For example, although the chapter on the Negro college has been modified somewhat in light of a rebuttal by a group of Negro college presidents, it still contains some controversial contentions which those long associated with the Negro college feel cannot be substantiated. Jencks and Riesman say, for example, that almost half of all Negro undergraduates attend predominantly white colleges yet in a footnote on the same page they say that between 50 and 60 per cent of all Negro students will probably be in Negro colleges. Since the number of graduate programs in Negro colleges is extremely small, in all likelihood Jencks and Riesman are wrong on this point. The conclusion and postscript to this chapter, which documents the aftermath of the controversy surrounding the first publication of this essay, is an excellent apology for the position which the authors take. They rightly say, "One reason for publishing bad news is the hope that it will force men to examine the course of action that leads up to it." In the words of the present student generation they attempt to "tell it like it is." The greatest strength of *The Academic Revolution* lies in the thesis which the authors developed through the several hundred pages of this volume.

Several concepts run through these volumes on the future of American higher educational institutions. All advocate change, though some want merely for the institutions to evolve into what they have always contained the potential to be, while others want them to be radically different from what they have been. All of the studies focus on the weaknesses of the faculty and the necessity for curricular change. Taken together, they constitute a powerful argument for reform in American higher education.

BIBLIOGRAPHY

COLLEGES

Barzun, Jacques, *The American University: How It Runs, Where It Is Going.* New York: Harper, 1968.

Eurich, Alvin C. (Ed.), *Campus 1980.* New York: Delacorte Press, 1968.

Henderson, Algo D. (Ed.), *Higher Education In Tomorrow's World.* Ann Arbor: University of Michigan Press, 1968.

Jencks, Christopher, and David Riesman, *The Academic Revolution.* Garden City, N. Y.: Doubleday, 1968.

Martin, Warren, *Alternative To Irrelevance.* Nashville: Abingdon Press, 1968.

Woodring, Paul, *The Higher Learning In America: A Reassessment.* New York: McGraw-Hill, 1968.

STUDENTS

"American Youth: Its Outlook Is Changing The World," *Fortune,* January, 1969.

Committee on the Student in Higher Education, *The Student In Higher Education.* New Haven, Conn.: The Hazen Foundation, 1968.

Heist, Paul (Ed.), *The Creative College Student: An Unmet Challenge.* San Francisco: Jossey-Bass, 1968.

Katz, Joseph (Ed.), *No Time For Youth.* San Francisco: Jossey-Bass, 1968.

Trent, James W., and Leland L. Medsker, *Beyond High School.* San Francisco: Jossey-Bass, 1968.

Yamamoto, Kaoru (Ed.), *The College Student and His Culture: An Analysis.* Boston: Houghton Mifflin, 1968.

PART THREE

The Future

Section VIII

Guidelines
for Action

In the opening essay of Section VIII, Edmund Muskie speaks on behalf of active student participation in decision-making. "I view as reasonable," Muskie states, "the students' demands for participation in the major decisions of the university. . . . The idea of giving students a greater voice in the development of relevant courses and curricula makes sense." Muskie's hope is that we may, in the end, "restore the confidence of young Americans in the capacity of our society to resolve the problems which afflict it."

The second essay, by James Gavin, places higher education within a broad national context. For Gavin, there are three major dilemmas facing the nation. The first—"efficiency versus responsiveness"—demands for its solution a new kind of administrator: one who, in order to accomplish greater goals, is able to accept some "sacrifice in efficiency, order, and dispatch"; who believes in "a genuine sharing of decision-making prerogatives"; who has a "tolerance for uncertainty, delay, and failure." The second dilemma—"compensatory treatment versus equal opportunity"—calls into question the validity of our traditional standards of excellence, thus relating back to Hamilton's and Godard's essays in Section III. The third dilemma arises from "the knowledge gap." Often we have all the knowledge that is necessary to solve a prob-

243

lem, but we find that the knowledge is not effectively translated or implemented. (This point relates to higher education research, discussed in Section VII.) These three dilemmas, Gavin contends, "must first be resolved or at least lessened . . . if progress is to occur."

The title of the last essay of the volume ("No Promise Without Agony") by Robert McAfee Brown echoes the title of the book itself. If we are to move from agony to promise, Brown insists, there are four significant sociopolitical and spiritual shifts in American life which must be made: Our fear of overt violence must be countered by our recognition of the covert violence that pervades our society; our abuse of power must be countered by creative uses of power; our demoralizing materialism must be countered by a quite different kind of materialism; and our sense of academic detachment must be countered by a sense of moral compassion. Brown ends his essay by describing two qualities that he believes can help people accomplish the transition "from here to there."

JOSEPH AXELROD

～ 26 ～

OPEN THE DOOR TO PARTICIPATION

Edmund S. Muskie

We have believed that when man is free to grow and be himself, he will enlarge his intellectual and spiritual powers and he will make possible a more enlightened and civilized society. For nearly two hundred years, we have sought a society in which all men are free. Our goal has been a country where true equality would release the energies of a free people.

We have cherished the ideal of equality of opportunity. We have cherished the ideal that no one should live in poverty—that no one should go hungry—that each individual would be able to develop his full potential. We have an unbounded faith in our ability to respond to the pressures, challenges, and opportunities of our time. We are also a nation marked by an advanced state of technological progress which has made us wealthy. Our ability to send men speeding toward the moon at nearly 25,000 miles an hour is a miraculous scientific achievement. We have made our agricultural abundance available to starving people throughout the world. We have made strong commitments in the fields of education, civil rights, equal opportunity, and elimination of poverty. We have invested over nine billion dollars a year in some one hundred and eleven programs dealing with education. Never in the history of the world have so many young people continued their education beyond secondary school. We are making efforts to rebuild the cities, improve living conditions, expand job opportunities.

But we are now confronted by doubts as to our ability to solve our problems. The performance of our society has failed to live up to the promises we have made and the expectations which we have aroused. We have found that our anti-poverty programs have failed to lift as many of our people out of poverty as we had hoped. We have found that agricultural abundance is no guarantee against hunger. We now realize that civil rights legislation —however strong—cannot erase all barriers between black and white.

We see unparalleled prosperity, affluence, and national economic growth; yet we find ourselves torn by the questions of war, poverty, confrontations between black and white, student activists and authority. We live in an age of immediate mass communication which catapults us into the center of disturbing events. We are made painfully aware of the war in Vietnam, civil disorder, student rebellion, hunger, and poverty. At times the very structure of our society seems in danger of being overwhelmed by forces man has set in motion but seems incapable of controlling.

We are faced with the questions: Are our attitudes responsive and receptive to changes within the social structure? Are our institutions—government, business, education, religion—capable of finding a solution for lasting world peace; eliminating poverty; resolving racial tensions; renewing our decaying central cities; developing our human resources; managing and controlling our environment; conquering disease and malnutrition?

John W. Gardner has said: "I have had ample opportunity over the years to observe the diverse institutions of this society— the colleges and universities, the military services, business corporations, foundations, professions, government agencies, and so on. And I must report that even excellent institutions run by excellent human beings are inherently sluggish, *not* hungry for innovation, *not* quick to respond to human need, *not* eager to reshape themselves to meet the challenge of the times." The rebellion of the youth of this generation—the *now* generation—underscores the validity of Mr. Gardner's remarks.

College students today are sensitive to social change. They are deeply concerned about human values, human needs, and human rights. They feel that our generation has been less than sincere in our professed attitudes on war, poverty, and racial injustice. They are resentful of the slow response of our institutions to social protest. They see themselves, as did the founders of America, as ridding the nation of a tyranny that has become intolerable. They have a deep personal concern for the role of the United States in the world. A very real and important question is whether we can restore the confidence of young Americans in the capacity of our society to resolve the problems which afflict it. We will miss a unique opportunity if we do not act promptly. In our accelerating world, it may be our only chance. To do this will take courage, the courage to face their criticisms squarely, to reexamine our national policies, our goals, our attitudes toward society and our institutions.

The true task of social change, as seen by John Gardner's Twenty-third Century scholars, is "to design a society (and institutions) capable of continuous change, continuous responsiveness." We must develop lines of communication with our young people and open the door to participation rather than confrontation. Together we must determine the direction our nation will take. This will involve a close examination of our weaknesses, our strengths, the purposes and the goals of our institutions.

I have witnessed student action in the political arena. Their frustrations have been understandable and their action consistent with the intensity of youth and the enormity of our problems. But the increasing incidents of campus confrontation and violence are perplexing phenomena for me and many other college graduates reared in more conventional times. My own knowledge of these incidents is limited to newspaper accounts, and from these I hesitate to make any firm judgments. I would, however, like to share some of my impressions with you.

The first is that many university administrations have not been sensitive enough to the changing characteristics of students, and have not listened closely enough to what they have been say-

ing. My own view is that college students today are more sophisticated than ever before, and have a greater capacity for maturity
and responsibility. They have demonstrated these qualities in
war, politics, social service, and other endeavors. It does not seem
unreasonable that they should seek similar opportunities on the
campus. If a university is to encourage its students to be active
and participating members of society after graduation, that university should make it possible for students to contribute to the
enrichment of campus life before graduation. My impression is
that many of the grievances and demands made by students are
reasonable, in light of the injustices within our society and in
light of their own capacities to contribute.

Tom Wicker summed it up recently in the *New York
Times* in these words:

> This is a brilliantly informed generation that sees with youth's
> harsh clarity how the wealth and the technology of America
> could make the reality of its life conform far more nearly to
> its ancient boasts. . . . In their outrage and contempt as well
> as in their vision, the best of them really are trying to tell us
> something—that we are not living up to the best that is in us.
> If older and sadder persons know that men seldom do, it is
> still a message that palpably and shamefully has seldom been
> so true as in today's myopic and contorted America.

Universities have traditionally been the fountainhead of ideas for
social progress in our nation. It would be wasteful now not to
give this generation of college students an opportunity to participate meaningfully in giving new relevance to our universities.
And so, I view as reasonable the students' demands for participation in the major decisions of the university which affect so directly the lives of the students. The idea of giving students a
greater voice in the development of relevant and selected courses
and curricula makes sense.

I am not suggesting that the university administration and
faculty abandon their responsibilities and I am not prepared to
support the idea of totally autonomous and segregated programs.
But the concept of student initiation, planning, development, and
even teaching of appropriate courses is healthy. Such programs
are not uncommon on campuses across the country, and they are
proving successful. My point is this: a university education should

not be an isolated experience, in terms of the relevance of learning as well as the opportunity for citizenship. In spite of efforts to open their doors and windows on the world, universities are nearly complete communities within themselves, and thus once removed from the outside world. This makes the problem of relating the life of faculty, students, and administrators within a university to the outside world far more difficult than many would admit. But a hothouse arrangement will deprive the university of the creativity and vitality of youth, and prevent the students from developing self-discipline, maturity, and judgment.

When I look at the role of students in the university dilemma, I do not find a faultless record. To many Americans outside the world of the university, it appears as if their leaders are a small band of students with little regard for the rights and safety of others. I am distressed that these students appear so ready to risk violence in pursuit of their objectives, regardless of the consequence of their actions. I cannot condone violence on campus or anywhere else as a reasonable substitute for negotiation or for the several other methods available to students to dramatize grievances and demands. The picture of National Guardsmen and police stationed on campuses to maintain order is abhorrent. If intelligent men and women of student bodies, administrations, and faculties cannot resolve their differences without bloodshed or the presence of an armed militia, then there is no hope for the rest of civilization. At the least, student violence represents intimidation of the administration, of other students, and of members of the faculty. In the last analysis, anarchy under the banner of intellectual freedom or university participation is still anarchy, especially when the rights of others are ignored, and when the processes of democracy are bypassed.

Now I understand that most students today, no matter how committed they may be to the concept of a more participatory university, are not provoking the kind of confrontation I am talking about. But it does seem to me that they do have an obligation to demonstrate their independence from those who would incite or risk violence. What concerns me most is the prospect of increasing conflict on our campus. At stake is the quality of higher education across the land, because no university can function under convulsion and siege.

As our universities work themselves out of the current crisis of confrontation, the biggest danger may be an instinct to withdraw from those issues which gave rise to disruption on the campuses. Nothing could be more dangerous for our institutions of higher learning, or for society itself.

~ 27 ~

OUR DOMESTIC CRISES

James M. Gavin

With repetition even the most ominous of statistics lose their urgency, the direst of prophecies their chilling impact. A recitation of the facts underlying our domestic crises has by now the dull familiarity of a liturgical chant: The gap is widening between the incomes of whites and blacks. Hard-core unemployment remains constant even in the face of accelerating inflation and acute labor shortages in many parts of the country; and the unemployment rate of black, Puerto Rican, Mexican-American, and Indian youth is more than twice that of white youth. Of the underemployed, two million can find only part-time work, but this figure does not begin to reflect those who are working below their skill level. Welfare costs are spiraling upward at a dramatic rate: New York City's welfare budget is projected for $1.7 billion for the next fiscal year, an increase of 29 per cent over this year.

The infant mortality rate in the United State is about the highest of any major, industrial nation and our longevity rate is among the lowest. Indeed, the infant mortality rate in the Mississippi Delta is only about a tenth of one per cent below that of India. Thousands of Americans suffer from malnutrition and even starvation in spite of our tremendous agricultural productivity and a variety of subsidies and controls. The social, psychic, and economic costs of crime are escalating.

Commercial interests continue to encroach upon those of conservation and recreation. Precious and irreplaceable forests, watersheds, lakes, and beaches are being ravaged and lost. Environmental pollution is a national disgrace and approaches crisis dimensions in many sections of our country. "Quality of life" issues are emerging as important concerns of more and more citizens, young and old. But our youth, in particular, are pointing up the conflict between the humane values espoused by our society and the impersonal, bureaucratic, often materialistic characteristics of individuals and institutions importantly influencing the quality of life in our society.

Beyond such a listing of domestic problems, there are facts that are difficult to quantify but that must be reckoned with just the same: the facts of frustration, impatience, and thinly repressed rage. Terms such as *alienation* and *anomie* have been transformed from sociological esoterica into Sunday supplement cliches.

When National Guardsmen patrol the streets of an American city for nine continuous months—as they did in Wilmington, Delaware, following the riots there in April, 1967—we realize how acute our sense of helplessness has become. Riots and even political assassinations have lost the character of unique and isolated events and instead have come to be seen as recurrent symptoms of a deeper malaise. Indeed, one of the greatest tragedies of the times may be a lessening in our capacity for outrage, and ultimately, for compassionate and responsive action. It is difficult for those who feel themselves disestablished—whether they be minorities such as the Appalachians, blacks, and Puerto Ricans, or majorities such as those under twenty-five—to accept the torturous rate of observable progress. And it is equally difficult for those in positions of power and for the average citizen to accept the irrationalities, extremism, and sporadic violence that are symptomatic of any period of ferment and change.

The business corporation, the university, the government agency—institutions which to a large extent govern our well-being and determine the direction of our society—seem infinitely complex and remote. The need to make bureaucratic structures more humane and democratic—to keep them accessible, flexible, and responsive to our needs—has emerged as the central problem of all modern societies, East and West.

Our past attempts to deal with our domestic problems have brought into focus the problem of bureaucratic insensitivity. The urban renewal program, designed to replace slum housing, destroyed in its first decade of operation far more low-income housing than it created; it had a dismal history of subsidizing down town real estate development in the name of public interest and with little consideration for residents. Even where we have built public housing, the projects generally have been depressingly custodial in character, and the potential tenants rarely consulted in their design. We have recently come to realize how city welfare systems—no matter how well intended and generous in their provisions—tend to perpetuate dependency, discourage stable family life, and rob the recipient of what little dignity he has.

Where there have been provisions for citizen participation, (public hearings, for example) they have often been elaborate charades, designed to legitimize decisions that have already been made by planners and politicians in the privacy of their conference rooms. Even where sincere, they have generally consulted the people after the fact rather than in the process of exploration and planning.

The poverty program, with its requirement of maximum feasible participation of the poor, made a genuine effort to incorporate client views at all stages of project planning. However, it confused the role for citizen participation in policy formulation and project design with that of day-to-day project administration; the results were several well-publicized incidences of mismanagement that did much to reduce popular support and discredit the program in Congress.

Ultimately, however, it was the violent summer of 1967 that exposed the inadequacy of past programs—not only in terms of their magnitude—but in terms of the process through which they were developed and implemented. In particular, the rioting in New Haven and Detroit—cities pointed out as models for the entire country for the way in which federal poverty and renewal funds could be used—shocked many dedicated public servants out of their complacency.

How sensitive have the inhabitants of university presidents' and deans' offices, city halls, and government agencies become to the suspicion and hostility with which even their best intentioned acts are viewed by large segments of our population? At least some of our institutional leaders appear to be responding positively and constructively to such indicators. In dealing with domestic problems today, there *does* seem to be a greater willingness to experiment with new organizational forms and procedures: to re-think the relationship between various levels of government and their constituents, and to make allowance for more meaningful community involvement.

Urban renewal procedures have been revised to include the neighborhood more directly in project planning and to mini-mize dislocations. Emphasis has shifted away from slum clearance and commercial redevelopment toward the rehabilitation of resi-dential areas and the preservation of community values. The De-partment of Transportation has instituted new requirements to insure that decisions on highway locations and design are more open to public scrutiny. New concepts such as civilian review boards, community development corporations, consumer coopera-tives, neighborhood mayors' offices and city halls, are further examples of a movement toward direct accountability and toward innovation from the bottom up. The Model Cities Program repre-sents the most ambitious current effort in the urban area to con-centrate the energies and resources of all levels of government and to find a workable balance among politicians, planners, and neighborhood spokesmen.

Despite all this ferment and activity—the pilot projects, demonstration grants, and so on—many of us have the sensation of treading water, while the currents of change carry us even further from solid land. We are aware that all our social programs taken together alter only a few lives in significant, constructive ways, and that our environmental programs affect only a small percentage of the homes and acreage developed each year. Our most ambitious efforts—new Towns, for example—create desir-able options for a few, but their total impact remains negligible. Yet most social commentators agree that our worst problems—at least those we understand, such as air and water pollution, inade-

quate housing, hard-core unemployment—could be virtually eliminated at a price our society can easily afford.

What explains this impasse; why have we been unable
simply to muster our collective will and proceed to do the job?
I think this inhibition can largely be explained in terms of three
dilemmas that must first be resolved or at least lessened in their
severity if genuine progress is to occur.

The first dilemma: efficiency versus responsiveness. The
first dilemma emerges from the simultaneous demands upon our
institutions for both greater efficiency and greater responsiveness.
Swift and measurable progress on our domestic problems will obviously require more efficient delivery of action programs. I use
efficiency in the broad sense of a clear ordering of priorities, an
appropriate level of investment, and effective management of
available resources. In many areas we can not wait two or three
generations. We need results and we need them now.

Yet, the more responsive an institution is to its clientele,
the more protracted is the execution of its programs. More alternatives will be explored, more views considered before any decision
is made. In some instances irreconcilable differences in interest
will be exposed that might otherwise have gone unnoticed and
unresolved. An inherent problem of community participation is
that people can more easily be mobilized to stop something
threatening than to work for something desirable. Broader and
more intense citizen involvement—whether in the city or on campus—invariably means some sacrifice in efficiency, order, and dispatch; and it also entails a genuine sharing of decision-making
prerogatives.

If mayors and college presidents are serious about increasing opportunities for participation, then this means developing a
higher tolerance for uncertainty, delay, and failure. Conflict must
be accepted as the price of revitalizing our institutions and, in
some instances, as a good in itself. In my thinking, perhaps the
best indicator of vitality in civic life today, is the growing political
sophistication of the lower- and lower-middle income groups.
Compared with four or five years ago, ad hoc protest groups form
with amazing rapidity when neighborhood interests are jeopar-
dized by the proposals of municipal planners and highway engineers.

As we explore ways to incorporate fuller citizen participa-

tion in project planning and execution, we must make sure that
it does not paralyze public action altogether. Above all, we must
distinguish the degree and nature of participation appropriate
for each type of policy area. (By "we," I mean both those in positions of official responsibility and those assuming advocacy roles
on behalf of community groups.) In a project designed to increase
the well-being of a particular neighborhood—a housing rehabilitation plan, for example—it may well be appropriate that local
residents hold a high degree of control over the final design. It
may also be advisable that residents be hired wherever possible
to share directly in the project's implementation, even at some
sacrifice of efficiency. And we might still rate the program a success
if its only outcome is to raise the level of community concern and
engender a sense of community efficacy without producing a physically tangible result.

In the design of a city-wide transportation system, on the
other hand, it is not desirable that neighborhood groups hold a
veto over the final plan. Narrow local interests in neighborhood
conservation must be traded off against community-wide interests
in greater mobility and economy. We need procedures to assure
that legitimate neighborhood interests are fully protected, but
these interests should not dictate the final outcome.

In other areas the problem is still too much particularism
rather than excessive standardization. The inflated cost of new
housing provides an instructive example. In many metropolitan
areas, new housing is commonly beyond the reach of not only
lower-income groups but middle-income groups as well. Here the
need is not simply for more efficient technology as is so often assumed; construction labor, for example, represents only about 15
per cent of the retail value of the typical new home. Instead, the
difficulty is really one of removing a series of institutional constraints that impede the extension of modern industrial methods
and organization to housing production: obsolete building codes,
restrictive lending practices, union work rules, land speculation,
and the property tax system, to cite just a few of the major im-
pediments. The same businessmen who rail against the growth in
federal bureaucracy would welcome greater federal power if it
would result in more standardized regulatory practices, such as
a nationally promulgated building code.

At the federal level, President Nixon has declared his intention to check the growth of welfare statism and to decentralize federal activities while continuing to attack social ills. He intends to do this in three ways: first, by encouraging volunteer social service; second, by enlisting the profit motive of private industry in urban problem solution; and third, by substituting block grants, primarily to the states, for the direct provision of federal services. The first of these—voluntarism—is praiseworthy but it is likely to have minimal long-term, sustained effect. The second —increased reliance on the private sector—could possibly direct substantial resources into those problem areas that can be defined in market terms. We have already seen major ventures by the aluminum industry in the housing field, the petroleum industry in New Town development, the electronics industry in educational hardware, and the aerospace industry in urban transportation. Westinghouse, General Learning, Litton, and others have managing Job Corps camps on a profit-making basis.

It is still too soon to tell whether these and similar efforts will bring a substantial level of investment into areas of high social priority and be characterized by an increased rate of innovation.

One potentially powerful device for attracting large-scale private investment into areas of social concern is the use of tax incentives. Tax incentives are politically attractive because they may avoid the need for yearly congressional appropriations. In 1967 the late Robert Kennedy submitted the most elaborate legislative proposal to date recommending the use of this approach to encourage private investors to rehabilitate or build low-rent housing and to locate new industrial capacity in the ghetto. Similar incentives might also be granted to businesses that install air pollution control equipment or hire and train the hard-core unemployed.

A major source of opposition to the Kennedy plan and other tax incentive schemes has come from the Treasury Department. Even though tax breaks are now available to activities as diverse as grain storage and oil drilling, the Treasury seems to be steadfastly opposed to further erosion of the tax base, especially for what it considers a narrow social purpose. Backers of incentive plans argue that, even accepting the Treasury's definition of "narrow social purpose," the present structure of the tax code is so riddled with special exemptions that, without thoroughgoing revisions of the code, housing for poverty groups surely justifies this further exception.

Block grants and tax-sharing plans have both been discussed for several years as stratagems for checking the growth of federal bureaucracy. Block grants would transfer federal funds to the states or cities for some broad social purpose, for example, for preschool education. The federal agencies would no longer undertake a project-by-project review, but would simply evaluate the state's or city's overall performance in administering the funds. This approach holds promise of expediting domestic programs provided three conditions are met:

The first condition is that strict performance criteria are applied to ensure that priority is given to those most in need. Harold Howe, on leaving office, raised this concern when he said: "I seriously question the wisdom of transforming present federal aid programs into a block grant system which ignores a special focus on the needs of the disadvantaged and the handicapped." [1]

A second condition for the success of block grants is that they be administered in such a way as to demand and result in increased competence at the state and local level. One reason for expanding federal programs in the past has been a lack of competence in some state education departments. In the long run, a combination of greater funding, administrative development programs, and broader responsibility should improve the ability of state and local agencies to recruit and effectively utilize good talent.

A third condition is that a move toward block grants be accompanied by expanded government spending for social purposes. No matter how successful block grants might be in building grass roots control over social expenditures, federal taxation and funding will remain the primary means for redistributing wealth from affluent suburbs to where it is needed in central cities and rural counties. Metropolitan government with new taxing powers would be a more efficient way of achieving the same result, but it does not seem feasible in the immediate future. Unfortunately, the most likely circumstance under which true metropolitan government may come into being is as a reaction to the prospect of

[1] Annual Meeting of Council of Chief State School Officers, Salt Lake City, November 18, 1968. Reprinted in *Vital Speeches,* January 1, 1969.

blacks gaining control over the machinery of central city government and over the patronage that such control entails.

*The second dilemma: compensatory treatment vs. equal
opportunity.* The second dilemma emerges from attempts to give
compensatory treatment in terms of both training and recruitment
to persons from disadvantaged backgrounds. The concept goes
far beyond equality of opportunity—the treatment of each individual on the basis of merit alone. It insists on preferential
treatment for certain groups until they have the means to effect
proportionate influence on the institutions that manage our society. This often means bypassing someone with superior quali-
fications to choose someone in greater need.

This principle has received legislative acceptance in several
government programs: in the Concentrated Employment Program
and other manpower development programs, and in Titles I and
III of the Elementary and Secondary Education Act of 1965, for
example, as well as in the recruitment practices of private industry,
public agencies, and educational institutions. But there are strong
inhibitions against applying the principle on a significant scale,
and the government programs have received only token funding.

The demands from the have-nots for preferential treatment
have created psychological and normative problems for the haves.
A labor leader may, at least in principle, acquiesce to the concept
of first come, first served as the admission policy for union membership. However, he is likely to reject the idea of jumping minority groups to the head of the line as undemocratic and unfair.
Robert Coles has written extensively about the feelings of the
large low- and middle-income white sections of our cities; he
describes how they, too, feel overlooked and powerless in their
dealings with the city bureaucracy, and resent compensatory programs as a reverse form of racial discrimination in which whites
are victimized or ignored.

The resistance to compensatory efforts raises more complex
issues in the higher echelons of business, government, and education. An untrained black or Puerto Rican will perform equally
well as his white counterpart in a union apprenticeship program—the quality of riveting or carpentry will remain unchanged.
However, most colleges undertaking ambitious black recruiting
programs have encountered strong faculty anxiety about the lower-

ing of academic standards. Businesses have similar concerns about performance as they extend their recruiting efforts beyond mere tokenism. This is why most admissions offices and personnel departments still limit themselves to discovering the fully qualified minority member who could clearly make it on his own, but for some reason has not been aware of his opportunities.

Despite some absolute gains in the last decade for blacks, Puerto Ricans, and other poverty groups, the relative distance between them and the white majority is widening in terms of employment, median incomes, infant mortality, and education. These gaps can only be closed through even greater favoritism. The failure of our institutions to accept the necessity of compensatory action—and I mean accept it wholeheartedly—can only result in an even more divided nation.

To apply this on a significant scale will require patience and imagination. Institutions will have to reexamine not only their employment and admission criteria, but their entire style of relating to employees or students. For example, once young blacks are on campuses in large numbers, they often have a catalytic effect on tradition-bound institutions. Instead of being humble and grateful, they often start asking provocative questions, challenging the status quo, and demanding significant change. Their demands frequently include the admission of more black students, new or radically changed programs and courses, and greater participation in policy decisions. Such demands challenge the structure and the value systems upon which most of our universities are based. How is an institution to respond constructively to such challenges and confrontations? It would appear that the faculty that deals with these issues honestly might have to reevaluate its concern for maintaining those characteristics that traditionally have been the basis of its "academic reputation." And will it not also have to reexamine the attitudes and values that determine how status and prestige are distributed within the academic community? Will staff members who commit themselves to experimental programs receive the same share of promotions, special grants, honorary degrees, endowed chairs and other rewards as those who publish regularly and work only with the most promising graduate students? Institutional commitment to the accommodation and compensatory treatment of the disadvantaged will obviously require significant change in the sociology and engagement processes of those institutions.

Perhaps the most ambitious effort so far to hire black workers has been undertaken by the automotive industry. In the past year, it has hired forty thousand workers from the ghettos of Detroit. To accomplish this, companies have opened recruiting offices in the ghetto, provided special door-to-door transportation, ignored most prison records, offered special on-the-job training, tolerated a high degree of absenteeism, and, in some instances, have virtually gone to the worker's home to coax him to work. The automotive industry reports that about 65 per cent of those hired have stayed in the jobs—about the same retention rate as for other newly hired workers.

The difficulties of reaching the hard-core unemployed suggest that first priority among all compensatory programs should be assigned to preschool and elementary school education. We cannot, of course, simply abandon the thousands of unemployed blacks who have reached maturity as victims of inadequate diet, education, and health care and shackled by attitudes formed in an era of limited opportunity. However, long-range efforts should center on ensuring that the generation still in its infancy will have the skills and motivation necessary to make and capitalize upon their own opportunities.

The third dilemma: the knowledge gap. The third dilemma I see inhibiting effective action to resolve our domestic ills is the disparity between what we know and what we must do; or where we have the answers, our inability to communicate this knowledge to those in a position to apply it. Since it is here that higher education has such tremendous and relevant resources and capabilities, I shall discuss this dilemma only briefly; but perhaps some perspectives from an outsider might be useful.

With the endless proliferation of urban symposia, hearings, task forces, pilot projects, demonstration grants, urban reviews, it often seems that the issues have been overstudied, if anything. Black community groups now actively resist being studied, diagnosed, and restudied. Voltaire once remarked that "the art of medicine consists of amusing the patient while nature cures the disease." I sometimes feel the same could be said of urbanology—that amorphous profession which has grown up around problem-solving in our cities. But there is an apparent need for accurate knowledge of what really works in actual practice, and an even greater need for guidelines on how best to utilize what we have discovered in implementing constructive action on a broad front.

For example, if we listen to urban school administrators' criticisms of the products of teacher-training institutions, we must conclude that either we do not yet know how to educate the slum child or that if we do, such knowledge is not being effectively translated and implemented. Differences in the behavior and in the effects of the behavior of various administrators suggest that many of them are not profiting from what has been discovered in applied psychology and group dynamics. Public, professional, and certainly legislative reaction to obvious examples of needlessly duplicated research studies and innovation efforts seems to signal the need for more effective dissemination of research-related information and possibly for more effective coordination of efforts to develop, evaluate, and diffuse significant innovations.

Such feedback information probably is of considerable importance to institutions of higher education as well as to the many diverse groups which depend upon your actions, capacities, and products. Is there not a need for the invention of new forms or styles of interaction with the several publics which our institutions must serve? Should there be more purposeful differentiation of roles among institutions of higher education? Do we not need more effective linking agents between researchers and practitioners in order to better capitalize on what is being discovered and developed? Do you see a need for an improved system of disseminating the results of research and evaluation projects?

I submit that if we are to close the "knowledge gap" many such improvements are needed, and that institutions of higher education will be looked to for leadership and resources to satisfy such unmet needs.

I have discussed three dilemmas inherent in our current inability to act with resolve and constructive effect on societal problems of the utmost urgency. The first of these dilemmas is the frequent incompatibility of demands for swifter and more massive results with those for more citizen involvement. Greater

participation inevitably means surfacing conflicts that would otherwise be glossed over. I noted that those in positions of responsibility will need to accept greater controversy and uncertainty
where neighborhood interests are of paramount concern. But we
also need to recognize and define those areas of public policy
where local veto power is clearly inappropriate.

The second dilemma is centered about conflict between the
need for preferential treatment of certain groups and the deep-
rooted American ethos of equal opportunity. This is why we have
had so much trouble moving beyond the legalistic, civil rights
phase in combatting the problems of poverty and racial inequality.

The third dilemma emerges where we feel compelled to
act without the knowledge or the tools necessary to deliver results.
Here again government is cast in the undesirable role of the tease
or coquette, frequently arousing expectations it cannot fulfill. The
principal effects of so many well-intentioned but piecemeal programs in the past have been to supplant the abject fatalism of
the poor with active and focused hostility and to precipitate criticism of unsuccessful efforts.

If we are going to have action on a scale truly proportionate
to our domestic needs, each of these dilemmas will have to be resolved. We will need new institutional forms and procedures that
will enable us to set clear priorities and to apply resources where
they are needed most, yet at the same time permit us to satisfy
demands for more responsive processes of government. We need
new techniques for building consensus while insuring that all
legitimate related interests are recognized and accommodated. We
need broader recognition among both the intelligentsia and the
middle class, that without massive discrimination in favor of
blacks, Puerto Ricans and other poverty groups, present dispari-
ties will split our nation. And we need more research that asks
intelligent and pertinent questions, new linkages between theorists
and practitioners, and more attention to evaluating innovative
efforts and disseminating such results.

In the past we have demonstrated our ability as a nation to
concentrate our imaginations, technical capabilities, and resources
in order to meet urgent societal needs. The Manhattan Project
of World War II is an example of just such an effort.

Charles Haar, former Assistant Secretary for Housing and

Administration, speaking on the subject of the urban university, has observed:

> Involvement and commitment; a respect for the pragmatic; a willingness to engage in and with community issues—few urban universities would rate high marks in such tests. By contrast, consider the contribution of the land-grant colleges to the development of American agriculture. From fertilizers to fox-farming to family nutrition, they led and pushed and persuaded that most obdurate of objects, the American farmer, to an unequalled productivity.[2]

Unfortunately, in our urban ghettos, in the Appalachian valleys, and on our nation's campuses we are confronted by problems that defy neat technical formulations; rebuilding a sense of community in this country will prove far more difficult than harnessing the atom or convincing Nebraskan farmers to plant hybrid corn. In the process of solving our problems through public and private action, we must reform the problem-solving process itself. We need brains and we need money, but above all we need new ways of working together.

2 "The Urban University: Challenge and Response," Lake Erie College, Painesville, Ohio, February 28, 1968.

~✕ *28* ~

NO PROMISE
WITHOUT AGONY

Robert McAfee Brown

In the old days, the preacher spent most of his time telling good decent people what a terrible state the world was in, and how they'd better hop to it before Satan got a stranglehold on the future. Both preacher and analyst could afford the luxury of announcing doom. But that's not news any more. We do not need to be reminded that 1970 might be worse than 1969. Our most extravagant hope is simply that it will not be too much worse. Furthermore, no educator has to feel guilty any more that he has fled from the "real world" to the "ivory towers of the university." Everybody knows about the agony. We do not need a description of that. The real question is: Is there any promise? Can we believe in more than the agony?

I am going to suggest that if there is any promise for America, it will be only as we go through, and not try to circumvent, the agony. President Nixon, in a curiously contradictory metaphor in his inaugural address, said, "The American dream will not come to those who sleep." Somewhat intoxicated by that figure of speech, I respond that the American nightmare, in which we are now caught, will be creatively appropriated only by those who are wide awake, and who can, from the very midst of the nightmare, see from within it some pointers to hope. No promise, then, without agony.

Let me suggest some shifts of perspective through which we must go if we are to discover signs of promise in the midst of the agony, centering on the words *violence, power, materialism* (in the treatment of which I hope to surprise you), and *compassion,* and keeping two further prescriptive words up my sleeve for the conclusion.

The first shift involves a deeper analysis than we usually make of the quality of contemporary life that usually scares us most. Our fear of overt violence must be countered by our acknowledgement of covert violence.

When I refer to "the fear of overt violence" I am pointing to something all too real to the middle-class white American. If he has not yet been the victim of violence he fears that he soon will be. Even if he is on a campus, he fears a sit-in, maybe in his office, during which his files will be destroyed. If he is in a computer center, he fears what might be called a smash-in. If he is in a classroom, he fears a disruptive teach-in. If he is white, he is scared silly when he sees as many as three blacks with Afro hair styles, black jackets, and dark glasses, moving in his direction. He is sure he is about to be clubbed. When he hears angry rhetoric by members of any minority group, he is sure that the verbal overkill is just about to escalate into the unveiling of hitherto hidden knives, clubs, and guns.

And this is not just a white middle-class hangup. The protesting student cannot but fear the stock-in-trade of his opposition —mace, billy clubs, and tear gas, used to put down what the student thinks are the legitimate concerns for which he is protesting—fearing, if I may say so, the kind of treatment his fellow students got in Chicago in August, 1968, or in Berkeley in May, 1969. The black or the Puerto Rican or the Mexican-American has every reason to fear the violence that may be perpetrated against him if a cop or a white gang happens to catch him in a secluded spot.

But I suggest that we will not advance from agony to promise, until we recognize that such an analysis of violence is super-
ficial. Our fear of overt violence must be countered by our
acknowledgment of covert violence. By *covert violence* I mean
something more subtle and destructive than physical violence,
terrible as that is, and the common threat that links together the
two kinds of violence I am describing is the denial of personhood.
The violence manifested when Sirhan Sirhan squeezes the trigger,
and the violence manifested when a white man denies a job to a
black man, are finally cut from the same cloth. In each case, the
perpetrator of the violence is saying, "You don't count. I will get
you out of the way." When a city re-zones its school districts to
make sure the black students will not get into the good schools
and thus "lower standards," that is covert violence. When land-
lords pile up tremendous profits from rat-infested slums, that is
covert violence. When society gives a dole to minority members
but will not restructure itself to provide jobs for them, that is
covert violence. When we send an eighteen-year-old to jail for five
years because he says, "I refuse to kill Vietnamese peasants," that
is covert violence.

The report of the World Council of Churches' Geneva
conference commented, "Violence is very much a reality in our
world, both the overt use of force to suppress and the invisible
violence (*violencia blanca*) perpetrated on people who by the millions have been or still are the victims of repression and unjust
social systems . . . the violence which, though bloodless, con-
demns whole populations to perennial despair." That unfortunately describes America. We are not only committing overt
violence in Vietnam, but we are committing covert violence in
Oakland, Chicago, Memphis, Detroit, Seattle, Jackson, and Boston.

What has come to be called "institutional racism" is a
particularly telling example of covert violence, illustrating that
even though as individuals we may be very open and understanding and unbigoted, we participate in institutions whose very
structures guarantee that they will perpetuate the things we think
we are opposing. Individually as educators, we believe in a fair
shake for all students, regardless of race, color, or creed, but our
entrance examinations have tended to cater to middle-class, white,
suburban Americans, so that de facto it has been exceedingly
difficult for members of minority groups to gain admission by our

"normal" standards. That is covert violence. In principle, we believe that military service should not exempt certain classes of
people, and yet we condone a Selective Service system that de facto
discriminates in favor of white middle-class kids who lived in good
enough parts of town to get good enough high school educations
to get into colleges, and whose parents can pay the tariff to keep
them there, so that those who actually get drafted are more likely
to be the disadvantaged who do not have enough education to
get a 2-S deferment that will enable them to dodge the draft for
four years. That is covert violence.

Until we see the agony in such terms as these, we will be
in no position even to begin to look toward any promise.

A second shift is called for, if we are to find signs of promise in the midst of agony. This is the recognition that the abuse
of power must be countered by the creative use of power. Let
nobody in this day and age try to argue that power *per se* is evil
—or good. Power is what we make of it, and the choice is in our
hands. And it is the abuse of power that has led not only to the
overt, but also to the covert, violence we have been examining.

Why are students so turned off by the older generation?
Surely a major reason is their feeling that we of the older generation have engaged in a monstrous abuse of power. Without turning this talk into a panegyric against the American presence in
Vietnam, let me use that simply as the most glaring example of
the point, since it is the event most responsible, I believe, for the
great disaffection the young presently feel for the old (and for
"old" read "anyone over twenty-six," which is when you become
non-draftable). How does the student view our presence in Vietnam? He sees the most powerful nation on earth using overwhelming force to pummel one of the tiniest nations on earth.
He sees incredible technological resources being used almost solely
for destruction—pellet bombs timed to go off sporadically and
destroy civilians, napalm melting the flesh indiscriminately of
young and old alike, biological ingenuity being used to defoliate
tens of thousands of acres of verdant jungle, half a million men
being deployed eleven thousand miles (40 per cent of whom have
been injured), more explosives being used in a single day than
were used in the entire North African campaign of World War II,
political and economic and military resources being used to shore
up an oppressive dictatorial regime in Saigon, the verbal overkill

of the former President and Vice-President being used to justify it all in the name of "moral commitments"—the student sees all this and he cannot help thinking, "Here is power, all right, and it is power that is being terribly abused."

And then he looks back over the last half decade and asks, "Who was opposing all this? Were the Catholic bishops? Or the Protestant preachers? Or the businessmen? Or the Congressmen? Or the trade unions? Or the educators?" And after citing the few brilliant exceptions—the Bishop Shannons, the William Sloane Coffins, the Eugene McCarthys, and the William Fulbrights—he has to say that the older generation has *not* been opposing all this. And the student verdict, justifiably, has become: America has abused its power, and become so intoxicated by the exercise of it that America has lost all sense of proportion and moral value.

But from that point on the answer is not to disavow power, though some, students included, tend at least temporarily to think so, and to move in that direction. But flower power will not feed starving peoples. No, the answer is to move from the abuse of power to the creative use of power. To some, such talk may sound utopian, but wearing both of my hats—that of educator and that of clergyman—I respond that if between them the universities and the churches and synagogues cannot begin to work toward the creative use of power, we might as well throw in the sponge.

What would this involve? It would involve setting some new priorities, saying in effect, Very well, we *do* have the most power in the world, how are we going to use it? It would involve recognizing that the most important use of power in which we could engage would be the sharing of it. Suppose that instead of using our foreign aid to shore up corrupt dictators in Southeast Asia and South America and the Caribbean, we were to use our resources to help the economies of younger nations get on their feet? Suppose we took seriously the very minimal goal that the Pontifical Commission for Justice and Peace, and the World Council of Churches, have recommended—the contribution of 1 per cent of our Gross National Product to an international monetary fund, the resultant pool to be available to developing nations for use in making their own economies more self-sufficient? Suppose we did that? We would at least be making the first beginning steps toward using power responsibly and creatively. Suppose that instead of spending 87 billion dollars a year on the military budget, and 30 billion dollars a year on Vietnam alone, we rethought our sense of priorities and realized how grotesque it sounds to the black man when in the face of those expenditures we tell him that we cannot find 6 billion dollars a year to implement the Kerner Commission Report? When our own increase in Gross National Product in one year is more in dollars than the total budgets of all the countries of South America combined, do we have any right to expect the South Americans to look at us in any but the most distrustful terms? Is it a creative use of power to be spending billions of dollars on moon shots and space exploration of other planets—exciting though those may be—when on this particular planet two-thirds of the peoples of the world will go to bed hungry this very night?

And I submit to you that if educators and churchmen are not willing to dedicate the finest hours of their lives to emphasizing the incredible reallocation of priorities that is called for by our present abuse of power, we have no reason to believe that anything less than holocaust and revolution will result. We either shift from the abuse of power to the creative use of power, or we face Armageddon—and possibly in our own lifetimes.

A third shift that is called for is from a misplaced materialism to a transformed materialism. It is a cliché both political and clerical that we have lost our sense of "eternal values" and that we must "recover the spiritual." Now I have nothing against eternal values, but my point just now is that they are expressed in and through the material. Thus if somebody talks about "the eternal value of the human soul," I want to remind him that in both Judaism and Christianity, persons are not viewed as having eternal souls and transitory bodies, but as possessing a kind of psychosomatic unity of body and soul, indivisible. This means that if you talk about a human being as having eternal or infinite worth, you are cheating on the evidence unless you are just as concerned with whether he has enough to eat as you are with whether he has experienced a presence that disturbs him with the joy of elevated thoughts. We have no right to be more concerned with a person's soul than we are with whether or not he has soles on his shoes. It is interesting that in Jesus' parable about the Last Judgment, the questions that are asked are not: Have you had a religious experience? Did you go to church regularly? Were you baptized? Can you recite the creed?, but quite simply: Did you feed the hungry? Did you clothe the naked? Did you care for the sick? Did you visit the imprisoned? Did you, in other words, concern yourself with the neighbor in need? That is the criterion for the life acceptable to God. Our neighbors' material concerns, if we may so put it, are our religious obligation.

And for reasons hard to fathom, an incredible proportion of the material goods of this world has been entrusted to the United States of America. For the first time in the history of the world, we now have the technological knowhow to see to it that nobody in the world needs to starve or be cold. For the first time in history! And if you want a job as educators, if you want a challenge, look for ways to put all that information and technique to work. Let us train scientists who will increase our technological expertise to grow food and thus get greater productivity per acre; let us train economists who will find better ways to make capital available to underdeveloped nations; let us train political scientists who will help to develop regional economic and political alliances to increase trade within the third world and between the third world and us; let us train teachers who will instill the vision of the one family of man in our young; let us train politicians who will lead us rather than simply follow where the latest poll suggests the rank and file want to go. Let us do these things so that, as the richest nation on earth, we can shift from a misplaced materialism, dedicated to providing luxury items we do not need (complete with built-in obsolescence), into a transformed materialism dedicated to the task of sharing the goods of this earth with the two-thirds of the world that is ill-fed, ill-housed, ill-clothed, so that such clichés remain clichés no longer, but merely epitaphs of a world we refused to accept and were determined to transform.

All of which leads to a fourth shift through which we must go if we are to transform the agony into the promise. This is a shift within the educational enterprise from academic detachment to moral compassion. It is high time that, self-consciously and determinedly, we addressed ourselves to the question "Education for what?" and indeed "Education for whom?" and that we took very careful stock of the ends to which our knowledge is being put. I take my cue for the moment not from the humanists and theologians but from the scientists. On Tuesday, March 4, 1969, scientists participated in a Day of Concern. By the hundreds, they left their classrooms, laboratories, and field assignments to ask the question, "For what and for whom are we doing this work?" They are rightly disturbed that biologists are being paid by the government to do research in germ warfare, that physicists are hired to provide us with more efficient antiballistic missile systems, that money that could be going into cancer research is being diverted into poison gas research, that medical expertise that could be ministering to a ghetto is being hired to research more hideous forms of napalm. They are saying, "It is time we took a long, hard look at what society is telling us to do with our knowledge."

I hope their example will force the rest of us to take a similar look at what we are doing with our knowledge. There is a moral question to be asked of political scientists who devote their energies to devising new methods of counterinsurgency, when those methods will be used to stifle peoples' revolutions against tyrannical regimes. There is a moral question to be asked of educators who promote a school system in which students come to believe that the right of dissent must be stifled when it goes against the status quo (and I hope all Californians will fight the attempts of a governor who would take academic policy decisions away from professors and hand them over to politicians).

Do not misunderstand me. I am not making the specious plea for "instant relevance," which says that I need not complete a book if it does not immediately turn me on, or says that history is a waste of time because only the twentieth century is important, or claims that every experiment, every discussion, every lecture, must equip me instantly to go outside the classroom or the laboratory and cope. Rather, I am pleading for the breadth of vision that can enable us to see that any study of any significant body of material will make us more usefully equipped citizens to cope with a world that continues to multiply problems even as we study. It is particularly true in our day that those who ignore history are doomed to repeat it. I am pleading for study that is infused with moral compassion—and I remind you that that word *compassion* means "to suffer with," to be alongside the other, in his misery as well as in his joy, in his terror as well as in his triumphs, in his agony as well as in his promise. Let us not be embarrassed by this concern; let us rather see the nobility of it, and realize that it is the sense of compassion that makes us human, that makes us brothers, that separates us from the animals and from the machines.

Those, then, are four shifts that will be needed, if we are even to begin to move from agony to promise: (1) our fear of overt violence must be countered by our recognition of covert violence, (2) our abuse of power must be countered by the creative use of power, (3) our misplaced materialism must be countered by a transformed materialism, and (4) our sense of academic detachment must be countered by a sense of moral compassion.

All well and good, you may say, but how do we get from here to there? Let me, to conclude, suggest two qualities that I think could help us in that transition.

The first of these qualities is conveyed by the Greek word *metanoia*. This means an about-face, a turning in an opposite direction, or, as theology has translated the word, a conversion. Do not be turned off by the word, I beg you. For nothing less drastic will suffice. It will simply not do to say to rich, contented, and unconcerned Americans, "Just go on being more of the same." No, what is called for is a change of direction, a fresh start. It means, "Take a fresh look at *violence*. You are so afraid somebody will beat you up that you don't realize that you are beating people up all the time." It means, "Take a fresh look at *power*. If you continue using it so destructively it will destroy you as well." It means, "Take a fresh look at your *materialism*. As long as you keep it for yourself you build up a head of steam that will soon explode and destroy us all." It means, "Take a fresh look at *education*. You are so busy describing life that you are stifling peoples' power to live." And at this point at least, we could afford to take a leaf from Karl Marx, appropriate his final thesis on Feuerbach, and see it as an indictment of ourselves: "Philosophers [for which now let us read "educators"] have interpreted the world in various ways; the point, however, is to change it."

To all of this, the plea for *metanoia* means, "You are on the wrong track, or at least you are going the wrong way, a way that leads only to mounting agony. You may be fooling yourself, America, but you are fooling nobody else. The rest of the world sees through your rhetoric, your self-justifying talk, your cloaking of your own vested interests in the name of pious double-talk."

Can education demand conversion or force it? Of course

not. But what education can do is to force people to confront choices, to point out the consequences of given courses of action, so that a decision can be made to turn about, to begin again, to make a fresh start, to undergo (and I do not apologize for the phrase) a conversion experience. Will we learn from Vietnam that backing a dictator is no way to liberate a people, and that destroying a city is no way to save it, so that we do not make the same mistakes in Latin America? Only as we become wiser than we were before Vietnam. Will we learn from the escalating race riots in this country that white people cannot indefinitely coerce and maim and destroy black people without a day of reckoning finally coming? Only as the lessons of Watts, Detroit, Newark, and a dozen other brutal realities are learned more quickly than we have learned our lessons in the past. Can we move from agony to promise? Only by measuring the agony full scale, with no illusions and no sentimentalities, and then committing ourselves to a new direction, again with no illusions and no sentimentalities, recognizing that we undertake great risks, but that they are risks infinitely worth taking, for they commit us not to narrow nationalism, but turn us about to the whole family of man.

And where do we find the vision and power to do that? Here I suggest a second quality. Let me sneak up on it by suggesting that perhaps the opposite of agony is not, as the title of this book suggests, promise, but (as the title of Irving Stone's biography of Michelangelo suggests) ecstasy. Ecstasy is a situation in which one is in *ex-stasis*, or "standing outside oneself." That is to say, it is the situation of having perspective on oneself, of seeing oneself in relation to whatever is beyond oneself. It is the quality of—and here I must employ another theological word—it is the quality of transcendence. Now by this I am not insisting upon the image of a Great Big Being off somewhere in the sky, and I immediately remind you that Herbert Marcuse, whom nobody is about to accuse of being a theologian, can use the word to describe engaging in what he calls "the great refusal," the unwillingness to accept things simply as they are, the repudiation of one-dimensionality, the recognition that we make a judgment about the present in terms of something that is not in and of the present.

Maybe this could be described simply by saying that we are called upon to have a sense of humor about ourselves, to apply to ourselves the reminder Kierkegaard wished he could have suggested to Hegel, namely the comic fact that he who thought himself the infinite surveyor of all that is, had occasionally to turn aside from his manuscript to sneeze. The thing that most frightens me about the New Left, or the radical right, is not that they threaten middle-class values. Middle-class values need to be threatened. What frightens me about them is the absolute humorlessness of their crusade. I do not mean this in a condescending manner. Quite the opposite. I mean simply that there is something terrifying about the crusader who is never for a moment aware of his own shortcomings, the partiality of his insights, the finitudes of his being, the actual narrowness of his angle of vision—for he has no resources to guard him against the fanaticism of taking himself with such utmost seriousness that it would be beyond his capacity to admit that in any particular instance he had been wrong. This ability to laugh at ourselves, to see something slightly comic in our pretensions, is a blessed gift, for it is an acknowledgement of some standard of judgment or value, beyond ourselves, in the light of which we can cut ourselves down to size.

And when we can do that, then we can experience *metanoia,* turning about, conversion. People describe this over-againstness, this "other" that judges them, in many ways. I am not saying you have to be a Christian or a Jew to experience it, though I have found that in my case it helps. But I am saying that this sense is what makes one a human being—a person—and that only because of it, only because we feel confronted by it, can we know either agony or promise—or ecstasy.

W. H. Auden captures this mood in the closing chorus of his poem, *For the Time Being.*[1] And although in it he is describing the pursuit of the Christ child, his theme is applicable to every quest on which we are called in this day and age. So make your own translation, into your own idiom, of the direction Auden offers us today, through agony to promise:

> *He is the Way.*
> *Follow Him through the Land of Unlikeness;*
> *You will see rare beasts, and have unique adventures.*
>
> *He is the Truth.*
> *Seek Him in the Kingdom of Anxiety;*

[1] W. H. Auden, *Collected Poetry* (New York: Random House).

*You will come to a great city that has expected your return for
  years.*

He is the Life.
Love Him in the World of the Flesh;
And at your marriage all its occasions shall dance for joy.

Index

B

BARZUN, J., 236, 240
BEARD, R., 221, 223
BENNETT, A., 216, 224
BENNIS, W., 139
BERDAHL, R., 215, 224
BERGER, L., 220, 224
BLOCK, J., 222, 224
BLOLAND, H., 215, 224
BOCOCK, J., 221, 224
BOULDING, K., 141, 238, 240
BOWEN, H., 31–32
BOWMAN, D., 217, 224
BOWMAN, J. B., 26–27
BREWSTER, K., 119
BROWN, E. R., 221, 224
BROWN, N. O., 207
BRUNER, J., 193
BUTLER, N. M., 149

C

Campus culture: drug use, 113–122; environment and student unrest, 123–135; music, 201–204; sexual behavior, 105–112
Campus governance (see Governance, campus)
Carnegie Commission on the Future of Higher Education, 26, 30, 214
CASSIRER, E., 190–191
Center for Research and Development in Higher Education, University of California (Berkeley), 214
CHAMBERS, M. M., 216, 224
CHARDIN, P. T. DE, 76
CHASE, J., 216, 224
Christian values, 270–276; and psychedelia, 206, 208–209; and sexual behavior, 106, 112
CHURCHMAN, C. W., 143
CLARK, R., 217, 224
CLEAVER, E., 86, 164
COLES, R., 259
Colleges and universities (see Universities and colleges)
COLVARD, R., 216, 224
Community college, 51–55
Counseling, 127–131; current research in, 217

COUSTEAU, J., 24
COX, L., 214, 224
Curriculum relevance, 59–76; to Black society, 69–76; Experimental College at San Francisco State College, 133–135; faculty control over curriculum, 72, 155; program at Free University of Berlin, 218; responsibilities of higher education, 51–68
CUTLIP, S., 26

D

Demonstrations, 123–135; guerilla tactics, 96 (see also Student protests)
DEMOTT, B., 210
Department of Health, Education, and Welfare, Committee on Federal Support for Higher Education, 30–31
Disadvantaged students, 74–77, 215–217, 220–221; admission, 74; federal survey on campus racial discrimination, 215–216; impact on other students, 75–76; open-door policy toward, 75–76; remedial work, 75–76; research on evaluation of, 217, 220–221
Domestic issues, 251–264: conservation, 252; hard-core unemployed, 261; hunger, 45, 60–61, 252; infant mortality in U.S., 46, 251–252; manpower development, 257, 259; violence, 266–273
DRESSEL, P., 219, 224
Drug abuse, 114–122; Drug Abuse Control Amendments of 1965, 114; drug legislation, 114, 118–122; and findings of First International Symposium on Psychodysleptics and Pharmacopsychoses, 121 (see also LSD; Marihuana; and Psychedelia)
DUMKE, G., 93

E

Education, higher: and academic